What Others Are Saying

What a great gift and purposeful use of a legacy to take your dad's teaching notes on the book of Acts and make them available to the public. Thank you, Jennifer, for this great act of honoring; thank you, Brother Jones, for over twenty-five years of faithful ministry on our Bible college campuses, and thank you, Reader, for diving into the book of Acts and experiencing the Holy Spirit in fresh and new ways! Grab your Bible and this commentary and enjoy the journey.

Doug Clay
Assemblies of God General Superintendent

Iron sharpens iron, and this commentary on the book of Acts accomplishes just that! This work will enable the reader to see the book of Acts with new eyes and gain fresh perspective. It isn't just information, but an exhortation to walk closely with the Holy Spirit. As we do this, we will not only be transformed ourselves, but He will empower us to transform the lives of others.

Tahnya M. Abraham
Human Resources Faith Church

For anyone intrigued by the Holy Spirit's role in the launch of the church, God's Power Unleashed is for you. This book is a compilation of a lifetime of study by Professor David L. Jones and will be a wonderful resource for learners of all levels. You will be encouraged and enriched by his insights into the book of Acts.

Mark Dean
Superintendent, Minnesota District Assemblies of God

David Jones was a special individual. I first learned of the Jones family through some very old Pentecostal leaders I had first met when I was a student at the British AG Bible College in the mid 1970s. In fact, when one of these leaders heard that my wife and I intended visiting the US, they asked that we visit Mrs. Jones, David's mother. Little did I realize that many years later I would be the President at Trinity Bible College and Graduate school in Ellendale, North Dakota, where David taught. David was a force in the classroom. He is still quoted regularly today by his students. His raw, down-to-earth, no-nonsense approach to ministry and leadership is evident in his exegetical work. His life, spirituality, and practicality make this an excellent book, and I give it my hearty endorsement.

Paul R Alexander, PhD,
President, Trinity Bible College and Graduate School, Ellendale, North Dakota

God's Power Unleashed would be a great addition to your study library. Jen Courtney has gone to great lengths to not only honor the legacy of her late father, but to also make his teaching notes on the book of Acts available to another generation. Her unique observations prior to the notes of each chapter give us a window into the character and personality of her father.

I had the dual privilege of not only knowing Brother Jones, but of also sitting under the teaching of his father, T. J. Jones. As I read his insights on the power and practice of the early church, it was as if I were back in the classroom again being challenged and inspired to believe God for greater things.

Rev. Clarence St. John
Former Minnesota District Superintendent

The Jones name is royalty at North Central university here in Minneapolis. David Jones's father, TJ, has his name inscribed in bold letters over the pillars of our library. Sent here from England as a young man, David Jones set in motion the very book you are holding. You hold history, depth, and the very best of God's kingdom in your hand. This exciting new book, *God's Power Unleashed*, will lift and embolden your faith and leadership.

Dr. Scott Hagan
President, North Central University

God's Power Unleashed comes from the classroom notes of respected Bible scholar and university professor, David L. Jones. His roots date back to his father's relationship with the late Smith Wigglesworth. The narrative within the pages of this commentary will motivate its reader to become a Book of Acts Christian.

Dr. G. Craig Lauterbach
Founder & President, Lifeword Publishing

GOD'S POWER *Unleashed*

A Book of Acts Journey with PROFESSOR DAVID L. JONES

Jennifer L. Courtney

LifeWord Publishing
Post Office Box 201
Pipersville, PA 18947 USA

ISBN: 978-1-7363911-9-8 (Print)

979-8-9879724-0-3 (E-book)

Printed in the United States of America.

I dedicate this book to the co-author, my Dad. This whole project is due to his lifetime work and devotion to studying the Bible and imparting its truth to his classes and congregations with excellence, power, and, of course, British humor. This is for you, Dad! To God be the glory!

Acknowledgements

To those who got me started with this project and helped me finish.

Professor Nathan Walstad at Trinity Bible College, a student of my dad's, messaged me to ask if I had any of Dad's teaching notes from his Acts class. Nathan was teaching that same class years later at the same college. His request got me thinking that maybe I should do something with this storehouse of wisdom I have in the form of teaching notes and sermons and make it accessible to more people. Thank you, Nathan, for helping me get the ball rolling on this amazing project!

Jo Clements, my friend and mentor for over twenty years prayed for me, supported me, and was almost as excited as I was about this project of getting Dad's life's work published. Thank you for letting me be real on the hard days and rejoicing with me on the good days!

To my husband, Dan. Wow, babe, I could never have done this without you! You invested time and money, quiet space for me to work, and fountain Diet Dr. Peppers when I needed a little pick-me-up. Whenever I asked for your help with some tough wording or an idea for a story, you dropped what you were doing to help me. Every single time! Not only is it special to me that you believed that I could do this, but I also love that you wanted to honor my dad and God's Word, believing that this project was worth all the investment. Thank you, babe. You're the best in the whole wide world!

Contents

Foreword

David L. Jones is quite possibly the most beloved professor in the history of Trinity Bible College (now Trinity Bible College and Graduate School). His success was the combination of his great British wit, his rock-solid theology, and his vast experience in both the pulpit and the lectern. He was the type of professor who didn't just teach the Bible—he *was* the Bible. He was as important to his students outside of the classroom as he was in it. Numerous times in his twenty-five-plus years as a professor, he talked students off the proverbial ledge by saying something that only he could get away with, like, "When are you going to stop being stupid?" or "Well then, knock it off!" When he said it, you knew it was encouragement from a godly man that you better take to heart.

This is the first book in a series that comes straight from his teaching notes as he taught hundreds of future pastors to rightly divide the Word of God. I had the privilege of taking these classes from him, but I also had the privilege of working under and alongside of him as his youth pastor. His daughter, Jen (my wife), has beautifully captured his wit and some of the amazing stories from both classroom and pulpit. Get to know this General of the faith and learn about the amazing power of God through this book—and the others to come!

And to my amazing wife, your father was proud to know you were passing on his works, and he would be very proud of your finished product here.

Although he joined the church triumphant before he could see this project completed, he will live on through the students he taught, through the parishioners he pastored, and now through these books. May God bless you, as you discover the wit and wisdom of Rev. David L. Jones.

In Christ,

Pastor Dan Courtney
Crystal Hills Assembly

Forward

Prelude

David Lancaster Jones was born on February 8, 1938, in London, England. He lived a life full of family, spiritual heritage, British patronage, Bible studying and people loving, preaching and teaching, and lots of humor. He parted ways with this world on September 17, 2021, in Minneapolis, Minnesota after eighty-three years, seven months, and nine days of faithful service to the Lord. As Psalm 90:10 says, "Seventy years are given to us! Some even live to eighty" (NLT). So, you could say my dad had a good long life, the promised years in the Bible plus three! When it's your loved one, it never seems like enough time; however, I find joy in knowing three things:

1. My dad is now in the presence of HIS Father
2. How much of a difference he made to so many people that I've talked to over his years of ministry
3. That he knew his life's work was in the process of getting published

I was working on chapter five while sitting vigil by his bedside during his last days. I shared with him the stories that I wrote at each chapter's introduction, and he always smiled. Sometimes he would give me a thumbs up too. I will forever be thankful that I started this project when I did, and that he knew that his life's work would live on and continue to impact others with the glorious truth of the gospel!

Introduction

If I come to your church and you're not preaching the Word of God, I'll burn your house down!" "The Antichrist can have my house. My car is paid for, but he can have it too." "And the angel said, 'Get up, Peter!' And Peter said, 'Ugh, leave me alone; I'm sleeping.'" If you have been in a classroom or congregation of my dad's, you can *hear* these *Jonesisms*, can't you? I know I am biased, but I cannot think of another preacher who so eloquently marries reverence with relatable silliness! It's a gift that I have enjoyed my whole life. Whatever your childhood was like, you don't often realize the uniqueness of it until you experience life a little, and I know that I am one blessed lady!

I am the fourth out of five kids in the Jones family, and I have been given the great gift of a ministry calling, thus inheriting the treasure of my dad's sermons and Bible class notes—as well as many books from the libraries of my dad and my grandpa (the renowned T.J. Jones). My grandpa was an Assembly of God ordained minister in England and America, then my dad in America, and now me. I am in awe of my biblical heritage and am very thankful for it! I have said often, "I have AG blood coursing through my veins," as I continue the one hundred plus years of a Jones in full-time ministry, and with that, a reverence for the Word of God and the high calling of ministry.

If you knew my dad at all, you know that he revered his British heritage almost as much as the Bible—almost! He was the fifth of five boys born to T.J. & Doris Jones, hailing from Wraysbury, England. Having been born in February 1938, his earliest memories involved wartime sights, sounds, and smells, as he lived just outside of London at the time. My grandma raised five boys by herself in England during WWII and remained strong in her faith! Where was my grandpa during that time, you ask? Early in the summer of 1941, with a reference letter from renowned British preacher Smith Wigglesworth in hand, Grandpa sailed to America to preach at some good ol' fashioned camp meetings. While preaching in America, the war reached England and all domestic travel across the pond was suspended. My dad had great stories to tell about learning to swim in the Thames, eating lard sandwiches, seeing German soldiers, and cuddling under the dining room table during air raids so the ceiling plaster would not hit them on the head! Meanwhile, my grandpa, stuck in America during the whole war, had to make a living and find a place to put down roots. For him, that became Minneapolis, Minnesota, where he taught preaching and Bible classes at North Central Bible College (now North Central University). After the war ended, my grandpa went back to England to snatch up his family and move them to his established place of residence: Minneapolis. But the British heritage remained strong. I have memories of my dad pulling out his British accent on occasion, getting up at 5:00 a.m. on July 29, 1981, to watch Prince Charles and Lady Diana wed in St. Paul's Cathedral, and the annual traditions of wassail punch and British crackers at our plate setting for Christmas dinner.

Thanks to my spiritual heritage, I don't remember not being in church or knowing about Jesus. Church and Jesus were accessible to me; and for that, I am very thankful. I can be myself around church and Jesus because of my dad. He made it all approachable, handleable, and relatable to me. His drive for representing the Word of God in all its glory and accessibility made it searchable for me. It made me want to know and experience more of God and His truth.

I recall many times coming around the corner of the TV room and catching my dad asleep in his La-Z-Boy with Bible notes open on his lap as he simultaneously studied, napped, and watched the Weather Channel or History Channel. There he would be in all his British sophistication—his silver-streaked, jet-black hair ruffled, white button-down shirt partly untucked, and laying as flat as the recliner would allow, with his mouth wide open in a snoring frenzy. The mouth-wide-open in slumber is a family tradition; we call it "the Jones look," and it has been passed down through the generations. I participate with pride, on occasion, usually while experiencing my best sleep! When we would catch Dad deep in "the Jones look," the goal was always to quietly snatch the remote and change the channel to something a little more exciting. His sleepy response was always the same as he arose from his delicately balanced napping environment with a meteorologist or historian droning on: "Hey, I was watching that," he would say. To which, we would either laugh or roll our eyes and relinquish the remote so he could go back to napping—I mean "watching." But always in that scene were either his Bible, his class notes, or some Bible class papers that he was grading, on his lap. His devotion to his students and church members understanding the glory of God from the Word of God was a normal part of his life, and it was contagious. It is something I am honored to have caught.

My dad's fifty plus years of pastoral/teaching ministry took him throughout the Midwest (Minnesota, Wisconsin, North Dakota, and Nebraska), but his legacy has gone all over the world through the hundreds of students that soaked up his biblical gems and enjoyed his British wit, which sometimes took you off guard a little! My husband and I are just two of those students who sat in his Bible or Preaching or History classes at Trinity Bible College in Ellendale, North Dakota, where his charismatic teaching style spanned over twenty-five years. So many stories on that campus involve my dad. One of them is about the beloved wooden pulpit, which now sits in the prayer chapel on Trinity's campus, dedicated to my dad with a plaque. His admiration of this pulpit was, like many things with my dad, funny and reverent at the same time. I think his appreciation for the solid, wooden pulpit (as opposed to the clear, plastic pulpit) was a symbol of what he wanted his students to catch and run with—the Word of God is a solid foundation. There was one Principles of Preaching class (you know who you are) who hid that clear, plastic pulpit around campus in an effort to support my dad's passion for the solid, wooden pulpit. Well done, class! I don't recall if anyone got in trouble, but I know it filled my dad with reserved British delight!

At the end of his teaching career at Trinity, my dad was affectionately referred to as "Pope Jones."Retiring at seventy-five years old, he then resided in an assisted living home near Minneapolis, Minnesota. At eighty-three, he anticipated going home to be with Jesus, and my mom who went to heaven in July 2019; and, as I sat with him, his faith never wavered! Some days were difficult for him to communicate or to get around, but if you asked him to pray for you, the glory still fell! I wish everyone could know the covering of a father's prayer over them; the memories of his prayers always bring tears to my eyes now. His life seemed small in his room at Waterford Manor, whittled down to necessities, memorabilia, and some family pictures hanging on the wall, but his influence for Jesus spans the globe. And I inherited the seed of that influence in the form of his notes and books. What an overwhelming treasure!

That treasure came to me in a box, a moving box to be precise. At first, that box sat at my sister's house in a Minneapolis suburb until we had the chance to transport it home to Pennsylvania. Once home, the notebooks and sermons made their way onto a bookshelf. I would read a sermon or leaf through his Bible study notebooks every once in a while, always blessed by the wisdom I gained. In these quiet moments, I truly appreciated the scripture, "For the word of God is alive and active" (Hebrews 4:12, NIV). To think that some of his sermons or notes were written sixty years ago, and yet, they still have spiritual impact, is amazing.

One winter afternoon, my husband and I were out for a Sunday drive and were talking about our future. We were in a middle ground of sorts, an in-between stage in our ministry life, and we were sharing our hearts with each other about what we knew God had called us to do, and with all He had entrusted us. As the conversation meandered through our experiences and callings, the topic of my dad's notes and sermons arose. I will never forget where we were when the calling to publish my spiritual heritage downloaded into my heart and soul. We were in my husband's white diesel truck, on a cute, residential street in a sleepy, small central Pennsylvania town where the big-porched houses are so close to the sidewalk that a front yard doesn't have a chance! We were turning right, onto a different street with a big white house on the corner, and I started weeping as the profound weight of the calling to get this truth out into the world filled me up. I have no doubt that God positioned and called me to not only carry on my dad's legacy, but to encourage today's spiritual leaders to impart truth to the next generation.

So, here I am, looking at my bookshelf with his Bible commentary notes and sermons—some handwritten, some typed on a typewriter, but all rich with godly wisdom and his dry British wit that made the Bible come alive with power and relevance. And now, it is my turn. It's my turn to pass on this torch of biblical reverence, Holy Spirit revelation, and relatable practicality to you, the reader, whether you are a past congregant of his or a previous student in one of his classes at Trinity, or simply a learner who wants to broaden their understanding of Scripture. May you hear my dad's heart and voice almost as much as you capture the heart and voice of God as you read.

One thing you need to know before you partake of this scriptural feast is that my dad unapologetically loved the King James Version of the Bible. Especially if you've been in a Bible or preaching class of his, you have heard his amusing rants about how the King James is the only version that is worth our time. Is this KJV adoration strictly because he is British, and it was translated for a British king? Ha ha! That is not his reason; however, it did make him all the more pleased to be British himself. The reason for this singular Bible version focus is because it is the first English translation taken directly from the original languages of Hebrew (Old Testament) and Greek (New Testament), therefore being the most accurate English translation of the original text. So, when the Acts scripture is quoted in the text of this book, it will be in King James because I am using the actual notes my dad used as he prepared for his college Bible classes. Sometimes he used other versions to make a point, and those are noted accordingly. I've done my best to stay true to his original intent and thoughts as I paraphrase and compile his life's work into books and make them accessible to anyone who has a hunger for the Word of God.

There is one other thing to note before we dive in. You will find in this book two different names used to denote the third person of the Trinity: Holy Ghost and Holy Spirit. To avoid confusion, allow me to explain. The King James Version of the Bible uses the term "Holy Ghost" because it was translated in 1611, and in old English, that was the wording of the day that was used to describe "an immaterial being." As language changed throughout the centuries, this word morphed into the word "Spirit." So, because the King James Version is used throughout the book, but other translations as well, and also because my dad would use "Holy Spirit" in his notes, you will see both names used. But rest assured, "Holy Ghost" and "Holy Spirit" are interchangeable, and both refer to the third Person of the Trinity.

I suggest having a Bible with you to follow along, and reading each chapter in the Bible before reading the corresponding chapter in this commentary. It will make so much more sense to you. Or you can follow along on a Bible app on your phone or device; I recommend YouVersion or Blue Letter Bible.

So, grab your Bible or open your app, and get ready to eat some meat!

Promise, Prayer, and Pragmatics

Acts Chapter 1

My dad was Pentecostal, but he was also proper and level-headed when it came to things of the Holy Spirit. He was known for saying, "I don't care how high ya jump (in relation to an outward manifestation of the presence of the Holy Spirit) as long as you walk straight when you come down." In other words, you can hoot and holler all you want when you feel the Holy Spirit move, but when you come down from that spiritual experience and land in your normal, mundane life, job, and tasks, you'd better be sensible about things and walk with integrity.

Acts chapter 1 is a perfect mix of a spiritual experience and the practical side of life. This chapter opens with Jesus giving His followers the promise of the Holy Spirit with some instruction, and then, His ascension into heaven. Talk about a spiritual experience! In verse 13, the action moves to the upper room, where His followers wait and pray for this promise. In the midst of the ten days of waiting, they take some time for practical things and replace Judas in their group of twelve apostles: promise, prayer, pragmatics.

At 7:30 a.m. on a chilly September day in North Dakota, the second day of class at Trinity Bible College, David L. Jones was open for business with his briefcase, Bible, and British wit! The first day of class is always the go-through-the-syllabus day, but on the second day, we sink our teeth into the book of Acts! He opened this first day of teaching with a rousing, "Good morning, folks!" A few students mumbled a "good morning" back to Brother Jones, as he was affectionately called. "Did you all have your coffee this morning? I've had my cup of tea, which is better than coffee, so WATCH OUT, I'm wired," he would say with a chuckle. He so often amused himself, which inevitably amused others; it's a good connection.

And that was part of his charm—that connection and amusement. Students never quite knew what was going to come out of his mouth next, whether it would be something that would make you chuckle along with him, something that would make you think deeply, or something that would touch your soul with wisdom. He kept everyone on their toes in the classroom, office, or hallway.

So, join me as we enter the classroom, his office, or a hallway where any of these scriptural truths could be on his mind and out of his mouth at any moment.

* * *

Promise Acts 1:1-11

Luke is no doubt the author of Acts. "The former treatise" is a strong indication of his authorship because the literal translation of "former" is "first of two." Luke was the first of two letters written by Luke; Acts was the second. Also, Acts 1:1 mirrors Luke 1:3 in that he addresses Theophilus in each book's beginning.

"O Theophilus" (v. 1). Theophilus means "beloved by God" or "the friend of God" and thus could be applied to any Christian reading the book of Acts. It is supposed that Theophilus was a gentile convert who lived somewhere other than Palestine. He must have been a man of integrity and held in high esteem by Luke, as well as others, because Luke addresses him as "most excellent Theophilus" (Luke 1:3).

> The former treatise have I made, O Theophilus, of all that Jesus began both to do and teach. (Acts 1:1)

The word "began" in this verse is noteworthy, for it is the token of Luke's writings. It occurs thirty-one times in the Gospel of Luke and ten times in the book of Acts. AND THERE IS A RICH TRUTH HERE! What Jesus began to do here on earth, He has never ceased to do; He just shifted His headquarters and mode of operation. Great works shall ye do by the acts of the Holy Spirit!

Notice the order here: first, He DID, and THEN, He taught. How unlike the Pharisees who "say and do not" (Matthew 23:3). Christ perfectly exemplified His own doctrine. He did what He said; and so must we.

The book of Acts merely takes up where the gospels leave off, when Christ was received up and His work was done on the earth. How He carried it on through His disciples, energized by the Holy Ghost, is the grand subject of the book of Acts.

Notice Jesus's dependence upon the Holy Spirit in His earthly ministry: "After that he through the Holy Ghost had given commandments" (v. 2). He found it necessary to depend upon the Holy Ghost, from His mighty works to His instruction of the disciples. The apostles were chosen by Him for a distinct ministry of the Holy Spirit and, in the same sense, so are we chosen of God for a distinct ministry of the Holy Spirit.

The theme of Acts, Christ is risen, comes to the forefront in verse 3: "To whom also he shewed himself alive after his passion" (His suffering and death). It was this revelation that began to change the spiritual attitude of all the disciples. This is why we see these wonders done. It is on these two factors, His atoning work and His resurrection, that rest the validity of the church today.

Now, to alleviate any doubt, Jesus showed Himself "by many infallible proofs" for "forty days" after His resurrection (v. 3). He taught them of the kingdom of God. He opened the Scriptures to them (Luke 24:45-47), commissioned them as "sent ones," and charged them to preach repentance. Then, He commanded them to wait for the anointing of the Holy Ghost because they would need the power of the Holy Ghost to accomplish this.

Verse 4 shines a light upon the latter instruction of Jesus to wait. "And, being assembled together" indicates the closeness of their relationship with their Lord and with each other. And how important THAT is!

He commanded them (or charged them, is the wording of Jesus here), and it is significant. This word "commanded" is the Greek word παραγγέλλω, pronounced parang-gel-lo, and it is used two other times in Acts. Acts 10:42 reads, "And he commanded us to preach unto the people," and Acts 17:30 says, "But now commandeth all men every where to repent." So, these strong commands in Acts were to wait for the Spirit, to preach the gospel, and to repent of sin. This little study on the word "command" illustrates to us the importance and the seriousness of our relationship with God. THIS IS NOT A GAME!

With respect to the command to wait for the Spirit, it is because they were not yet fully equipped for service. They needed what the Father had promised, as Jesus taught them in John 16:7-15. He said that He must go away so the Comforter and Guide could come to them.

The promise is communicated in Acts 1:5, "Ye shall be baptized with the Holy Ghost." This promise is also given in each of the Gospels: Matthew 3:11, Mark 1:8, Luke 3:16, and John 1:33. It seems that God placed a real importance on a personal experience with Him, and of His power to carry on what Jesus had begun, because of the expediency of the promise, "Not many days hence." That was the expectation because the day of Pentecost was not fully come, but the message to us is: BE FILLED NOW! We do not have to wait like the disciples did; we have access now. Praise God! To quote my dad, "That almost makes this British preacher jump and shout in excitement!"

The disciples' question in verse 6 reflects the limitation of their spiritual understanding: "Wilt thou at this time restore again the kingdom to Israel?" They were concerned with a Jewish monarchy when Jesus was trying to establish a spiritual monarchy in their own hearts. This illustrates the carnality of our desires in the light of God's desire for us. The truth is that they needed the Holy Spirit to completely revolutionize their thinking concerning God's purpose and plans.

As to their question, Jesus answered, "It is not for you to know" (v. 7). It is most gratifying to realize that what God wants me to know, He will reveal to me as I open my heart to His truth. Now the rest of His work I must take by faith. In verse 8, He brings them back again to the real issue—THEIR REAL NEED—they needed the power of the Holy Spirit: the power of God! Their response showed that. God knows what we need, even when we don't understand our own needs.

Let's take a look at the two words translated "power" here in (vv. 7–8). They are two different words, which may help us relate to that which God gives us here in Acts. Verse 7 uses the word "power," speaking of the "authority" of the Father. The word in the original Greek is *exousia*, meaning the absolute, unrestricted power of God. This word can also be translated to mean "denoting the freedom of action or the right to act."[1] In verse 8, the word "power" in the original Greek is *dunamis,* pronounced *doo-nam-is*. This refers to the manifestation of God's power.[2]

Thus, the baptism of the Holy Spirit does not make us "little gods" to act as we will; it gives us the ability and the right to manifest God's power. The power and authority is with God; the manifestation is with us. The key word of the book of Acts is POWER, and specifically, showing God's power; thus we are His witnesses. "Ye shall be witnesses unto me both in Jerusalem, and in all Judaea, and in Samaria, and unto the uttermost part of the earth" (v. 8). The apostles being witnesses in Jerusalem, where they live, is portrayed in Acts chapters 1-7; and in Judaea and Samaria, the places beyond

1 James Strong, "1849, Exousia," Strong's Greek: 1849. Εξουσία (Exousia)—power (Bible Hub), accessed September 17, 2022. https://biblehub.com/greek/1849.htm.

2 James Strong, "1411, Dunamis," Strong's Greek: 1411. Δύναμης (Dunamis)—power (Bible Hub), accessed September 17, 2022. https://biblehub.com/greek/1411.htm.

where they live, is shown in Acts 8:1-11:18. That order, first where we live and then beyond where we live, is still God's order for us today.

After the promise had been given to the apostles by Jesus, it was time for Him to ascend to His heavenly home. The ends of the Gospels give some details of His exit plan: Luke 24:50 states, "And he led them out as far as to Bethany, and he lifted up his hands, and blessed them." After this blessing, He was taken up (v. 9). They were eyewitnesses of His ascension. Think about it, folks; WE may be eyewitnesses of His coming again!

Verse 9 continues: "And a cloud received him out of their sight." This was no ordinary cloud, but a prophetic picture of what WILL be: "And they shall see the Son of man coming in the clouds of heaven with power and great glory." (Matthew 24:30)

At this point in the class, my dad would bang the lectern (partly for impact and expression, and partly to wake up any student who happened to nod off) and say, "BELIEVER! He will come as He went." And then he would chuckle at himself for his wit and the pure enjoyment of truth being uttered. He might even call out, by name, the kid that he had just woken up!

So, how did the disciples respond to His ascension? Verse 10 answers that question: "And while they looked stedfastly." "Looked stedfastly," in this verse, means with intense and earnest gaze. When was the last time you were intense or earnest? It wasn't the angels, "Two men stood by them in white apparel," that speak to us here, but the "gaze" of the disciples. As they saw Him go, let us look for Him to return—with that same intensity and earnestness.

The angels spoke to the disciples, "Ye men of Galilee," they began (v. 11). The mention of their nationality, as in Acts 2:7, where the Jewish devout men in Jerusalem at that time marveled at the way those Galilaeans were speaking, emphasizes their lowly place from a worldly point of view. It also serves to magnify God's grace and power. He manifests His power through yielded, committed, human vessels, no matter what their lot in life. The angels go on to say to them, "Why stand ye gazing up into heaven?" The angels were saying that Jesus would return, but a period of time would pass. Their message was, and is, that in this interval, the presence of the Holy Spirit is to be the pledge of His return. Ephesians 1:14 calls it "the earnest of our inheritance." Jesus taught that the ministry of His Holy Spirit attests to His return. PRAISE GOD!

Prayer Acts 1:12-14

Verse 12 shows obedience in motion: "Then returned they unto Jerusalem from the mount called Olivet, which is from Jerusalem a sabbath day's journey." There is a study here on the matter of obedience to the Lord in the particular demands that He may make of us. There was no real significance in the fact that they should tarry in Jerusalem, except that it was a center of activity. And there was no spiritual significance unless it was the fact that the Holy Spirit would descend upon them in the same locale from which Jesus ascended. So, the real issue in their necessity to return to Jerusalem was that it was part of the command of Jesus to "wait for the promise of the Father" (v. 4). It could just as well have been Bethany or Jericho, but Jesus commanded them to wait in Jerusalem. It is significant to mention here that the Lord means what He says. We tend to forget that in our permissive society. Also, it seemed necessary at this initial outpouring that the apostles be together. Thus, the command to wait in Jerusalem.

> And when they were come in, they went up into an upper room, where abode both Peter, and James, and John, and Andrew, Philip, and Thomas, Bartholomew, and Matthew, James the son of Alphaeus, and Simon Zelotes, and Judas the brother of James. (Acts 1:13)

Whether they were in Jerusalem or Jericho did not matter; where the upper room was is beside the point. The important matter is that they were obedient to the command of Jesus to tarry (wait) until the Holy Spirit endowed them all with power. And they were all there; all of the apostles, except Judas Iscariot. Even doubting Thomas was there.

I know that with the advent of the Holy Spirit, the theological need of "wait for His endowment of power" is done away, but let us never become so matter-of-fact about the ministry of the Holy Spirit in our lives that we never come to appreciate those times of waiting in His presence. There is too much matter-of-fact ministry happening today, without the weight of a life lived in His presence!

This is a great spot, as his daughter, to speak of my dad's "waiting in His presence." My dad, having been born in 1938, was a teenager in the 1950s (lucky guy!), and he tells stories of a downstairs prayer room in their church building in Minneapolis, then called "The Tab." It was a room strictly set aside for prayer, and it was customary for groups to go down to the prayer room just to wait in God's presence. Oh, what a rich treasure my dad got to take advantage of; time set aside just to wait for God to make His presence known! He was a teenager, so was every single time he went down there filled with pure, godly motive? Probably not. In fact, he also talks about the cute, blue-eyed blonde who would also be down in the prayer room: my mom!

However, the presence of God was known in thickness, and the art of waiting was demonstrated, appreciated, and learned. There is a little plug for taking your kids to church! Fast forward fifty years, and add a daughter and son-in-law in ministry with him in North Platte, Nebraska. My dad planned Saturday evening prayer meetings in preparation for Sunday ministry to take place the next day. I didn't always go due to young motherhood or youth activities, but when I was present, I was always moved by my dad's praying. It wasn't the eloquence of words; it wasn't the length of the prayer; it was hardly even English. But every once in a while, he would utter, "Glory to God," in his deep, only-when-praying voice. What moved me so was the evident presence of God that his praying brought. It was almost a groaning (the word travail comes to mind). His desire for God to show Himself to his congregation the next day was the cry of his heart. Much like the word travail connotes, his prayers were birthing the manifest presence of God to be evident the following day in that place. His hunger for God's presence inspired me and made me want more of God in my own life. As a minister, it also taught me the unquestionable need to depend on the Holy Spirit and not my own efforts. This is a part of my spiritual heritage for which I am very thankful!

We pick back up with verse 14 and another key theme in Acts, and for the church today. "These all continued with one accord" is one of the most significant statements in the New Testament. It is THE key to the Acts of the Holy Spirit manifesting in and through the church. The disciples had a oneness of mind and heart. There was a unity unexcelled in all of God's creation.

Listen, for God to work in power through the church, there must, of necessity, be this accord! There was accord of supplication or purpose (Acts 1:14), accord of expectation (Acts 2:1), accord of consecration (Acts 4:24), accord of separation (Acts 5:12), and accord of cooperation (Acts 15:25). Thus, they continued. And for every mention of this oneness of heart and mind, there was a demonstration of the ministry of the Holy Spirit of God.

The word "continued" in verse 14, in its original language, is a very strong word indicating a tenacious endurance. The actual Greek word translated "continue" here is προσκαρτερέω, pronounced pros-kar-ter-eh-o, literally meaning, "steadfastly continuing, to give unremitting care to, to wait on continually."[3] Thus, in this attitude, they

---

3 James Strong, "4342, Proskartereho," Strong's Greek: 4342. **Προσκαρτερέω** (proskartereho)—continue (Bible Hub), accessed September 17, 2022, https://biblehub.com/greek/4342.htm.

continued in prayer and supplication to God. Listen folks, it was not cut and dried recitation. It was a heartfelt cry to God for His promise, "Pour out of thy Spirt, O God!" And a similar attitude must be ours today for a continual outpouring of His power and blessing.

Pragmatics Acts 1:15-26

The ten days between the ascension and Pentecost were days of orientation in many respects. Peter was the leader now, even as it seems he was during Christ's earthly ministry. Remember, Peter had received a special commission from Christ for this post-ascension/church age, directed now by the Holy Spirit.

There were about 120 people gathered in the upper room. This did not represent the whole company of disciples; some were resident elsewhere or absent. Actually, it was only a minority that waited together for the promise of the Father. Sadly enough, there are still those who, for various reasons, fail to seek the Holy Spirit for power in their lives. First Corinthians 15:6 states this truth from the apostle Paul's pen: "He (Jesus) was seen of above five hundred brethren at once; of whom the greater part remain unto this present, but some are fallen asleep." However, the promise of the Holy Spirit is for "all flesh."

Peter's reference to Psalm 41:9 in verse 16, "Even my close friend, whom I trusted, the one who shared my bread, has lifted up his heel against me" (BSB), shows their faith in the inspiration of Scripture. Peter says, "This scripture must needs have been fulfilled, which the Holy Ghost by the mouth of David spake." Their awareness of the Holy Spirit's ministry was becoming more keen. Compare this with previous times when Peter was completely unaware of the Spirit's ministry. Peter attests to the work of the Holy Spirit throughout Scripture when later, in 2 Peter 1:21, he writes, "Holy men of God spake as they were moved by the Holy Ghost." David, who wrote the psalms referenced here in Acts, was one of that number of holy men. And the reference was fulfilled before their eyes, even down to the details in the upcoming verses.

The end of verse 16 speaks of "Judas, which was guide to them that took Jesus." The word translated "guide" here is always used of unholy men in the New Testament. Matthew 15:14 and 23:16, 24 speak of blind guides. Romans 2:19-27 warns us of sinful guides. Here in Acts 1:16, it has the connotation of a traitor guide. Thus, Judas, who should have guided sinners to know and accept and follow Christ, instead, guided the wicked to take Him as prisoner. The worst part of the crisis of Judas is in the next verse, "For he (Judas) was numbered with us" (v. 17). Here's some truth for you: it is possible to be numbered among God's own disciples and have nothing of the love and compassion of Christ Himself. Flip over to the book of Hebrews in your Bible and read this passage: Hebrews 6:4-6. It contains sobering truth about turning away from God. This passage describes the fate of one who has tasted the things of God and then rejects Him. Sadly, Judas is an example of one such person!

The end of verse 17 says, with regard to Judas, "And had obtained part of this ministry." He had received by special divine appointment an important office: apostle. But Judas failed to take the responsibility that constituted personal development. Let this truth hit you hard: having an official position, or knowledge of God and His goodness, is no insurance in itself against failure and betrayal.

Verse 18 gives the awful account of Judas's end: "Now this man purchased a field with the reward of iniquity." This was Judas's own purchase from the money he had embezzled from the treasury of the apostles. The verse goes on to say that Judas, at that place he resorted to, committed suicide, "falling headlong." Upon hanging himself, apparently the rope subsequently broke, and he fell upon the jagged rocks and "burst asunder."

Why the detail and attention upon Judas at this point? It is to emphasize the horrible consequences of his sin. He had known the Savior, and was chosen by Him; yet, still he was deceived. So terrible was the consequence of Judas's act that all the countryside knew of it. They called the area the "field of blood" because of the suicide of Judas, who had betrayed Jesus.

Verse 20 concludes the mention of Judas with Peter quoting Psalm 69, which appears extensively in the New Testament for its prophetic words of Christ and His ministry. Peter demonstrates, once again, the apostles' dependence upon the inspired Word of God.

Acts 1:20 quotes Psalm 69:25, "Let his habitation be desolate." Habitation can be translated in various forms to mean sheepfold, farm building, or military camping place. These are all expressive of Judas's ministry as an apostle, but no more would he be God's shepherd, husbandman, or soldier. The end of verse 20 moves the group of apostles to take action and replace Judas: "And his bishoprick let another take." His place was desolated. Judas became a "has been," but the ministry he was chosen for would continue on. Let Judas's example be a warning to us of the false security of Christian fellowship. That alone does not secure our sanctification and personal relationship with Jesus.

The end of Acts chapter one completes the pragmatics of the apostles filling Judas's vacancy, as it defines the qualifications of an apostle in verses 21 and 22. It is a specific position or office; an apostle is a witness of Jesus. But more than that, he is a witness of the life of Jesus; and also of all He said and did from where His ministry began with the baptism by John to His resurrection and ascension. There are two possible exceptions to these qualifications: Judas and Paul. Judas disqualified himself from seeing the resurrected Jesus by ending his life. Paul was taught everything he needed to know by Jesus and was called by Jesus directly. See 1 Galatians 1:11-12 for reference to Paul being taught by Jesus Himself.

The apostolic ministry continues yet today, even though we are not eyewitnesses of Jesus Himself, as verse 21 dictates. There is a lesson for us here in continuing the apostolic ministry, and that is that a similar experience of personal conviction of the crucified, risen, and ascended Lord be ours. Personal association with Christ is an indispensable qualification in any ministry. The original apostles were both a personal witness of Christ and a witness of continuing ministry. We are now witnesses of the continuing ministry of apostleship as the church continues. Verse 23 shows us how the remaining apostles interpreted the instructions from the book of Psalms, "And they appointed (nominated) two, Joseph called Barsabas, who was surnamed Justus, and Matthias." Notice the order of their introduction: Joseph and then Matthias. Perhaps it was that they thought Joseph was the one to be chosen. But man's choice is not always God's choice. This choosing is a study in the sovereignty of God in human affairs.

Now to ascertain the divine choice, in verse 24, they prayed: "Thou, Lord, which knowest the hearts of all men, shew whether of these two thou hast chosen." This is the first recorded prayer, in public, of the church. When I imagine the scene, I envision Peter leading out in prayer. "Thou, Lord, which knowest" indicates they were convinced that He had already chosen one to fill this place of ministry, as He had originally chosen the Twelve. It is good to know that He knows. They asked Him to make His appointment by showing His choice. They prayed that they might know His will, as to not alter it.

We are again reminded of the tragedy of Judas in verse 25: "That he may take part of this ministry and apostleship, from which Judas by transgression fell." Judas went from the light of the Savior's presence to the darkness of his own place; his choice was in harmony with his character, and so was his end.

Some interesting truths arise out of this account: "And they gave forth their lots; and the lot fell upon Matthias" (v. 26). There is an absence of organization. Perhaps

Matthias was appointed neither by the apostles nor by the church, but directly by the Lord. Although some do believe that Paul was God's choice for the twelfth apostle since we never hear about Matthias after this mention of him in Acts, I leave it to you to ponder.

There is no mention of the laying on of hands or the gift of the Holy Spirit, for "the Holy Ghost was not yet given" (John 7:39b). This method of casting lots, adopted for learning the Lord's will, is thoroughly in the spirit of the Old Testament.

> He is to *cast lots* for the two goats—one lot for the LORD and the other for the scapegoat. (Leviticus 16:8, NIV)

> Be sure that the land is *distributed by lot*. What each group inherits will be according to the names for its ancestral tribe. (Numbers 26:55, NIV)

This method disappears after Pentecost; henceforth, the apostles are not guided by external signs but by the indwelling Spirit.

This incident concluded the preparation for the Holy Spirit to descend. The Lord prepared the way through His death, resurrection, and ascension. The church was prepared organically by the completion of the apostolic order according to Scripture. The individuals were prepared inwardly by the spirit of prayer. The same order follows today! The first two, the Lord and the church, are sealed, and the last preparation is up to each generation and every individual.

The Spirit's Descent and Impact

Acts Chapter 2

This would be the day that my reserved and dignified British father might get a little excited in class. "The promise delivered!" he would shout, as he entered the sleepy 7:30 a.m. class with his teaching Bible triumphantly lifted above his head. "Get ready, folks, this one will definitely keep you on the edge of your seat today," he would say; knowing full well that some well-meaning freshman would accidentally nod off, despite the glory of that day's lesson.

Imagine the disciples: the Spirit of power, yet meekness, that they witnessed in Jesus for three years was now alive in them. They probably did not even completely comprehend what that empowerment meant to them, but they felt it, and it changed them forever.

Remember that Jesus promised the disciples in John 14:12, "Very truly I tell you, whoever believes in me will do the works I have been doing, and they will do even greater things than these, because I am going to the Father" (NIV). Boom! He said it, and then He delivered. Wow! That's enough for this reserved, half-British/half-Scandinavian woman to shout, "Hallelujah!" and scare her dog that is loyally lounging on the ground next to her!

I think I heard the bell, and Dad has taken his place at the lectern. Let's listen in.

* * *

The Spirit's Descent Acts 2:1-4

This chapter introduces the advent of the Holy Spirit "upon all flesh." St. Augustine marks this event as the birth of the church. The day of Pentecost is the focal point of Acts. Without it, the book of Acts would never have been written. Note how the coming of Jesus and the coming of the Holy Spirit upon Jesus's ascension complement one another. When Jesus came, it was "God WITH us"; when the Holy Spirit came, it was "God IN us."

Thus we see the promise fulfilled, "When the day of Pentecost was fully come" (v. 1). The day of Pentecost, in Jewish tradition, was celebrated on the fiftieth day after the presentation of the first harvested sheaf of the barley harvest. It was fifty days from the first Sunday after Passover. This was the second of three great feasts between Passover and the Feast of Tabernacles. In the Old Testament, the day of Pentecost bears the names: "Feast of Weeks," "Feast of the Harvest," or "Day of First Fruits." It marked the close of the wheat or grain harvest—not of all the harvest, but a part of it (the first fruits). The complete harvest was celebrated by the Feast of Tabernacles.

To emphasize this feature of the Feast of Pentecost, a special offering was appointed apart from the other sacrifices: two wave loaves. Leviticus 23:17 gives the instruction, "From wherever you live, bring two loaves made of two-tenths of an ephah of the finest flour, baked with yeast, as a wave offering of firstfruits to the LORD" (NIV). It is important to note that, in the days of the apostles, Pentecost was the best attended of the Jewish feasts. Therefore, it is a most appropriate time for the descent of the Holy Spirit, as a great many people would be assembled in the city. A great many people were assembled, and as the "Day of First Fruits," it is significant that 3,000 souls were the first fruits of a greater harvest. Thus, the Passover found its fulfillment on the day of Pentecost (3,000 souls were added to the church). God's timing is perfect.

Only the Feast of Tabernacles awaits fulfillment, when the harvest of men shall be gathered in at His coming! "Was fully come," as verse 1 opens, was fulfilled according to Israelite law. Preparations were made to offer sacrifices to God. Verse 1 also tells us that "they were all with one accord in one place." The phrase "one accord" occurs eleven times in the book of Acts. The Greek word for this is *homothumadon.* Broken down, *homo* means "same" and *thumos* means "mind."[4] The church still needs this today. We must be of the same mind! Paul said in Philippians 1:27, "One spirit, with one mind striving together for the faith of the gospel." This holy accord is still the common denominator of Holy Spirit power.

"And suddenly there came a sound from heaven as of a rushing mighty wind" (v. 2). As God often does, this mighty work on the day of Pentecost occurred suddenly. And we can be sure of that which comes from heaven. As James puts it in chapter 1, verse

4 James Strong, "3661. Homothumadon," Strong's Greek:3661. ὁμοθυμαδόν (homothumadon)—with one mind (Bible Hub), accessed September 17, 2022, https://biblehub.com/greek/3661.htm.

17 of his book, "Every good gift and every perfect gift is from above." And the gift of the Holy Spirit that was given on the day of Pentecost surely does come from above; it filled the whole house. It is significant to note that it is the SOUND of a rushing, mighty wind. It is not wind, but a sound. Now, the word used here is not the usual word for wind, but rather, it is usually rendered breath, i.e., violent breath, or a blowing or blast. LISTEN! It was a holy breath from heaven. Wind is expressive of God's demonstration. In John 3:8, Jesus told Nicodemus about the freedom of wind, and He compared it to "every one that is born of the Spirit." Another example of God using wind to express His power is found in Ezekiel 37; God told Ezekiel to prophesy to the wind to breathe upon the dry bones that they may live. As sound naturally speaks of invisible energy, so the sound told of the energizing divine Spirit.

Acts 2:3 shows that the manifestation of the Spirit Himself was visual, as well as audible: "There appeared to them tongues of fire, distributed and resting on each one of them" (RSV). Again, it was not necessarily fire itself, but "tongues like as of fire." Nevertheless, the fire represents the divine presence of God, as in Exodus 3:2 when God appeared to Moses in the form of a burning bush that did not burn up. It also complements the account of John the Baptist's prophecy found in Matthew 3:11 and Luke 3:16: "He shall baptize you with the Holy Ghost, and with fire." It is an emblem of the Spirit's power. Also, fire is significant because of its cleansing, purifying, and sanctifying power. The form of tongues does not go unnoticed; for He had come to empower them to speak with boldness.

"And they were all filled with the Holy Ghost, and began to speak with other tongues" (v. 4). It is important to note the focus, the sign, and the Source of the power they received. The focus was on being "filled," the sign was "speaking with other tongues," and the Source was the Holy Spirit. This experience was visual, audible, and experiential, whereas wind and fire were the emblems (external evidence) of the manifestation of the Spirit Himself. Tongues being spoken by the 120 in the upper room was a sure sign that the Holy Ghost indwelled them as well, not just the apostles.

The Holy Spirit took entire possession of them and imparted to the fullest extent of their capacity His grace and power. Thus, we are yet in the divine age of the Holy Spirit! God manifests Himself and waits to indwell EACH OF US. The speaking in tongues was a "title deed," not the property of the empowering of the Holy Spirit. A title deed is the proof, or the evidence, of the possession of real property. The title deed itself has no actual value. It can also be said then that speaking in tongues was the proof, or evidence, of the Holy Spirit's indwelling. The real value is the indwelling of the Holy Spirit. So, they were praising God and magnifying Him. Thus, tongues became the first evidence of the Holy Spirit's empowering and can rightly be regarded as the initial evidence of His coming today.

The most important happening, outside of Calvary and the resurrection, that has changed the course of the world, happened on the day of Pentecost. The simple description in those first four verses of chapter two is still making an impact upon the world today. And it made its impact on me in that downstairs prayer room at *The Tab*, short for *The Tabernacle*, back in the 1950's. It wasn't all Elvis and sock hops in the '50s, folks! We experienced the Holy Spirit in a simple prayer room in the basement of a church in Minneapolis. And all because we sought to know Him. Do YOU know Him?

The Crowd's Reaction Acts 2:5-13

Verse 5 begins with some setting details of this story: "And there were dwelling at Jerusalem Jews, devout men." The crowd was there because it was feast time; in fact, the most popular feast on the Jewish calendar. They were people whose dispersion went back for centuries, but whose religious heritage was so vital to them that they came back to Israel for this feast. They were devout men; this is evident from the fact that they were at the prescribed feast. LISTEN, the church could use some of that sort of devotion TODAY! The verse goes on, "Out of every nation under heaven." Jews were found in practically every civilized country. Now the verse becomes more than a historical account, but is illustrative of God's Word and His desire to reach all men with the truth of the gospel.

"Now when this was noised abroad" is a reference to the different tongues being spoken freely by Jesus's followers. When the people heard them speaking in tongues, "the multitude came together." The crowd's response then was confused amazement: "and were confounded, because that every man heard them speak in his own language" (v. 6). Pentecost was disturbing and arresting. There was a power resting upon them that was evidenced distinctly by this sign. Hear this, the reaction to the manifestation of the Holy Spirit will always be similar to the reaction of that day. First Corinthians 14:22 upholds this: "Wherefore tongues are for a sign, not to them that believe, but to them that believe not." The miracle of Pentecost always draws attention to the message of Pentecost—Jesus Christ Lives! They were confused, to say the least, and this phenomenon continues in our day: men speaking in tongues unknown to them, but understood by others.

"They were all amazed and marvelled, saying one to another, Behold, are not all these which speak Galilaeans?" (v. 7). Thus, not only the miracles, but the considered Source of the miracles. These Galilaeans profoundly confused the whole matter because the Galilaean dialect was easily recognized. Various pronunciations were peculiar to them, and they were a despised people; a lowly class. Hence the statement, "Are not all these which speak Galilaeans?" All of this greatly confused the issue but built the case for the miracle.

Allow me to take a moment to tell a well-known Trinity secret on my dad: He can pull out his British accent at a moment's notice. Do you want to know why he didn't keep his accent, while my grandma did until her death? Picture ten-year-old David Jones in his British knickers, the youngest of the five Jones boys, arriving in America on Christmas Eve 1948; fresh off the boat, a snowy New York City holiday greets him in his proper attire. I am sure he was chilly and felt out of place. Several days of travel found the family in their new home in Minneapolis, Minnesota. His new surroundings were quite different than his familiar London. It was America, but the Midwest at that, and with Scandinavians all around him. No longer looking or sounding like everyone else, he had to lose his accent for sheer grade school survival! What a shame, as the British accent has such a distinguished and recognizable lilt.

Let's pick back up in verse 8, "And how hear we every man in our own tongue, wherein we were born?" It was a miracle indeed. Now, this passage has become a stumbling block to some, and misinterpreted. Because they spoke in various understood languages, it is declared that they had the gift for the purpose of preaching. But it was Peter who did the preaching (vv. 14-40). The ministry of tongues in the public setting was as it is today: to draw attention to the message of Christ—to glorify Jesus.

Luke then lists in verses 9-11 several places represented by men in the crowd who heard their language. "We do hear them speak in our tongues the wonderful works of God" (v. 11). And THAT is the function of public tongues today. It drew this reaction: "They were all amazed, and were in doubt, saying one to another, What meaneth this?" Others, mocking, said, "These men are full of new wine." Now, in these two verses, Acts 2:12–13, we find two opinions of Pentecost that still exist today! And every one of us falls into one category or the other. One expresses interest, "What meaneth this?" The other, ridicule, "These are drunk." It is important for us to constantly evaluate our spiritual reactions. I believe that those who were interested were filled with the Holy Spirit, but others simply said, "They are drunk." Paul later exhorted with this illustration in Ephesians 5:18, "Be filled with the Spirit." And this is the ultimate of it all! It is not the tongues; they are merely a sign. It is the intoxication of the Spirit that we need. The possession of every fiber of our being by God's Holy Spirit—the fullness. Let that be our desire.

Peter's Preaching Acts 2:14-41

Peter's message on the day of Pentecost may be the greatest message the world will ever hear because it exalts Jesus Christ. The passage before us constitutes Peter's introduction of the Holy Spirit and the validity and credentials of Christ's ministry, ending with the response of conviction by its first-century hearers. It is an explanation to the assembled multitude, of the phenomena taking place. In this introduction, Peter first answers the reckless charges against the disciples and then explains the sign.

Luke indicates that he spoke with dignity and authority. He "lifted up his voice" and said, "Hearken to my words." Note the marked difference in Peter, in particular, from the pre-Pentecost days. Peter says, "For these are not drunken, as ye suppose." He denies this charge of drunkenness by applying a bit of logic: it was 9:00 a.m. "It is but the third hour of the day." The Jewish sabbath was from sunrise to sunset, making 6:00 a.m. the beginning of the day. Now, devout Jews customarily ate nothing until about the fourth hour, and some waited until noon. It appears that they, the Jews, drank wine only with their evening meal. Thus, the charge of drunkenness had no foundation, and Peter appealed to their universal custom to show this. After showing what it was NOT, in a very short, direct manner, Peter preached a whole message explaining this distinct work of God. Christians need to learn from that today. Listen, we don't need to defend the Holy Spirit message today; we need to demonstrate it, preach it, and explain it.

Peter's explanation begins with a reference to an Old Testament promise: "But this is that which was spoken by the prophet Joel" (v. 16). It is interesting to note that of the 431-word summary of Peter's message, 225 words were scripture quotations. And that must still be the heart of the Holy Ghost message today—the Word of God.

Quoting the prophet Joel, "And it shall come to pass in the last days, saith God." Joel actually used the word "afterward." There is no mystery here. Peter is simply more specific and indicates the time between the first and second comings of the Messiah—the church age. More scriptural indications of this movement are found in Hebrews 1:2, "Hath in these last days spoken unto us by his Son," and 1 Peter 1:20, "Was manifest in these last times for you."

Quoting Joel here in verses 17-18, Peter listed things that would transpire as a result of the outpouring: prophecy, visions, and dreams. And for emphasis, prophecy is mentioned again. Actually, all of the predictions belong to all the subjects; there is no distinction. The Spirit is to be poured out "upon all flesh." The term "pour" is significant, for it expresses the readiness of the Spirit to fill waiting hearts. It speaks of the abundance of God's provision. He does not ration us.

Peter then continued Joel's prophecy, in verses 19–20, to show how long the Holy Spirit will be poured out, as this word suggests a multiplied fulfillment. All that Joel spoke of did not occur that day, but it was fulfilled, it is being fulfilled, and it will be fulfilled. It is interesting to note the comparison between the description of the end times given by Joel and that given by Jesus in Luke 21:9–11, 25–26. Joel speaks of a move of the Holy Spirit on everyone; but Jesus warns of wars, natural disasters, and fear. Note also that John the Baptist spoke of the outpouring of the Holy Spirit, and immediately after, of the final judgment (Luke 3:16–17). Peter's message was that signs and wonders would occur before the day of the Lord.

The redeeming promise is stated here, "That whosoever shall call on the name of the Lord shall be saved" (v. 21). And all this time, salvation's door has been open. In essence, he was saying that this was the purpose of the outpouring. What a mighty invitation this is! What a message we have: Whosoever. The Lord. Delivered. That'll preach!

When Peter had secured their attention and explained the phenomena, he followed with a masterful statement concerning the validity of Christ's ministry. This was especially important in the Jewish world; and it is equally important today when false christs shall appear (Matthew 24:24). Three verses directly and pointedly set forth this message: Jesus is approved of God (vv. 22–24). Peter highlights this message in three ways: Jesus is approved of God by signs and wonders, crucified by Jews and raised again from the dead. Later, Peter declares Christ to be the Exalted One at the right hand of the Father, having sent forth "this, which ye now see and hear" (verse 33). Thus, he quickly outlines his message to his hearers. The logic and proof were without contest.

Peter, anointed by the Spirit, proved the infallibility of his message conclusively. And the message is still the same: Jesus—a man approved of God by miracles and wonders and signs (v. 22). The divinity of Jesus had been proven and accredited in their own midst by supernatural manifestation. No doubt many in the crowd had seen—there was no denying these works of God by Jesus. The whole Jewish world was witness of this proof of Jesus! Nicodemus, a Pharisee, recognized the significance of these works,

"We know that thou art a teacher come from God: for no man can do these miracles that thou doest, except God be with him." (John 3:2)

Also, the man born blind that we read about in John chapter 9, "Herein is a marvellous thing, that ye know not from whence he is, and yet he hath opened mine eyes... If this man were not of God, he could do nothing" (John 9:30-33). Jesus Himself had appealed to His works as grounds for their belief, "But if I do, though ye believe not me, believe the works: that ye may know, and believe, that the Father is in me, and I in him" (John 10:38). Thus, Peter firmly established the divine approval of Jesus as Christ the Messiah. He then touched on the predestined character of the death of Christ, showing it to be fixed in the plan of God. Note Acts 4:28 as proof of the determination made beforehand by God: "For to do whatsoever thy hand and thy counsel determined before to be done." According to the determinate counsel and foreknowledge of God, Jesus was "delivered" to the Jews to be crucified. The thought here is that Jesus could not have been crucified had God not permitted it. What Peter implies here is that they, the Jews, killed Jesus without restraint. "Ye have taken, and by wicked hands have crucified and slain, whom God hath raised up" (v. 23-24). Now, the contrast here seems to be in the way God set Him forth as Messiah (He came to reign) and the way the Jews in opposition opposed Him.

Peter then affirms that God raised Him from the dead, saying, "It was not possible that he should be holden of it" (v. 24). In bringing salvation, God overruled the wicked deed and raised Jesus from the dead. He is the firstborn from the dead; He is the proof of a future resurrection. To prove this assertion of Christ's resurrection, Peter appealed to them with David's writings, quoting the last four verses of Psalm 16:

> I have set the LORD always before me: because he is at my right hand, I shall not be moved. Therefore my heart is glad, and my glory rejoiceth: my flesh also shall rest in hope. For thou wilt not leave my soul in hell; neither wilt thou suffer thine Holy One to see corruption. Thou wilt shew me the path of life: in thy presence is fullness of joy; at thy right hand there are pleasures for evermore. (Psalm 16:8-11)

Again, he turns to Scripture, and Peter declares that David prophesied the resurrection with confidence. There is a grand lesson for us to rest in hope and be anxious for nothing—not only from a death and resurrection standpoint, but in our daily living. May our flesh rest in the hope of the soon return of our Lord.

"Thou wilt not leave my soul in hell." Christ, in the words of the Psalm, expressed His confidence in God that His soul would not be completely abandoned. Hades is the abode of departed spirits; the place into which men pass after death. The word itself literally means "the unseen." And into this realm, all depart at death, though the state of the saved and unsaved is entirely different. "Neither wilt thou suffer thine Holy One to see corruption." "Holy One" means not only holy, but actively affectionate toward God.

"Thou hast made known unto me the ways of life" (v. 28). As Peter continues to quote David from Psalm 16, there is little doubt that, in reference to Christ, it means resurrection life and the path thereof: trial, test, hardship, suffering, death. Jesus knew what He had to face. "Thou shalt make me full of joy with thy countenance" (v. 28). This, in effect, is the outcome of "I have set the LORD always before me" (Psalm 16:8). Thus, Peter sets forth Christ—who He is and what He has accomplished for us.

Dad taught the Principles of Preaching class for many years at Trinity Bible College; he taught my own husband how to preach. Like preachers of old, my dad used the adage "three points and a poem" for sermon structure and presentation. Read any of his, mostly, handwritten sermons and you will find three points to it. At this point in Acts class, Dad would say in his "tongue-in-cheek" but "I'm serious" way that, like any good preacher, Peter goes on to the third point of his three-point message. In the process of establishing the validity of Jesus as the Messiah, the Son of God, Peter shows that the verses he quoted from the Psalms do not refer in fullness to David. But they are perfectly fulfilled in the Son of David, the Lord Jesus Christ.

Verse 29 opens with, "Let me freely speak unto you of the patriarch David." Freely means literally "with boldness of speech," and such is essential when giving a testimony of Christ. David, Peter says, both died and was buried; therefore these words of Psalm 16 refer to someone else: Christ. It did not refer to David or Solomon, or any other king of Israel: "For David's sepulchre is with us unto this day."

Peter also quotes Psalm 132:11 directly, which states the promise of God to keep a descendant of David on the throne (v. 30). And 2 Samuel 7:12 gives more proof by explaining God's covenant with David, which points to the promise of God to David of a coming King. This maintains that Peter refers to Jesus. David saw by prophetic vision that the Messiah would come through him, and even that He would be raised from the dead. Quoting from verse 31, "His soul was not left in hell, neither his flesh did see corruption." Thus, we have the clear, consecutive, and forcible declaration of Peter from Psalm 16 that Jesus is the Messiah.

The words of Psalm 16 refer to a "Coming One." They cannot refer to David because he died and saw corruption. All Jews acknowledged that the Messiah was promised as Prince of the house of David. Therefore, this Psalm refers to the Messiah. Jesus was raised from the dead, and He is the expected Messiah. Now, all of the preceding verses, Acts 2:25-31, constitute the argument for the messiahship of Jesus.

In verse 32, we see Peter jump back to where he left off in verse 24 and continue his case: "This Jesus (emphatic sense) hath God raised up, whereof we all are witnesses." This truth is that upon which the gospel message depends. It implies the consumption of the Savior's atoning work, His power, and His influence as the living Lord. Furthermore, not only was He raised up, but He also ascended to the right hand of God, and what you see and hear from Peter is validation of that exaltation. The practical, everyday truth for us is that when Christ is exalted in our lives, there will, of necessity, be a demonstration of miracles in our lives. And the world will know it also; some will even say that we are drunk. They may call us "holy rollers," but others will ask, "What shall we do?" Glory to God!

Now, once again from Scripture, Peter proceeds to prove that Christ's exaltation was clearly predicted, as he quotes Psalm 110:1 in verse 34, "For David is not ascended into the heavens: but he (David) saith himself, the LORD said unto my Lord, sit thou on my right hand." "The LORD said unto my Lord," or Jehovah speaking to Christ, clearly announces the exaltation of Christ. It denotes Christ at the throne of divine power and authority.

Verse 35 continues with the Psalm 110 quote, "Until I make thy foes thy footstool." This implies ultimate victory! It is an illustrative term. To plant the foot upon the neck of a fallen enemy is a symbol of complete victory (see Joshua 10:24; 1 Samuel 17:51; 1 Corinthians 15:24-27).

"God hath made the same Jesus, whom ye have crucified, both Lord and Christ" (v. 36). Note that the lordship of Jesus is the ultimate test of His divine nature. As we have seen, the Psalms declare Him Lord of all. But so do Philippians and Hebrews, mirroring this verse in Acts. Philippians 2:9 says, "Wherefore God also hath highly exalted him." Hebrews 2:8b-9a declares, "We see not yet all things put under him. But we see Jesus." He is Lord, crowned with glory and honor! And then, our text points out that God hath made Jesus both Lord and Christ. He IS Lord. The obvious message for us humans is to make Him *our* Lord! Have you today?

With the awesome declaration that Peter emphatically proved, the messiahship of Jesus, then comes the power-packed punch of the altar call, or the challenge. Verse 37 opens by telling us the reaction of the crowd, "Now when they heard this, they were pricked in their heart." Here is plain evidence of the power of God's Word presented under the anointing of the Holy Spirit! The word in verse 37 that draws our attention is the word "pricked." It is an unusual word used only this one time in the New Testament. It means literally "pierced or penetrated, as with a needle or a sharp instrument." They were literally "broken in heart," as in Psalm 109:16, where the Hebrew meaning gives emphasis to a true sorrow in the inner man. And the truth is that sin is not a skin disease; it is a gross malady that requires the surgery of the Word of God. And this is exactly what began to happen here—the Word started to cut. Thus, the Holy Spirit fulfilled Christ's promise in John 16:8-9: "When he is come, he will reprove the world of sin." That is why people react the way they do; the Holy Spirit is ON THE JOB. Their reaction proved the truth of Peter's message. "What shall we do?" they asked each other (v. 37).

Paul asked the same question in his reaction to Jesus on the Damascus Road, "Lord, what wilt thou have me to do?" (Acts 9:6). The Philippian jailer also asked in Acts 16:30, "Sirs, what must I do to be saved?" These responsive questions imply true repentance. The declaration is basic; they were ready for the instruction of the disciples, or Jesus, in the case of Paul's experience. They were submissive to God's Word. Some Christians, though they have put their faith in Christ as Savior, have not gone beyond that. If this applies to you, please repent and ask the Lord to reveal His next step for you.

Peter's response was direct—He gives two requirements and two promises (vv. 38–39). The first requirement was: "Repent." Now, this is the door of the gospel. All of the blessings of the good news begin with our repentance. Repent means a change of mind, which will inevitably result in a change of conduct. What is the difference between false repentance and true repentance? The former fears only the consequences of sin, whereas the latter has an aversion to sin itself because it separates us from God.

The doctrine of repentance is mentioned often in Acts (3:19; 5:31; 8:22; 11:18; 13:24; 17:30; 19:4; 20:21). Confession is good for the soul! We need to practice repentance. It is one of the last great messages to the church in the book of Revelation—the church in Pergamos, to be exact. Revelation 2:16 gave a warning to that church, and subsequently to us—Repent—followed by a severe consequence. Of the seven letters written to churches in the book of Revelation, repentance being an admonishment given is something we need to take heed of as Christians.

The second requirement, following right after the first in verse 38, was, "Be baptized every one of you." This was to be the outward sign of an inward work. It was a public declaration of their faith in Jesus Christ as their Savior. Repentance, or turning from sin, must be followed by the definite acceptance of Christ; and baptism by immersion is the divinely appointed manner in which such faith is publicly expressed. Some of Jesus's last instructions to the disciples were to baptize those that believed on Him (Matthew 28:19-20 and Mark 16:15-16). "Every one of you" denotes the individuality of this work. Jesus is a personal God.

The promises are also declared in verse 38. The first promise is the remission of sins. That is a positive assurance of what God will do. The payment for our sins was already provided through Christ at Calvary. And WHAT A PROMISE THAT IS! We had an insurmountable debt upon us called sin. There is no way to pay, BUT repentance (true heart repentance) will cause Him to stamp PAID IN FULL on our account. Hallelujah!

The second promise is, "Ye shall receive the gift of the Holy Ghost" (future tense). This promise is to the same ones who had said, "His blood be on us, and on our children" (Matthew 27:25). Peter says that this gift shall be yours with repentance and obedience. And it is for all, even your children, as it states prophetically in Joel 2:28. Peter extends this to "all that are afar off." That promise can be fulfilled in every life no matter what the location, or dispensation, or heritage.

Peter wraps up his message with an emphasis on salvation (v. 40). He urges the crowd, in light of Christ's message, "Save yourselves from this untoward generation." It suggests that if we are to maintain our testimony and affect the world for God, we need ALL that God has for us. The church's first altar call ends triumphantly in verse 41, "And they that gladly received the Word were baptized." It implies that some may have already put their belief in Jesus. Nevertheless, 3,000 responded that day. Hallelujah!

The Church's Beginning Acts 2:42-47

The first church unfolds in verses 42-47 of Acts 2. These verses reveal the social and spiritual temperature of the church. They continued steadfastly and they had concern for one another; and as a result, they reaped a greater spiritual harvest. "They continued stedfastly" notes devotion and unwearied persistence. The word "stedfastly" is a key to the condition of revival that existed. The same Greek word is used elsewhere (Acts 1:14 and Mark 3:9) and translated "wait on Him." It is also used in Acts 10:7 with regard to Cornelius as "a devout soldier of them that waited on him continually."

The thought here illustrates our relationship to the Lord, which is to always be ready for His use. Isaiah expressed such an unwearied persistence as a great source of spiritual strength:

> Even the youths shall faint and be weary, and the young men shall utterly fall: but they that wait upon the LORD shall renew their strength; they shall mount up with wings as eagles; they shall run, and not be weary; and they shall walk, and not faint. (Isaiah 40:30-31)

In what did these new believers continue so steadfastly? The list is great: the apostles' doctrine, fellowship, the breaking of bread, and prayers. Apparently, the apostles had put together a system of doctrine, which they passed on to these new converts. It was vital for the growth of the church! Christ commanded in Matthew 28:19-20 to "teach all nations." Babes in Christ need to learn about their newfound Savior. We must KNOW what we believe. Fellowship is as vital as teaching, for the growth and development of the child of God. The breaking of bread refers to the eating of the evening meal, as in Luke 24:35. The evening meal for Christians was united with the Lord's Supper. The result was a unity of the believers. The same effect is ours today. The upper room unity continued through a same spirit of prayer, as they continued to pray together. Now, the truth of this verse is that the power of Pentecost touched every area of their lives! An outpouring of the Spirit in similar fashion will have an identical result today.

Verse 43 shows a feeling of awe among the people, "And fear came upon every soul." It was a renewed consciousness of God and His nearness, and interest in man; and this was further emphasized by what followed: "And many wonders and signs were done by the apostles." They acted on what Christ had taught them in Mark 16:17, "And these signs shall follow them that believe." And, folks, this is our promise too!

Those that were yet in Jerusalem pooled their resources and had "all things in common." How about that? A true picture of how a local church should function. It seems that this was a unique case, for it is not recorded in any other church in Scripture. Thus, here in Jerusalem, many of the believers were from a distance, and some were poor. The need of the hour, and the Spirit that prevailed, demanded such a reaction.

Verse 45 tells of this unparalleled generosity, "And sold their possessions and goods, and parted them to all men, as every man had need." "Sold and then parted" implies that they kept on selling and distributing from time to time, as necessity arose. Acts 4:32-5:11 give examples with Barnabas and Ananias & Sapphira. There was a common concern for one another's well-being, not only spiritually, but materially as well.

Verse 46 proves that with these words, "And they, continuing daily with one accord." Daily is the same word in the Greek as is used in verse 42 to show their devotion. They did not forsake the assembling of themselves together, as they were in the temple daily. Breaking bread from house to house was also a daily practice. The diligence of these matters points to the vitality of communion and fellowship: WE NEED ONE ANOTHER!

The last in this list describing the believers' behavior is "praising God." Pentecost is a message of joy and praise. Take the privilege of praise out, and we reduce our godward relationship to a cold form. It is often that in itself which melts cold hearts. It worked that way then, and it does still today.

The result of these actions by the first church is "the Lord added to the church daily" (v. 47). Now, the thought here is this: as the early Christians did their part, the Lord did His part. It is a basic principle of spiritual dynamic; and our hope is in the fact that principles don't change.

Healing for a Lame Man and a Sermon for the Jews

Acts Chapter 3

Is Brother Jones, as he is affectionally called, teaching or preaching? It's hard to differentiate since he easily goes back and forth between both, at either the lectern or the pulpit. You would walk out of the sanctuary or the classroom with equal amounts of biblical insight and personal application. And, of course, a joke or two; or as he called them in his Principles of Preaching class: "commercials." Without a doubt, this class or sermon would open with his iconic biblical humor, "This is the story of a man who asked for alms and got feet," he would say, and then get a kick out of his own joke…every single time.

So, pull up a chair in Acts class today, and let's count the times we are inspired by a biblical nugget of wisdom, along with the times he cracks a joke!

* * *

Healing for a Lame Man Acts 3:1-11

Although the believers had "favour with all the people" (Acts 2:47), these conditions were not to last long. The forces that opposed Christ and sent Him to the cross, would not remain hidden. This miracle brought them into the open once again and is the first recorded miracle of healing in the church. From the "many wonders and signs" noted in Acts 2:43, Luke is led by the Holy Spirit to select this one and to give the details concerning it. This miracle was significant because it was a turning point in the early development of the church. It resulted in a great gathering of souls and also aroused the Sanhedrin to its first opposition.

The first detail of the miracle noted by Luke here is the time of day. It was the ninth hour, or 3:00 p.m. Peter and John were on their way to afternoon devotions. Inspiring to think that even though they were taught by Jesus and newly filled with the Holy Spirit, they still needed this daily prayer meeting. They kept to their old rituals, for they found much ministry there and continued daily in the temple.

At the Gate Beautiful sat a man lame from birth. He sat at that accustomed place day after day, and was apparently well-known there because after the healing took place, many people recognized him. When he saw Peter, he immediately began to beg from him. Now, this story speaks to us of a lame world; he was unable to help himself. Since he was lame from birth, he truly was poor and could not provide for himself. Therefore, this story could be a bit of a rebuke to Israel based on the instructions given in Deuteronomy 15:11, "Open thine hand wide unto thy brother, to thy poor, and to thy needy, in thy land."

Peter's ready response to his request for money is a positive one, "Look on us" (v. 4). Having secured his attention, the man waited. Verse 5 puts it like this: the man "gave heed unto them, expecting to receive something." Peter went on, "Silver and gold have I none." His words were disappointing to the lame man, but the man's disappointment was short-lived because Peter continued, "But such as I have give I thee: In the name of Jesus Christ of Nazareth rise up and walk."

Now, let us speak of two vital matters here: the authority which was present and the lame man's expectation. The term "in the name" means "by authority of." Peter used this phrase in Acts 2:21-38. It recalls Jesus's statement, "These signs shall follow them that believe," in Mark 16:17-18. It speaks of all that Jesus was and is, the full revelation of Jesus Christ, alive and present in power. And Peter directed the lame man's faith to that Authority. In so doing, he was saying, "Jesus will heal you." The lame man's expectation teaches us a great lesson! What do you expect from God? His level of expectancy was low, really, but lest we judge until we consider our own level of expectancy. Some come to God expecting nothing. Some approach out of ritual half-heartedness in order to get a blessing. We need to expect God to probe us, and so work IN us that people see a difference in us. We will walk and leap and praise God as the lame man did in verse 8! What a different approach. Only the latter one allows Him to be Lord.

A Sermon for the Jews Acts 3:12-26

Here in chapter 3, Peter seizes upon another opportunity to preach the gospel—and the gospel ONLY. Here it is more specifically the gospel for the "men of Israel" (v. 12).

Now in this sermon, two new points of church doctrine are developed: the present power of the name of Jesus Christ (v. 16) and the hope of Israel, the coming of the messianic kingdom (vv.13-18).

The name of a person sums up everything we know about that person. So, to the Jews, the name of God was the sum of their revelation of God. And similarly, the name of Jesus Christ (the more they knew Him, the more they added to that name) would signify all that was contained in their revelation of God in Jesus Christ. Thus, in this name (Jesus) was preached repentance and forgiveness of sins. In His name, Peter raises up the lame man and works miracles. Thus, in speaking the name of Jesus, the apostles were unconsciously placing Jesus of Nazareth in the position of Jehovah of the Jews. And the whole sermon is marked by its numerous unfoldings of the different names of the Lord: Holy One, Just, Prince of Life, the Seed of Abraham, the Prophet, the Christ of God. Now this linking of names was important to the reception of Peter's preaching by those Jews. But more important was the fact that the special power of that Name was demonstrated by the miracles of spiritual and physical soundness—salvation. Hebrews 5:9 demonstrates this: "And being made perfect, he became the author of eternal salvation." It is no less of a fact of doctrine or a demonstration of truth for us today. Thus Peter used this miracle to show them, and us, the Source of such power.

To the Jews' amazement over the miracles, Peter basically says, 'Don't look on us, it is not us, IT IS JESUS!' Such a humble spirit should always motivate the believer. In verse 13, they give credit to whom credit is due: "God hath glorified His Son, Jesus." It was a fulfillment of Jesus's own teaching from John 14:13, "And whatsoever ye shall ask in my name, that will I do, that the Father may be glorified in the Son." The name is the key. It is the authorization—the guarantee. It incorporates the dual function of such a demonstration of God: power and purpose. Peter sums up this matter in verse 16, "And his name through faith in his name hath made this man strong, whom ye see and know: yea, the faith which is by him hath given him this perfect soundness in the presence of you all." Remember, a name declares the sum total of all a person is. And in our text alone, He is presented as Holy, Just, God's Christ, and the Prince of Life. These, among all the other names that are ascribed to Him, give us enough authority to move mountains for His glory and honor. His name is not a charm though. This name is a power to those who receive it, and it is He Himself who imparts faith to believe in His name. HIS NAME IS WONDERFUL!

In the second part of his sermon, Peter turns from the objective examination of the facts to the reaction of the crowd, specifically, the Jews. To that Jewish crowd, Jesus was still an itinerant Nazarene who had been crucified for blasphemy. BUT Peter's message set about to remove the offense of the cross and magnify Jesus as Lord. He did so first by declaring that the crucifixion was a deed of the Jews. Jesus was perfectly innocent. Verse 14 declares this: "But ye denied the Holy One and the Just, and desired a murderer." He had conquered death; and His suffering was but the gate to true messiahship, the lordship of all. It was the will of God that He should suffer and die, so that He could be glorified: "And (you, the Jews) killed the Prince of Life, whom God hath raised from the dead" (v. 15).

"But those things, which God before had shewed by the mouth of all His prophets, that Christ should suffer, he hath so fulfilled" (v. 18). To soften the blow of his blunt accusation, Peter assures them that they crucified Jesus in ignorance. Interestingly enough, it was an excuse that Peter could not claim for his own denial. The Jews had done it in ignorance; it was God's will in view of the lordship of Christ. But it did not absolve them from guilt; they needed to repent. Listen, although they did not know what they were doing, God knew what He was doing. As stated in Numbers 15:27-31, God put in place a provision for sin through sin offerings, and now, that provision is through Jesus, when we repent. Our only recourse to sin is repentance. And praise God, mercy is abundant and free! Repentance literally means to turn around, or to change one's mind—to line up (in this case particularly) with God's attitude toward Christ. It involves the whole thinking, feeling, willing self, and evidences a complete change.

Now, based on their repentance, Peter promised three things to them (v. 19). First of all, he says, "Your sins may be blotted out" (erased, smeared out, wiped out). When we repent, God forgives. And when God forgives, He forgets. Colossians 2:14 and Isaiah 43:2 uphold that truth:

> Blotting out the handwriting of ordinances that was against us, which was contrary to us, and took it out of the way, nailing it to his cross. (Colossians 2:14)

> I, even I, am he that blotteth out thy transgressions for mine own sake, and will not remember thy sins. (Isaiah 43:25)

The thought here in the word "repentance" is that only then is the sinner in the proper condition to receive divine forgiveness. It carries a literal meaning of "to comfort oneself." Thus, to repent is to bring peace and comfort to the soul.

The second promise Peter gave this crowd of Jews was that "times of refreshing shall come." Undoubtedly, this refers to the outpouring of the Holy Ghost, a divine visitation which God's people have known again and again in response to repentance and seeking Him. To the Jewish mind, it had a connotation of the final manifestation of the kingdom, but they were to find the times of refreshing to be vital and personal. Acts 2:38 follows this pattern: "Repent, and be baptized every one of you in the name of Jesus Christ for the remission of sins, and ye shall receive the gift of the Holy Ghost."

The third promise to the Jews in this sermon is that "He shall send Jesus Christ." Jesus Christ Himself, not just a make-shift, man-made kingdom. But in his message, Peter declared the return of Christ from the right hand of power, as exalted and reigning LORD. That was rich truth to those Jews. Verse 22 refers to Moses as a type of Christ—a prophet like Moses. Their hope was in the lordship of Jehovah; and Christ is that One!

Chapter 3 ends with a cherry on top for the Jews who were learning the real identity and purpose of Jesus. Christ is come to bless us in bringing us to repentance. There couldn't be a better promise to a sin-soaked world, or to the wayward Jews.

Opposition, Reaction, Prayer, and Growth

Acts Chapter 4

I want to take this chapter opening to highlight my mom, Mary Jones. She was as ladylike as the day is long. If you looked up the word "demure" in the dictionary, you would see a picture of my sweet, Scandinavian, blonde-haired, blue-eyed mother, with her hair and dress always in place. But boy, was she also fierce! Her convictions ran deep and strong, giving her children both a reverence for the things of God and a fear, I mean, healthy respect for her as our mother. Seriously though, the "you are in trouble" mom look originated with her! She didn't even have to discipline you; the look was enough. Maybe it was so effective because, otherwise, she was so sweet and accommodating. Whatever the secret, it WAS effective! I guarantee that the fear of disappointing my mother and her convictions kept me out of some avoidable trouble as a child and teen. And for that, I am forever thankful.

That strength of conviction gave me a solid foundation in my own "working out of my faith." Did I agree with her on everything? No. However, I knew that her faith in God didn't waver; or when it did, it was then that her fierceness kicked in! That gave me security. She was so sure of God's Word, and His specific movement in her and our family's life, that Dad often referred to her as "holy Mary, mother of God." Oh dad! Of course, he was kidding. However, there is a truth there because he leaned on her faith and assurance of God's words and workings when he had little or none, or used them as confirmation. What a great partnership they had!

I remember a story about my mom's faith from when I was about ten years old. This would be the early '80s: no cell phones, no texting, and barely answering machines to communicate with others. Pretty much just the good, ol' fashioned, connected to the wall with a long, curly cord, phone. I was staying with my eldest sister in Minneapolis, and her young family. I can't remember all the details now, but there was a lapse in communication between the four of us and my parents regarding our travel to my sister's home. We got to her house and got all settled in and slept soundly. My parents, on the other hand, were awaiting our call and never got it. They attempted to connect with us, but unbeknownst to my sister, her home phone was mistakenly off the hook. Thus, as those of you old enough to remember the old "connected to the wall with a long, curly cord" phones, that meant that on my parents' end of the phone, it just rang and rang and rang. So, understandably, in their thinking, we did not make it home, and they were worried. Well, my mom prayed, felt God's peace about the situation, and slept like a baby. My dad, not so much! In the morning, someone discovered the phone being off the hook and quelled my parents' fears with a phone call; my dad tired from a restless night's sleep, but my mom fully rested. Oh, the gift of the peace of God! And my mom knew how to access it.

Usually, at this point in the chapter opening, I ask you to join me as we enter the classroom or my dad's office to discover truth. But this time, join me as we enter my childhood home, where any of these scriptural truths could be present in my mom or dad at any moment.

* * *

The First Opposition Acts 4:1-12

Here in chapter 4, the theme again is Jesus. While the disciples were speaking, they were rudely interrupted. The religious leaders were very much annoyed at the presumption of the apostles in teaching the people as recognized rabbis would. They were also annoyed at the teaching itself: the resurrection of Jesus from the dead. The Sadducees did not believe in the resurrection. Now, wherever God's Spirit works, Satan tries to derail God's plan. The cross always accompanies the gospel. So, expect opposition!

Growing up in a pastor's home, I saw my parents face opposition and hard times. Even through the human response of wondering why something was happening and dealing with the stress of it, I saw my parents ultimately depend on their faith and their God to see them through. Then, when in ministry myself, I remember my mom sharing wisdom with me as we encountered our own opposition. In essence, she told me to watch for God to move when "bad things" were happening in the midst of a work for

God, since it was apparent that Satan wanted to derail it. How encouraging her faith was to me!

In this chapter, the priest, the captain of the temple, and the Sadducees were confronted by the apostles' teaching, as it was unsettling to them. The Sadducees were especially troubled! Now the Sadducees were the dominant party of the Sanhedrin, but they also seemed to have the most hang-ups religiously. They were the conservatives, and their religious guise was only self-righteous convenience. They discredited the resurrection of the body or any system of future reward. They did not believe in the spiritual realm: angels, etc. They believed that man is the master of his own destiny. And it was in this setting that Peter preached Christ. It is easy to see why they were annoyed. And, that time frame is not unique in such opposition. Wherever the Lord is preached, Satan seeks to thwart the gospel.

But many still believed the Word that Peter preached. Persecution, imprisonment, or excommunication cannot halt the truth. Paul says in 2 Timothy 2:9, "Wherein I suffer trouble, as an evil doer, even unto bonds." But the Word of God is NOT bound. Acts 4:4 tells us that there were about 5,000 men in attendance to hear Peter's sermon. This is the second mention of a number, and it marks the close of this introductory period of the young church; it was the last time people are numbered in the church in the Bible.

The next day, as recorded in verse 5, they appeared before the Sanhedrin, which was the governing body of the internal affairs of the Jews. This group, which numbered seventy-one, was made up of ten tightly knit groups; it was almost a family affair. So Peter and John stood before the court. The same scene as Jesus. The same place where Peter denied his Lord. This scene is no doubt a factor in his staunch defense of the faith, now before the Sanhedrin. Boldness seems to be the key word in this chapter.

Now, as the Jewish religious leaders often did, they shrewdly questioned NOT the good deed, but HOW the deed was accomplished. "By what power, or by what name, have ye done this?" they ask in verse 7. The question is conveyed with ridicule and scorn. The word 'ye' in this verse made reference to those disciples as unlearned and contemptible men. And that stance will always be so; when argument fails, ridicule follows. But intimidation cannot dampen faith and miracles. The witness for the defense was the lame man, NOW whole! The Sanhedrin, with their question, not only left themselves wide open, but they gave Peter and John the weapon and loaded it for them as well. They refused to be intimidated. What an opportunity!

Verse 8 begins with Peter's response: "Filled with the Holy Ghost." This scripture indicates that the Holy Spirit gave Peter a special enforcement of inspiration. Peter spoke as Christ had said they would in Matthew 10:18-20, Luke 12:12, and Luke 21:14-15. Peter's words imply a mild rebuke in reference to "good deeds done." For usually men are tried for evil deeds, and this is not the case here. In the very camp of the enemy of the gospel, Peter sends forth the truth. He who had once flinched before a maidservant of the high priest, now accuses the priests and rulers of having crucified the Messiah. Wow! What a difference the Holy Spirit makes!

He continues his rebuke (v. 10): "Whom God raised from the dead," and by that proved Him to be the Stone, i.e., a foundation stone, a cornerstone. Now the Jews were familiar with this analogy. Israel was the house of God; the temple of the Lord, and the rulers were the builders. But Peter's content was that the Chief Stone was the Messiah, or Christ. Now, this Stone had been laid for a foundation in Zion by God, but the rulers had laid Him aside. But then God lifted Him up from the rubbish heap where He had been laid, from the grave, AND made Him the "head of the corner." The head of the corner is the critical part of the building. Structurally, it is critical because here the side walls meet. In warfare, it is the vantage point of the defense; again, this speaks of its strength. And Jesus has that distinct function for us. He is our Sustainer. Later in the Scriptures, Paul declares this about Jesus in 1 Corinthians 3:11, "Other foundation can no man lay than that is laid, which is Jesus Christ." As cornerstone or battlement (the high point of the wall or tower), He is our Defense. And He is the only One who can be that for us.

Peter lays it all on the line with this proclamation in verse 12, "Neither is there salvation in any other." The words "salvation" and "saved" express so adequately the completeness with which He does His work in us. As the sermon illustration of the healed man testified FOR them in verses 9–10, Peter uses the words "made whole" and "whole" to describe him. No other name can make us whole, complete, healthy, or strong.

Reactions of the Sanhedrin and the Saints Acts 4:13-22

Now, prepare yourself for the glaring difference between the Sanhedrin and the saints. There are some lessons to be learned here of the power of God-directed witness. Boldness is the characteristic of the book of Acts. Verse 13 testifies of the undeniable change in Peter: "When they saw the boldness of Peter and John." They compared the Peter of a few days before and recognized this change. Their boldness of speech was beyond their own power; they spoke as men who were learned and schooled, but it was common knowledge that they were not. The latter part of verse 13 furnishes the key to this: "They took knowledge of them, that they had been with Jesus." They, no doubt, recognized them as followers of Jesus, but more importantly, they recognized the power and authority as being from Jesus. These men are just like Jesus. Now, this account speaks to us of the caliber of their boldness. It was not cold and calculated argument; it was not brashness or rudeness. It was holy boldness to the power and reality of Jesus Christ. And this ought to be the identification of our lives: do men see just us, our lives, and our goodness, or do they see Jesus?

Another fact the Sanhedrin could not ignore was that the lame man stood before them—the star witness! Witness, or truth, will always silence argument. The blind man in John 9 could not argue from a theological point, but his bold witness silenced the hecklers: "One thing I know, that whereas I was blind, now I see" (John 9:25). Notice, in this text, the two aspects of witness. Verse 13 was the verbal witness: "They spoke with boldness." Verse 14 was the silent witness: "Beholding the man which was healed standing with them." One is just as forceful as the other in God's time.

Verse 15 begins the Sanhedrin's response: "They conferred among themselves." That was their mistake; in the face of the miraculous, it is well for us to confer with God, not man. Verse 16 continues with their human response: "What shall we do?" Note the contrast of the same wording in this verse to that of Acts 2:37. In chapter 2, this response was out of conviction and confession, but in this verse in chapter 4, it is confusion. They recognized the miracle: "For that indeed a notable miracle hath been done," but they did not receive the Master. Yet, face to face with the power of God, they could not feel His power in their own lives. This should act as a warning to us of the need to cultivate a tenderness toward the things of God, not skepticism.

Their worry was revealed in verse 17, "But that it (the gospel) spread no further." How ironic that the very statement that was meant to silence them would only fan the flame of the gospel everywhere. Thus, it was the beginning of a persecution that fueled the worldwide spread of the gospel. It divided the real from the phonies, and sent them forth. The Sanhedrin continued with their "punishment" for the apostles and commanded them not to speak or teach in the name of Jesus. But that very order just motivated them more. It loaded Peter's guns of righteous indignation, and he brings out here a basic rule of Christian citizenship: Matthew 22:21, "Render therefore unto Caesar the things which are Caesar's; and unto God the things that are God's." Putting those so-called godly rulers on the defensive, he declared in verse 19, "Whether it be right in the sight of God to hearken unto you more than unto God, judge ye." Verse 20 is a classic response and ought to be the testimony of every one of us. "For we cannot but speak the things which we have seen and heard." There is a moral obligation upon each believer to give witness of the reality of God's power.

Note what they did in verse 21: "So when they had further threatened them, they let them go." It is proof to us of the power of testimony. The Sanhedrin were powerless to do anything in contrast to the power of God. In spite of their open defiance, they let them go, only repeating their threats. Thus, because of their testimony in front of the Sanhedrin, "All men glorified God for that which was done" (v. 21). ALL OF THAT because a shrunken, withered, helpless man yielded to the power of Christ.

A Holy Ghost Prayer Meeting Acts 4:23-31

Let me take you to a Holy Ghost prayer meeting. Here is a commentary on how to get the job done. Now immediately upon release of the apostles from the Sanhedrin, they returned to the other believers. After reporting to them what the council had threatened, their first reaction was to pray. That is a good response to spiritual opponents constantly at odds with the power of God.

Verse 24 begins their prayer meeting as they "lifted up their voice to God with one accord." Such praying is so very necessary at times. Note the content of their prayer; it makes a difference what we say. They began with "Lord/Sovereign Master." In the hour of real need, they rested their souls on the absolute government and power of God. Oh, what a place to begin! They continue, "Thou art God, which hast made heaven, and earth." That kind of recognition makes a difference in prayer. So much of our thinking is below that caliber these days. Let me say it again, "Sovereign Master, we come to Thee!"

Their prayers were like their preaching, saturated with God's Word. They quoted from Psalm 2:1-3, which shows the attitude of the godless toward the things of God. It is always a similar reaction, but triumph is the ultimate result! "The heathen rage," they prayed in verse 25. How illustrative of the crucifixion and of their appearance before the Sanhedrin. Such action refers to the conduct of an untamed horse: "The people imagine a vain thing," verse 25 continues. It is futile that man would fight against God, for He sets up kingdoms and He tears them down again.

Verse 26 continues from Psalm 2: "The kings of the earth stood up, and the rulers were gathered together against the Lord, and against his Christ." NOW, the victory of this text (Psalm 2) had its fulfillment in Christ, and they were still feeling some of the opposition. And SO SHALL WE. Still using Psalm 2 as a springboard for their prayer, verse 27 continues with the raging of men against Christ; but note the change now in their prayer. Read verse 28: "The people of Israel were gathered together for to do whatsoever thy hand and thy counsel determined before to be done." LISTEN to what they were saying in that prayer meeting; in summary, 'Lord, it's all in Your power and authority to do what is good.' They made their petition to God; and so can we! We can make our petition with that same assurance and knowledge of God's ability to do whatever we ask in His name. Thus, upon asserting His sovereignty and power upon the basis of His Word, they asked God to work miracles. And the whole thing is so wonderfully simple and effective.

Allow me the joy of celebrating my mom's faith once again. Zoom in on the Jones family in August 1978. You'll find Mom, Dad, Wendy, Becky, Heidi, and me: my mom was eight months pregnant with Adam, and we were on the verge of moving from Minneapolis to La Crosse, Wisconsin to pastor a different church. My sister Heidi, then eleven years old, came home from summer camp very sick. I was six, and we shared a room. At this point, all I understood about this sickness was that it was necessary for me to move out of our shared room and stay with my cool teenage sisters, Wendy and Becky. I loved sleeping in their room! However, I soon began to understand the severity of the situation when my dad and Becky took Heidi to the hospital after only a few days.

So, here is my mom: eight months pregnant, packing a house, helping four children (all at different life stages) say goodbye, saying goodbye herself to a church she has loved for nine years, and her adopted daughter is in the hospital with a blood disease. Aplastic anemia was the final diagnosis, and only a move of God kept her alive. I believe it was largely due to my mom's desperate prayers and her foundational relationship with God.

The weekend of our final Sunday at Bethel Assembly of God church in Minneapolis, instead of celebrating with her church family, my mom was in the hospital with Heidi. At some point, she prayed this prayer: "God, we are moving to Wisconsin and our daughter is sick, here, in Minneapolis. I am having this baby in less than a month. You're going to have to do something here because I am not going to be apart from my family, and I am not going to have this baby here while my husband pastors in Wisconsin. I am not leaving my daughter."

And do something, He did! Within a couple of days, my sister was released from the hospital. The doctors could not explain it. Our family moved all together, and our brother was born less than a month later in La Crosse, Wisconsin. God heard my mother's desperate and faithful cry! He heard her heart; it wasn't eloquent words; it was a mother simply pleading for a miracle from a God that she trusted completely.

Verses 29-30 finalize their prayer: "And now, Lord, behold their threatenings." "Behold"; how expressive they were of God's providential care. They were basically saying, 'Look down upon our situation, Lord.' Note that they did not ask to have the threats prevented, only to look upon them; and if He so desires, "to scatter them with His eye" (Proverbs 20:8). Also, they did not ask punishment for the Sanhedrin or protection for themselves. They only wanted boldness to go on preaching the Word. Listen, folks, God doesn't have anything to work with unless we speak His Word. In the midst of the arrogant unbelief and unconcern of the religious leaders, scorned and beaten, the new Christians prayed, "Grant unto thy servants, that with all boldness they may speak thy word, by stretching forth thine hand to heal; and that signs and wonders may be done by the name of thy holy child Jesus" (Acts 4:29-30). They asked to speak with "all boldness." They needed great boldness for a great purpose. And does this not echo our needs as well? All they wanted was boldness to go on preaching the Word, and it would come from continued miracles! They boldly asked for miracles. Again, here is the promise of Jesus to the disciples: "And these signs shall follow them that believe" (Mark 16:17). And that is still our rightful claim! Signs to follow and confirmation of the Word. It is not wishful thinking; it is the Word of God.

Verse 31 reveals the answer to their prayer; the place was shaken! There was a token of power in the physical sense, as well as the spiritual refreshing. The truth is this: when the inner-man is renewed, there will inevitably be a shake-up on the outside. They spoke the Word with boldness. May our praying net the same results!

The Church Continues to Grow Acts 4:32-37

"And the multitude of them that believed were of one heart and of one soul," begins this section in verse 32. It speaks of the reason for the results, and the prevailing spirit that was evident amongst them. The church was now comprised of a wide variety of people: young/old, rich/poor, common/aristocrats. And the most striking characteristic was its UNITY. There is growth in unity. The Greek word translated "heart" in verse 32 refers to the center of personality, i.e., the thoughts, the feelings, the will. That group of believers thought, felt, and acted as one. "Of one soul" in this same verse indicates that it was as if God had wired them ALL into His circuit and threw the switch. They possessed God, as a body of believers, and it so influenced their lives that it related to everything else they possessed. "Neither said any of them that ought of the things which he possessed was his own." The Amplified version puts it this way: "Not one of them claimed that anything which he possessed was (exclusively) his own." This principle of stewardship was not church law; it was taught and led by the Spirit. Not only did they themselves belong to God, but their goods (possessions) as well. And they held, administered, and released their possessions as needed. Now, this basic principle is still necessary today for the furtherance of the kingdom. Verse 32 ends with this sentiment: "But they had all things in common." While the practice of such may not be entirely practical, the underlying principle of such a way of life is a contributing factor to the growth they saw. Anything less will greatly reduce the power and the grace.

Let's take a gander at 1 John for some depth into their results in prayer and growth:

> Beloved, if our heart condemn us not, then have we confidence toward God. And whatsoever we ask, we receive of him, because we keep his commandments, and do those things that are pleasing in his sight. (1 John 3:21-22)

They had asked for boldness to "speak thy word with all boldness." It was a reaffirming of Acts 1:8: "And ye shall be my witnesses." And because of their heart's condition, there was unity amongst them. There was also no condemnation. Because of all this, they received what they asked for—POWER! As stated in verse 33, "And with great power gave the apostles witness of the resurrection of the Lord Jesus: and great grace was upon them all." Again, the Amplified version expresses it like this: "The favor of God rested richly upon them." Is that not our desire today? GREAT GRACE! Listen, they had discovered the truth of real stewardship: "Give, and it shall be given unto you" (Luke 6:38). They had given of themselves, and God gave of Himself. GREAT GRACE!

"Neither was there any among them that lacked," verse 34 declares. Now, there is more said here than meets the eye! It is more than benevolence. It suggests that if we give of ourselves, we ourselves will never be in want; it is a paradox of the Christian life. It reveals the love of Jesus. Second Corinthians 8:9 shows this amazing love: "For ye know the grace of our Lord Jesus Christ, that, though he was rich, yet for your sakes he became poor, that ye through his poverty might be rich." "Listen to me, folks," Dad would say emphatically, "There is never a lack in serving Jesus!" Psalm 23 shows us how the Lord is our Shepherd. And Philippians 4:19 puts it right out there with this declaration: "But my God shall supply all your need."

The last two verses of the chapter give us a specific example of this Spirit-led generosity. With regard to Joses, who by the apostles was surnamed Barnabas, he is set forth in the text as an example of this "great power" and "great grace." And also in a number of places, we find his exhibits of a Spirit-ordered life: with Saul of Tarsus in Acts 9:27, with a leader in the church in Acts 11:22-24, listed as a missionary with Paul in Acts 13 & 14, and at the Council of Jerusalem in Acts 15.

Thus, there is displayed for us here the possibility of believers with one heart and of one soul. Where do you stand in relation to such fellowship? For only such relationships will yield the greatness of God's power and grace.

Trouble, Progress, Persecution, and Trial

Acts Chapter 5

No one likes getting into trouble! Not only do you have to deal with the shame or guilt of getting caught, but you need to deal with the consequences of your actions—not fun, and sometimes disappointing, devastating, or even deadly. Chapter 5 opens with the deadly kind of consequence, but let me share one of my dad's favorite consequences to mete out when a student would dare fall asleep in one of his classes. This was shared via Facebook by one of his students, Brent Enget.

> The setting is a 7:30 a.m., Bro. Jones class, in the old Room 150 of the Administration Building on the campus of Trinity Bible College. I was up too late the night before with friends, and the next morning, as Bro. Jones started to teach, his deep bass vibrato voice soothed me into a great sleep with my head resting against a pole. My best friend, Michael Lapham, and I were in the same class. I mention that now because I don't know exactly what question he asked, as I was sleeping. Nor did I see the amazing aim by which the chalkboard eraser flew through the air and hit the pole right above my head and brought me back to consciousness, amidst a shower of chalk dust. I heard about it from Mike. However, I do remember giving the right answer and Bro. Jones laughing that I had gotten it correct. He then said that it would be good if I stayed awake for ALL of the class!

So, are you ready? Let's follow along with Dad as he dives in. Just don't fall asleep in class!

* * *

Trouble: Judgment at the House of God Acts 5:1-11

As we begin our study of chapter 5, notice what a contrast this story is to the story of Barnabas at the end of chapter 4. These two accounts of new believers' actions are examples of real consecration and false consecration. The opening word in chapter 5 is "But." With that one little word, Luke recounts for us the second of two illustrations that revealed some of the inner condition of the early church. One was inspired commendation, and the other was condemnation. Now, the great lesson of these verses, in the first section of chapter 5, is that the blessing of God demands holiness unto the Lord. The power of God THROUGH us demands the righteousness of God IN us. With privilege goes responsibility.

In Psalm 51:6, the psalmist captures this need for holiness. "Behold, thou desirest truth in the inward parts: and in the hidden part thou shalt make me to know wisdom." And these first eleven verses in Acts 5 emphasize the awesome reality of the Holy Spirit's presence in the church, and our responsibility to it. We're not at a picnic, folks! This is not a carnival! This is THE CHURCH OF JESUS CHRIST, and we have a responsibility to God to uphold the sanctity of it all.

The story of our text shows the realism of the Word of God. It reveals God's attitude toward hypocrisy for all time, regardless of whether or not judgment is immediate. It is a warning against the wiles of Satan, EVEN within the Spirit-filled church! Now, whether Ananias got his inspiration from God or Barnabas is unsure, but whatever the origin of his deed, sin filled his heart.

Verse 2 shows us the real nature of their sin: "And kept back part of the price, his wife also being privy to it, and brought a certain part, and laid it at the apostles' feet." Now, the suggestion here is that they sold their possession not so much because they wanted to help others as much as they wanted to elevate themselves. Interestingly, to further add to the tragedy of the event, their names meant "God is gracious" (Ananias) and "Beautiful" (Sapphira). But neither graciousness nor beauty are part of this story. "Kept back part of the price" literally means to put aside for one's self, particularly in a deceptive manner! He professed to give it all, and his wife conspired with him. Looking at Acts 4:37 and Acts 5:1-2, every outward act of theirs was similar to that of Barnabas: they sold something they owned and laid the money profited at the apostles' feet. Even though their outward actions were the same, "The LORD looketh on the heart" (1 Samuel 16:7). Ananias posed as devout and pious, but he was really a liar and a cheat.

Peter's response in verse 3 was full of Holy Spirit wisdom: "Ananias, why hath Satan filled thine heart to lie to the Holy Ghost?" Think about this—the heart that might have been filled with the Holy Spirit is seen in contrast to be filled with Satan. Ananias had every opportunity to be another Barnabas, but he chose to deceive. "Why have you allowed this" is the implication of Peter's question of Ananias. So learn from Ananias— it is not men that our ultimate dealing is with, BUT WITH GOD! Let that truth keep us and cause us to honor and glorify God in all that we do.

Verse 4 gives more detail as to the insidiousness of their sin. Ananias was not forced to sell his possession, but he did, and then retained part of it while pretending to be surrendering the whole. Thus, not only was he deceitful, but also blasphemous, in that he withheld what he had professedly dedicated to God. The lesson here is this: BEWARE OF A LACK OF FULL SURRENDER. Partial dedication is not dedication. This heart condition is an abomination to God.

While Peter spoke, Ananias dropped dead at his feet (v. 5). And no sooner had they buried Ananias when his wife came in with the same story. Verse 8 reveals the incredible deception of the human heart with Sapphira's agreement with their conspired lie. "The heart is deceitful above all things, and desperately wicked" (Jeremiah 17:9). Peter goes on to accuse Sapphira of putting God on trial, "How is it that ye have agreed together to tempt the Spirit of the Lord?" And her end was the same as her husband's: instant death. Take note: due judgment will overtake every sin, sooner or later, UNLESS the pardon of Calvary intervenes.

Verse 11 closes out this section with the reverence something of this nature deserves: "And great fear came upon all the church." Such fear of God is a testimony to the whole world of the reality of our God.

A Progress Report Acts 5:12-16

Notice the results of the judgment and reverence of God as Luke gives us a brief progress report in the middle of chapter 5. Verse 12 begins the report: "And by the hands of the apostles were many signs and wonders wrought among the people." These men were simply acting in accord with God's Word, as Jesus in Mark's gospel foretold, "And these signs shall follow them that believe; In my name shall they cast out devils; they shall speak with new tongues…they shall lay hands on the sick and they shall recover" (Mark 16:17-18). Note that they were not acting on some passive desire; they were acting on God's Word—AND IT WORKED!

Signs and wonders are characteristic of the book of Acts. These two words are usually used together for this reason: the pagan world also had wonders and miracles. In Egypt, Pharaoh's wise men and sorcerers performed wonders and miracles; and the Antichrist will perform wonders and miracles. However, they are not signs. They mean nothing when their source is outside of God's power. Wonders and miracles like this have no significance without pointing to God as their Source, and they can be deceptive. But the wonders done by the apostles were divine evidence of God's love and grace. There was no deception, only revelation. And the promise to us here is this: that God is still showing His love and grace through signs and wonders! The suggestion in this verse is that they simply placed their hands upon the sick and suffering, AND THEY WERE RESTORED!

Verse 12 continues, "And they were all with one accord in Solomon's porch." Now, there are two things worthy of our attention here: they still continued a unity of the Spirit, and they still maintained the boldness of the Spirit. Not only did they disregard the warnings of the Sanhedrin, but they did so right on Israel's front porch. And that is the way of truth; there is boldness to proclaim, and God will vindicate and prove Himself.

The next verse goes on with a bit of a contradiction in the reports of the people around them: "And none of these who were not of their number dared to join and associate with them" (Acts 5:13, AMP). It seems such a strange statement, but it illustrates the distinction of the true church from the unbeliever. "And what communion hath light with darkness?" (2 Corinthians 6:14b); "The friendship of the world is enmity with God" (James 4:4). The rest of verse 13 is the seeming contradiction: "But the people magnified them." (AMP)

In spite of Satan's attack on them from the religious leaders, there was respect for their stand for truth. And as a result of that stand, "Believers were the more added to the Lord, multitudes both of men and women" (v. 14). This is the only place in the New Testament where "multitude" is plural. It indicates many, many people! Thus, those who dared not associate with them because of their own sin obviously made things right with God.

Now, there are some simple lessons here in church growth. The Word of God must be the basis of our authority. There must be unity among believers. There must be an unashamed proclamation of the gospel of Jesus Christ. There is no room for compromise of our message. Listen, we have the best gospel this world will ever hear. "It is the power of God unto salvation" (Romans 1:16). And salvation's message is that Jesus Christ saves, heals, baptizes, and is coming again!

This message had such an impact on everyone that they all came to the apostles with their sick: "That at the least the shadow of Peter passing by might overshadow some of them" (v. 15b). And the indication is that they were all healed. The shadow provided a point of contact, or a stimulant to faith. There is much teaching of this kind of "faith quickening" in Scripture. Matthew 9:20-22 gives us the story of the woman who was healed by touching the hem of Christ's garment. In Acts 19:12, handkerchiefs and aprons were taken from the body of Paul and sent everywhere as a tool for healing. Wherever Jesus went, the crowd sought to touch Him or the garment He wore (Mark 6:56). And the indication is that as many as touched Him WERE healed. Also, the hands of the apostles, and the oil, served the same purpose. Faith was activated and miracles were performed. The last verse in this section (v. 16) records the first extension of the gospel beyond Jerusalem: All of those people were healed.

The Second Persecution Acts 5:17-25

Verse 17 begins with the account of the second persecution against the early church. The condition of the young church was miraculous according to the brief progress report in the previous section. The church was growing (v. 14), miracles were the order of the day (vv. 15–16), news spread to the surrounding cities, and the church was growing in popularity (v. 16). Now, the religious leaders tolerated it for a time, but Satan began to unleash his fury. "Then the high priest rose up, and all they that were with him...and they were filled with indignation" (v. 17). They were jealous of the popularity of the apostles and jealous of their prestige and authority. Literally, they were filled with "hot steam." They couldn't take it any longer, so they tried to put an end to their teaching. When God's Word is having its greatest success, Satan will unleash all the demons in hell to try and stop that success. But Isaiah 59:19 gives us a great promise: "When the enemy shall come in like a flood, the Spirit of the LORD shall lift up a standard against him." He will rally the faithful.

The truth behind this persecution of the apostles is that God allowed it to manifest His glory and His name more than ever! Just like the story of Joseph at the end of Genesis, Satan meant it for evil, but God allowed it for good. In this story, the evil was that the apostles were thrown into prison: "And laid their hands on the apostles, and put them in the common prison" (v. 18). Not just Peter and John, but all of the apostles this time. Just think, they were imprisoned just for preaching Jesus.

The good part of this story is what happened next: "But the angel of the Lord by night opened the prison doors, and brought them forth" (v. 19). The irony of this prison break was that the Sadducees denied the very existence of angels (Acts 23:8). WHILE they were plotting against the apostles, one of these "non-existent" beings came and set the apostles free. The angel OPENED THE DOORS of the prison. Now, what an encouragement to our faith that is. We may never be imprisoned for our faith, but amid the blessings of spiritual life, we may find ourselves imprisoned by doubts, fears, or uncertainty. Listen, encourage yourself with this: "The angel of the Lord opened the prison doors!" But the apostles' freedom was not for naught. Think of this, most people want to be free from their prisons so they will feel good, but there is a higher calling.

The commandment of the angel makes the act of freeing them most significant, "Go, stand and speak in the temple to the people all the words of this life" (v. 20). Listen, folks, the angel's message is this: we don't need to back down for anyone! Romans 1:16 gives us the authority: "I am not ashamed of the gospel of Christ: for it is the power of God unto salvation." The angel specifically told the apostles to speak "all the words of this life." What a wonderful description of the gospel message. This life fills with glory, detests the devil, heals the sick, opens blind eyes, sets at liberty them that are bruised, and delivers from prison, literally and spiritually. Do you have this kind of life? The second part of the angel's message to the apostles was, "Go, stand and speak." I don't think they needed much prodding.

"They entered into the temple early in the morning, and taught" (v. 21). Meanwhile, there was a meeting of another nature convening. The religious leaders were about to bring judgment upon the apostles. Verses 21b-22 tell what happened. The high priest sent (the religious leaders) to the prison to have them brought to him, but when the officers came, they did not find them in the prison. Listen, if He can come forth from the dead, He can bring the living from prison!

Verse 23 and following tells of the religious rulers' bewilderment after the officers who were sent to get the apostles from prison gave the report, "The prison truly found we shut with all safety." It implied that the doors had not even been unsealed. The rulers were surprised by their report and "doubted of them where unto this would grow" (v. 24). They were concerned that others would hear of this miraculous event. The truth is simply this: God's ways will always confound the unbeliever. Psalm 70:2, "Let them be ashamed and confounded that seek after my soul." But God was working with the apostles and confirming the Word with signs following (Mark 16:20b).

Then the news came to the religious leaders that they were teaching in the temple again (v. 25). There was no way to deny this miraculous release; they could not explain it away! God was working—proving Himself. Thus learn, wherever we take a stand and speak all the words of this life, God will confirm it still today.

The Second Trial Acts 5:26-33

With the second persecution ending with the apostles being miraculously freed from prison, a second trial was necessary. So the religious leaders took extra precaution, and verse 26 records that the captain of the temple accompanied his officers to bring the apostles to the Sanhedrin. It was a peaceful arrest for fear of what the people would do if it weren't, because the apostles and their message were growing extremely popular. Now, this is not to demonstrate the martyr image; we're not martyrs, we're witnesses. The martyr image is to bring glory only to God, not us. And even when we are right, God will allow adverse circumstances in order to bring glory to His name. This may happen even as unrelated circumstances and seemingly unnecessary adversity come our way.

So again, they appeared before the council; and carefully, the high priest evaded the miraculous and asked, "Did not we straitly command you that ye should not teach in this name?" (v. 28). He referred to the strong reprimand he gave in Acts 4:18 to not preach about Jesus. It is interesting how they evaded the use of the name of Jesus though, referring to Jesus with pronouns. Verse 28 shows this disregard: "That ye should not teach in this name" and "intend to bring this man's blood upon us." John, the disciple, spoke of this in John 1:11, "He came unto his own, and his own received him not." The insult of all insults to God is when His own are unmoved by His message.

The scolding continues, "And, behold, ye have filled all Jerusalem with your doctrine" (v. 28). What was meant as a put-down was actually a praise. What a tremendous testimony to the power of that name and that blood. The literal meaning of the word "filled" in that verse is "and it continues to be full." Praise God!

So, what was the apostles' doctrine that was being opposed? It consisted of what they had seen in Jesus and heard from Jesus. Jesus Christ was their central theme, and their lives SHOWED IT! Note how the accuser sought to defend himself. The truth is this, he who seeks to examine Jesus, suddenly finds himself being examined. Listen to me, folks, the presence of Jesus Christ will either condemn or commend. The constant cry to the world is, "What will you do with Jesus?" or "What think ye of Christ?" Thus, confronted with His presence, these men were condemned and were indignant: "And (you) intend to bring this man's blood upon us."

Peter replied, "We ought to obey God rather than men" (v. 29). Let's collectively salute Peter, for obeying God is our highest duty. Now, we are not speaking here of some self-appointed, self-motivated duty. However, Peter was speaking of a Bible-oriented, Spirit-directed obedience. For example, if your standard of obedience is NOT in the Word of God, then it is misdirected. May I recommend a good treatise on Christian duty/civil disobedience? Check out this book: *A Christian Manifesto* by Francis Shaeffer.

Again, Peter begins to preach the contrast of Christ with the Sanhedrin's way of living. He pointed out that God raised up Jesus, but they killed Jesus. Peter includes them all in the statement, "The God of our fathers raised up Jesus, whom ye slew and hanged on a tree" (v. 30). He was saying to them, 'Do you see how contradictory your lives are? You say you serve God, but you deny His Son.' May our lives always be in conjunction with our message, both silent AND spoken.

This message of contrast continues. Peter says, in essence, 'You tried to defame Him, but God exalted Him.' Verse 31 says, "Him hath God exalted with his right hand to be a Prince and a Saviour, for to give repentance to Israel, and forgiveness of sins." Notice the order of the Savior's work in this verse: repentance and then forgiveness. And they must always come in that order.

Peter reflects the command of Jesus to the apostles, "We are his witnesses" (v. 32). So, he was saying, 'Because of that, how can we remain silent?' Think on this, folks: that mandate has not been repealed! Verse 32 continues with this caveat, "And so is also the Holy Ghost, whom God hath given to them that obey him." Obedience is God's condition for blessing.

Verse 33 records their response to Peter: "When they heard that, they were cut to the heart." When Christ is exalted, it brings men to a decision. And the Word of God will do the same today! Hebrews 4:12 points out the juncture that people are brought to by the Word of God: "Even to the dividing asunder of soul and spirit." The sad fact of those religious leaders was that they responded in the wrong way. The rest of verse 33 finishes with their decision: "And took counsel to slay them." Conviction brings conviction. What does the Word of God do to you?

Before the Sanhedrin Acts 5:34-42

This account closes the first chapter in the history of the church; it has predominantly been a time of peace and prosperity. During this time, the apostolic authority had become clearly defined, and above all, the body of believers emerged as the CHURCH. It is not the theocracy of Israel restored, but a whole new concept of reaching the world with the message of God's love.

In the previous section, the apostles stood before the enraged council who were ready to tear them apart. But God put forth His staying hand: "Then stood there up one in the council, a Pharisee, named Gamaliel." What a great example of the sovereignty of God! Proverbs 21:1 shares the wisdom of this characteristic of God: "Just as water is turned into irrigation ditches, so the Lord directs the king's thoughts. He turns them wherever He wants to" (TLB). And Isaiah 40:15 has this to say about it: "The nations are as a drop of a bucket." God is still in charge. And Gamaliel, a Pharisee, was used of God to work out His plan.

Gamaliel was a man of high regard; he "had in reputation among all the people" (v. 34). His fame also carried him in high esteem in the Sanhedrin. Although he was a Pharisee, and the dominant part of the council were the Sadducees, the Pharisees held more favor with the people. Gamaliel was a PhD but couldn't make up his mind about Christ. He was an expert in his field, but a failure in his life. Acts 22:3 records that Saul of Tarsus was one of his pupils. So, even though he was not fully persuaded in his own mind, he was nevertheless used of God to stay their execution. It is interesting to note that Acts 5 begins with a foe in the camp of God, but ends with a friend in the camp of the enemy.

Gamaliel addresses them in much the same manner as Peter had done previously in this chapter. He, in essence, says to them, 'Beware of making a mistake about these men; act cautiously and wisely.' He suggests a "wait and see" approach and then proceeds to give two illustrative reasons. In verse 36, he brings up Theudas, who had followers but amounted to nothing in the long run. His second example, in verse 37, is Judas of Galilee, who gathered some followers but then died, and his followers were dispersed. And on the basis of these two examples, he appeals to the Sanhedrin to give the apostles 'rope enough to hang themselves.'

"Refrain from these men," he said in verse 38; or in other words, leave them alone. Now, Gamaliel's advice seemed sensible, but actually it was a policy of indecision. A policy that, actually, could not be followed. For the truth is that there is no middle ground when confronted with Jesus Christ. You are either a saint or you are not. Gamaliel was faced with the most convincing evidence of Jesus being the Messiah. One cannot come this far in knowledge and then say, 'wait and see'; and yet he does. We must be on one side of the fence or the other. We will either serve God or mammon.

The penetrating truth of Gamaliel's advice is true today: "If this counsel or this work be of men, it will come to nought: but if it be of God, ye cannot overthrow it" (vv. 38-39). The outcome of this trial, recorded in verse 40, is that the apostles were beaten and commanded that "they should not speak in the name of Jesus." Then they were let go from the presence of the council, "rejoicing that they were counted worthy to suffer shame for his name."

Now this passage presents a vivid documentary of what is involved in living for Christ. First, it is contradictory to the age in which we live. Second, my testimony, experience, and fellowship with God is worth everything. I must guard it diligently. And my commitment to Christ is bounded by these demonstrations: always rejoicing, ready to suffer, and loving His name. They were honored that they were counted worthy to suffer shame for His name! And after all this, "They ceased not to teach and preach Jesus Christ" (v. 42).

Seven Deacons Chosen; One Deacon Accused

Acts Chapter 6

Chapter 6 has some similarities to chapters 1 and 2 with evidence of practicality and power! The practical aspect being the choosing of deacons when the problem of a practical system was needed due to their rapid growth. And the power aspect is displayed in the chapter as we see Stephen, "full of the Holy Spirit," defend the faith with endowment from on high! My dad was a great mix, as a church leader, of practicality and power. He knew that his strength and wisdom came from God, and he stood firm in that conviction as he showed his congregants and students alike how to walk with Christ in practical life situations.

My dad came up with an effective system of choosing church deacons, mixing the practical and the power. He shared it with his protégés along the way, one of them being my husband when he became a lead pastor, and we saw its effectiveness firsthand. The problem, sometimes, with elections of any kind, is that they can easily boil down to "popularity contests" or rely heavily on personality. That may work fine for Homecoming Queen, but that is not a great way to choose a church leader! We need to rely on the leading of the Holy Spirit, but we're also human, so having a metric to judge things by is helpful. Out of his experience, Dad came up with a great answer! The system is shared in the back of this book in Appendix A.

So why don't we join Dad, in the excitement of an annual church business meeting, and watch this process unfold.

* * *

Seven Deacons Chosen Acts 6:1-7

Chapter 6 begins with the account of the rapid growth of the church. A very short time had elapsed since the day of Pentecost, and estimates are that at this time, there were between 15,000 and 25,000 believers. Luke seemed to delight in interrupting with observations of growth (Acts 9:31; 12:24; 16:5; 19:20; 28:30-31). Steady, continuous growth is a mark of spiritual activity, but it was growth that caused the current difficulty here in this section: "There arose a murmuring of the Grecians against the Hebrews, because their widows were neglected in the daily ministration" (v. 1). It seemed that the church was impenetrable by outward attack. They defied the Sanhedrin to their face. So the work of Satan upon the young church began from within. It is Satan's chief offensive to stir up internal strife and discord. Note that if the disciples had not followed the leading of the Holy Spirit and quickly dealt with the problem, the church could have been torn apart!

Now, the problem was this, there was a grumbling against the Hebrews; the Grecian widows were not receiving a fair distribution for their needs. They were both Jews, but the Grecians were foreign born and thus looked down upon. Spiritual and social prejudice was the result. Oh, that men would learn that all are one in Christ Jesus. Jesus set the pace for this truth in the book of John: "That they all may be one; as thou, Father, art in me, and I in thee, that they also may be one in us: that the world may believe that thou hast sent me" (John 17:21). Other markers of being one with other Jesus followers are taking care of orphans and widows (James 1:27) and that we are known by our love for one another (John 13:35).

In verse 2, the apostles recognized two things: the ministry need that had to be addressed and what their priority needed to be, which was studying the Word of God. This is a great example of leadership in the early church. The apostles needed to focus on praying, leading, and properly applying the Word of God. They needed to be dedicated to the Word so the teaching of doctrine would be right, since the new Christians were "continued stedfastly in the apostles' doctrine" (Acts 2:42). Just like Jethro told Moses (Exodus 18:13-27), they could not solve all the problems in the church. So they appointed deacons to do that. The food program was important, but it wasn't the apostles' first responsibility or priority.

This important job couldn't be done by just anyone because it was bigger than just waiting on tables—it was dealing with disgruntled people. The qualifications for these deacons, listed in verse 3, were that they be men of honor and full of the Holy Ghost and wisdom. You don't need wisdom to bring food to people, but you need God's leading and wisdom in order to quiet the souls of disgruntled Jesus-followers. So the men followed the apostles' directions, and the problem was solved. They chose seven men "full of faith and of the Holy Ghost" (v. 5). Imagine the problems that could be avoided if we, as the church, just listened to our God-given leaders and did as they directed. These seven men were not chosen by the apostles, but by the multitude of the disciples. The reputation among the crowd, of these men, was paramount in the choosing. There was evidence to the multitude of spiritual maturity in them.

The commissioning of these men in verse 6 shows the importance of their ministry! Another reason they needed to be "full of the Holy Ghost and wisdom" is that the authority was being bestowed on them to deal with this problem and other problems that would come up among the new Christians. The people needed to see that these seven men had the apostles' authority to speak and lead in the church.

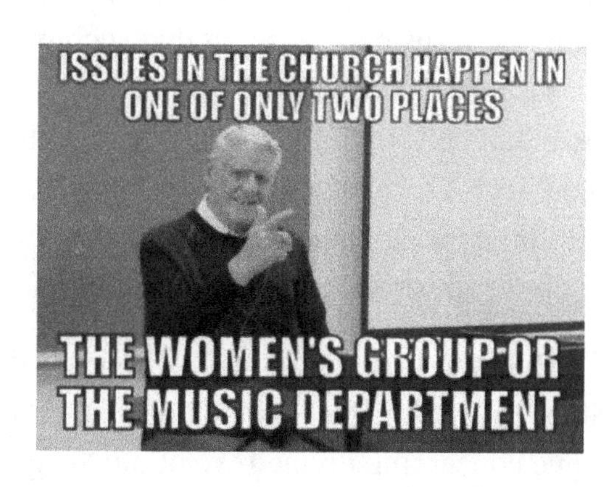

In verse 7, we see the results of following godly leadership. "The word of God increased" and "the number of the disciples multiplied in Jerusalem greatly." And even this, "a great company of the priests were obedient to the faith." Solving the problem expressed to everyone around them the love they had for one another, and resulted in the continued growth of the church. The first early church "grumble session" did not detain the work of God in Jerusalem. The leadership principles of priorities and empowerment squashed the work of Satan to try and tear them apart from the inside. It is much harder to deal with internal problems than external problems.

One Deacon Accused Acts 6:8-15

This section begins the highlight of the martyr, Stephen, who was one of the original deacons chosen. Verse 8 states, "And Stephen, full of faith and power, did great wonders and miracles among the people." Of all the deacons of that early church, Stephen seems to be the example to all succeeding deacons of any church. His qualifications and his character are previously listed, and Stephen is distinctly named as "full of faith and of the Holy Ghost" (v. 5). Let's compare the list of deacon qualifications to those in 1 Timothy:

> Likewise must the deacons be grave, not double-tongued, not given to much wine, not greedy of filthy lucre; holding the mystery of the faith in a pure conscience. And let these also first be proved; then let them use the office of a deacon, being found blameless. Even so must their wives be grave, not slanderers, sober, faithful in all things. Let the deacons be the husbands of one wife, ruling their children and their own houses well. For they that have used the office of a deacon well purchase to themselves a good degree, and great boldness in the faith which is in Christ Jesus. (1 Timothy 3:8-13)

Now the suggestion here in verse 8 of Acts chapter 6 is that God looked upon Stephen with special grace or favor, for this is the literal translation of the word "faith." Because of his great faith, and because of his devotion to the will of God, God honored his witness with great power! Stephen was not out of place, but he filled his place properly. Jesus made it plain that such ministry to witness was for ALL men, not only apostles, or even deacons. Again, I refer to Mark 16:17, "And these signs shall follow them that believe." Believing in Him is the only requirement to be used by Him. Ephesians 4:11-12, "and he gave some apostles; and some, prophets; and some, evangelists; and some, pastors and teachers; for the perfecting of the saints." The church needs all of these ministries, even deacons, to be full of faith and power.

But wherever God's work abounds, there will be opposition. They disputed with Stephen as to the messiahship of Jesus Christ. There will always be those who want to argue concerning divine revelation; "eggheads," I like to call them, whose knowledge is purely "enticing words of man's wisdom" (1 Corinthians 2:4). Flesh and blood hath not revealed it. The only real response is that which is found in verse 10: "And they were not able to resist the wisdom and the spirit by which he (Stephen) spake." Thus, the ministry of Stephen stirred up opposition, but his opponents were no match for him in argument. He was full of faith and had the Lord's promise of wisdom in such an hour of need. Let's take a look at Luke 21:15, "For I will give you a mouth and wisdom, which all your adversaries shall not be able to gainsay nor resist." Thus, Stephen merely claimed the truth of God's promise, and the religious unbelievers didn't know what to say!

Their retaliation is found in verse 11: "They suborned men, which said, We have heard him speak blasphemous words against Moses, and against God." The Amplified version says it like this, "They secretly instigated and instructed men what to say (against Stephen)." And the Living Bible puts it this way, "So they brought in some men to lie about him." The lowest form of dissension and accusation is lying, especially because, in this case, it was half-truth.

They charged Stephen with blasphemy. Now, the significance of this is that the Jewish heritage and ritual were most sacred. NO ONE spoke against Moses, the temple, or God. If he did, he was guilty of blasphemy. In this way, they sought to do away with Stephen because blasphemy carried the death sentence.

They "came upon him (Stephen), and caught him, and brought him to the council" (v. 12). The leaders stirred up the people with this aggressive action. Literally, they rushed at Stephen and took him, as an animal after its prey. And when we tell it like it is, the response will be the same today! The charge against him is announced in verses 13-14: blasphemy against the temple and its law, and against the sanctity of the messiahship. They figured that if one charge did not stick, the other one would.

The real problem for the religious leaders though, was not upholding the sanctity of the temple, the law, or the messiahship; rather, it was fear. They had a fear of change in their customs. They were in a rut, and they liked it. Look inside your heart and motives, folks; let not the custom and ritual of our lives come before the law of Christ! They would not accept Jesus, and so He was the focus of their contempt. Christ will always be a reproach or a stumbling block to some.

With the charges against him stated, verse 15 reveals something about Stephen as all eyes were fixed on him: And they "saw his face as it had been the face of an angel." He looked like he talked; his countenance showed his heart. He was not a holy grouch! And there was a look upon his face of one who was inspired, one whose soul was aflame, one who was not ashamed of Jesus, and one who was filled with the Holy Spirit. And the significance seems to point to the fact that it had eternal effect upon a young man named Saul.

So, with this inspiring account of Stephen, we must ask ourselves, 'How is my life witness?'

Stephen's Apology and Indictment

Acts Chapter 7

In this chapter, Stephen is before the Sanhedrin, not in defense of his life, but giving testimony of pure Christianity. He stands up to the religious leaders of his day in defense of the gospel of Jesus Christ, which he experienced firsthand. Let us be inspired by him and by the apostle Paul, who later declared in his defense of the gospel, "I am not ashamed of the gospel of Christ: for it is the power of God unto salvation to every one that believeth" (Romans 1:16). Stephen's courage and defense of the gospel leads him to answer the call of martyrdom. And what gives Stephen such courage to stand up to the Sanhedrin? The power of the Holy Spirit!

It's a Sunday morning in an Assembly of God church where Pastor Jones, with his slicked back, jet-black hair, sharply dressed in suit and tie, now pounds the pulpit and says with conviction, "We don't need revival; we need a continual burning in our heart daily! That is the only thing that will bring about the kind of conviction that Stephen shows us here."

So, put down your bulletin, don't read the Evangel now, but listen as Bro. Jones expounds on the Word of God. You might want to take notes, too, as his messages are always full of biblical insight.

* * *

Stephen's Arrest and Apology Acts 7:1-16

Stephen's arrest in this chapter is the third recorded opposition in the book of Acts. Peter and John's arrest is recorded in chapter 4, and all of the apostles were arrested in chapter 5. First, with Peter and John, they were warned; the second time, when they were all arrested, they were beaten; and the third arrest resulted in death. Here, in chapter 7, it seems that Stephen sensed the verdict of the Sanhedrin. He did not plead guilty, nor did he beg for an acquittal.

Actually, his defense was an apology in the true sense of the word. The word "apology" in its true meaning does not mean, "I'm sorry"; rather, it means a vindication of a certain thing, person, or thesis. Stephen was saying, in effect, 'I'm right, and here are my reasons.' Thus, his defense was not of himself, but of pure Christianity.

Now, the manner in which he called forth witnesses for the defense was magnificent, indeed! He built his case from the beginning of God's dealings with Abraham to the climactic incarnation of Christ. Stephen's historical survey covers every facet of God's dealings with Israel, with the theme of it being the perpetual rejection of God and His servants by His own people! And is this not man's biggest failing today, of both saved AND unsaved? Hebrews 12:25 gives us this warning: "See that ye refuse not him that speaketh."

Stephen's main arguments were as follows: God is not locally restricted, the problem with their religious rut, and the rebellion of Israel throughout history. Let's break those arguments down as Stephen so eloquently builds the case for the gospel. God is not locally restricted, and since Jesus's resurrection, He does not inhabit a material building. Rather, God inhabits us. He is Spirit. When you go to church, if you don't bring God with you, then as far as you are concerned, God is not there. Their religious rut had overshadowed their relationship with God. They thought more of their physical temple than they did of their God. In verse 2, Stephen points out the need for relationship over systems: Abraham worshipped God rightly before there was ever a place of worship. And it is true that sometimes men still think more of their ritual than of their relationship. How sad! Now, considering the rebellion of Israel, they rejected God's appointed man continually: Joseph, Moses, and, finally, Jesus. This brings up an interesting question: why the tendency for man to reject the truth God sends? Proverbs 20:17 sheds some light for us on this subject, "Bread of deceit is sweet to a man; but afterwards his mouth shall be filled with gravel." In light of this, Stephen earnestly appealed to them, "Men, brethren, and fathers, hearken" (v. 2).

He begins his apology with the historical account of Israel, beginning with Abraham's call from Mesopotamia, and with the call, the promise. And Abraham followed, first to Haran, until after his father died, and then on to Canaan. He punctuates that point in verse 4 by pointing this out, "(Canaan) this land, wherein ye now dwell." Thus,

Stephen links his hearers with the covenant of Abraham. To Stephen, it was significant that Abraham as yet had received no inheritance, "Not so much as to set his foot on" (v. 5). He had nothing to hold to but the Word of God, and yet he still believed. And the promise was sealed in the covenant which was consummated in Christ (see Hebrews 6:17, 20). LISTEN (my dad would shout), God gave Abraham the covenant before He ever gave him the land. And Stephen's point in this part of his apology was this: you have rejected Christ as the consummation of the covenant. NOW, if there is something to be learned here, let it be that we should take GOD AT HIS WORD!

Stephen continues with real insight in verse 9; he saw a comparison between Jesus and Joseph. Both were ill-treated, sold, not accepted, and unrecognized the first time, but God made them each a deliverer. It was futile for the Sanhedrin or sinners to oppose the purpose of God!

Further Apology of Stephen Acts 7:17-50

Thus far in Stephen's apology, we have observed his witnesses: first Abraham and then Joseph. And with each witness, the theme remains the perpetual rejection of God and His servants by His professing people. As Hebrews 2:3 warns us, "How shall we escape, if we neglect so great salvation?" And now we come to Stephen's third witness: Moses. It is at this point that Stephen refutes the charge of blasphemy against Moses and the law, which they accused him of in chapter 6.

> The false witnesses said, "This man ceaseth not to speak blasphemous words against this holy place, and the law: for we have heard him say, that this Jesus of Nazareth shall destroy this place, and shall change the customs which Moses delivered us." (Acts 6:13-14)

Here he honors Moses and gives him his true place in God's plan of deliverance. And with that, he once again drives home THEIR rejection of God's greater Deliverer, JESUS CHRIST! He brings out the fact that Israel might have stayed in Egypt had there been no change of dynasty and policy toward them.

> But when the time of the promise drew nigh, which God had sworn to Abraham, the people grew and multiplied in Egypt, Till another king arose, which knew not Joseph. The same dealt subtilly with our kindred, and evil entreated our fathers, so that they cast out their young children, to the end they might not live. (Acts 7:17-19)

It was during this time of oppression that Moses was born, and after three months he was cast out of his home only to be saved by Pharaoh's daughter. Thus, he was raised and educated as her son. He was "learned in all the wisdom of the Egyptians, and was mighty in words and in deeds" (v. 22). Stephen was simply pointing out that God was with Moses from the beginning and was simply preparing him for his great mission in the future. And although, through crazy circumstances, he was temporarily taken away from his own house, God had a grand purpose for him, AND for Israel (v. 35). And here's part of the comparison that Stephen is making; Jesus, too, nearly perished as a baby and was saved in Egypt. In Verse 23, Stephen brings up the desire of Moses to lead his people; at age forty, he felt the surge of leadership. He supposed that when he intervened as their deliverer, the people would recognize him as such, but they did not. Instead, the Israelites "thrust him away" (v. 27). Stephen, without a doubt, saw Moses as a type of Christ. John 1:11 gives evidence to this shameful principle: "He came unto his own, and his own received him not. But as many as received him, to them gave he power to become the sons of God." Jesus, too, was thrust away and not received, but He was and is our greater Deliverer.

At this point in his apology, Stephen, in order to emphasize that it was Moses, the very one who had been rejected, whom God had sent as deliverer, five times uses the term "this Moses" to drive home his message of rejection to the Sanhedrin. Peter used a similar phrase in Acts 2, 3, and 4 concerning Jesus: "This same Jesus." And Peter was speaking before the same body of men, the Sanhedrin. Then, Stephen, to press the analogy of Moses's/Jesus's rejection, points out that it was with a display of power that God affirmed Moses to Pharaoh and to Israel (v. 36). Likewise, with signs and wonders, Jesus was accredited by God. Then he quoted Moses's prophecy from Deuteronomy 18:15, "The LORD thy God will raise up unto thee a Prophet from the midst of thee, of thy brethren, like unto me." The significance of this is that Peter had applied the same prophecy before the Sanhedrin in Acts 3:22. Jesus alluded to it on the Emmaus Road with two of his disciples in Luke 24:13-35. Stephen drew the analogy together with all that Moses had done, as it was with Jesus, that Israel "In their hearts turned back again into Egypt" (v. 39). Stephen's summation then was this: WHO is guilty of blasphemy? And in the light of all the evidence, of course, ALL ISRAEL IS GUILTY! Stephen refuted the charge of blasphemy against the temple in Acts 6:14.

At the end of this section (vv. 44-50), he showed that the Lord placed no great emphasis upon the place of worship itself. Verse 48 shows that it was only a material shadow of a spiritual reality. It is Stephen's premise that "the most High dwelleth not in temples made with hands" (v. 48; see also Isaiah 66:1), but that true habitation of God is that which is "not made with hands" (Mark 14:58), but in the hearts of men. Thus, in concluding his apology, he answers both major charges concerning blasphemy against Moses/God and the temple. Concerning blasphemy against Moses/God, he showed that all Israel, and not he alone, must face that charge. We all must face that charge because "all have sinned" (Romans 3:23). Concerning blasphemy against the temple, he showed the attitude of God toward it as set forth in Scripture. And with this, he implied that he heartily agreed. Stephen defended the true church of Jesus Christ, and in so doing, called Christ-rejectors in every age, back to God.

Stephen's Indictment and Death Acts 7:51-60

Having addressed the charges of blasphemy, Stephen, without a break in his address, leveled an indictment at the Sanhedrin more severe than any recorded thus far. It summed up and applied all that he had just said, "Ye (emphatic) stiffnecked (obstinate, would not bend) and uncircumcised in heart and ears" (v. 51). They were stuck in the mud; they said, 'No one's going to tell us what to do!' This is not the first time Israel had met with this accusation; here are some examples:

> And the LORD said unto Moses, "I have seen this people, and, behold, it is a stiffnecked people." (Exodus 32:9)

> For the LORD had said unto Moses, "Say unto the children of Israel, Ye are a stiffnecked people: I will come up into the midst of thee in a moment, and consume thee: therefore now put off thy ornaments from thee, that I may know what to do unto thee." (Exodus 33:5)

> Understand therefore, that the LORD thy God giveth thee not this good land to possess it for thy righteousness; for thou art a stiffnecked people. Furthermore the LORD spake unto me, saying, I have seen this people, and, behold, it is a stiffnecked people. (Deuteronomy 9:6, 13)

Stephen's charge continued in verse 51, "Ye do always resist the Holy Ghost: as your fathers did." In essence, he was saying to these religious leaders, 'You say that you are godly, but you are not. You may give outward testimony, but there is no inward work. Thus, you are no better than the heathen.' Here, he classes the Sanhedrin with the fathers who had opposed God. He challenged them to name one prophet whom they had not persecuted and/or slain.

Then, in verse 52, he draws Christ into the picture and accuses them of murder! Wow, Stephen! No wonder he got stoned! You are the ones who have not kept the law, he says to them in verse 53. Before we go on, let us consider this matter of resisting the Holy Ghost. How can God's people be guilty of such a failing? To answer this question, let's acknowledge the fact that there are numerous scriptures of warning against this very thing; for example, "Quench not the Holy Spirit" (1 Thessalonians 5:19); and "Yield yourselves unto God" (Romans 6:13). In this particular verse, "yield" has the distinct meaning of "offer continually or surrender" or "to put yourself at God's disposal." God gave us these New Testament commands because He knows our tendency to fling ourselves in opposition to the Holy Ghost, not always in an active manner, but simply by reason of the fact that when we do not yield, we are in opposition. On this subject, Charles Finney has this to say, "Every Christian needs to be revived about every three weeks. But by a daily yielding to the Spirit, we can be revived daily, though our outward man perish."

Now, such accusations as these will bring a result, either good or evil. In this case (v. 54), it was evil. The religious leaders acted like animals. Satan had robbed them of all moral decency. Folks, that's what sin does; it's as simple as that. That's why we must yield to the Spirit! And in that moment, Satan unleashed his fury at Stephen.

Verse 55 gives Stephen's response. In that moment, because he was full of the Holy Ghost, through that awful experience, Stephen saw the glory of God, and Christ in His place of authority at the right hand of God. In the Sermon on the Mount, Jesus said, "Blessed are ye, when men shall revile you, and persecute you, and shall say all manner of evil against you falsely, for my sake. Rejoice, and be exceeding glad: for great is your reward in heaven" (Matthew 5:11-12). It is the persecutions against us for Christ's sake that prove us. And through that which stirred within him, he remained calm and controlled; a sure testimony to the power of a living Christ! The Holy Spirit enabled him TO SEE; it was not just in his mind's eye. He cried out, "I see…the Son of man standing on the right hand of God" (v. 56). Why was He standing when always before He is seated at the right hand of Power? Perhaps it is that Jesus arose to receive the first martyr! Perhaps Jesus arose in the court of heaven to testify for Stephen who had been condemned in the lower court. And thus it is, "Whosoever therefore shall confess me before men, him will I confess also before my Father which is in heaven." (Matthew 10:32)

And what was the crowd's response? Verse 57 shows us that the crowd could stand no more! There was no verdict, and mob violence broke loose. They reacted again like enraged animals. And again, we see men at the crossroads. Stephen's Spirit-anointed words would either bring them to Christ or cut to the heart. They did the latter, for they would not bow the knee. Can we learn something right here? YES! The lesson is to be tender and open to the Word of God. It will either reprove, rebuke, correct, or instruct. Verse 59 gives the final blow with the stoning of Stephen, while Saul looked on. The striking similarities of Stephen's death with that of Christ, except the manner of death, do not go unnoticed. The last verse of this chapter gives a final look into the purity of Stephen's heart, "Lord, lay not this sin to their charge." Thus we say, let this mind be in you which was also in Christ Jesus!

The Church Scattered and Philip's Ministry

Acts Chapter 8

It is here that we get our first real introduction to Saul of Tarsus, later known as Paul the apostle. Following the death of Stephen in chapter 7, and before Saul comes on the scene as an apostle, we catch a glimpse of the ministry of Philip. Philip's ministry in this chapter includes preaching to a crowd, Holy Spirit baptisms, fending off fake ministers, and having a one-on-one discipleship moment with an Ethiopian.

Dad was known for his great one-liners. He had the gift of making a possibly complicated truth of Scripture completely understandable in one fell swoop of a sentence; often with humor. Baptism in the Holy Spirit, let's face it, can be complicated to understand, let alone explain, since it is spiritual and not humanly manipulated. One student, and later colleague, of my dad's, had this to share of his first impression of my dad's preaching and famous one-liners. After hearing a refreshingly simple teaching, in sermon form, on the Holy Spirit, Chuck Vanasse (new to Trinity Bible College in the spring semester of 1991), went up to dad after the message and thanked him for helping him understand a sometimes puzzling subject. To which Dad's only response to Chuck was, "Well, the Holy Ghost ain't a spook, ya know!" True, Dad, so true.

Let's take a seat in today's class on Acts chapter 8 and see how many one-liners of wisdom we get to hear!

* * *

Saul Scatters the Church Acts 8:1-4

Up to this point, the church had made no effort to carry the gospel out of Jerusalem; there had been no direct missionary activity. Remember, the proclamation of Jesus included Jerusalem as the starting place, and from there it was to spread to "Judaea, Samaria, and to the uttermost part of the earth" (Acts 1:8). Now, the truth is, we cannot disregard the plain teaching of God's Word without repercussion. In this case, it was persecution. In other cases, there was death, sickness, and famine. One reference we can study in relation to this is 1 Corinthians 11 when Paul gives some instruction for communion; specifically verse 27, which speaks of drinking the cup of the Lord, unworthily. Thus, in the opening verses of chapter 8, Luke states the general condition that prevailed at the time of Stephen's death.

Verse 1 opens with the mention of Saul, "And Saul was consenting unto his (Stephen's) death." "He was approving, endorsing, taking pleasure with them in it ("heartily agreeing," Roth). The truth is that Saul not only agreed with the horrors; he became the prime motivator. And Stephen's death became the gate that introduced a flood of persecutions against the church. Now, consider a basic principle here that we have seen before: wherever there is a good measure of spiritual success, Satan will unleash all of hell to pull down that which God in His grace has built. We saw this in chapter 6 with Stephen. Now think of that principle in this way: this is a victory in itself, to realize Satan's tactics! There are two things that we must do in the face of such opposition: examine ourselves and go forward in the authority and power of God's Word.

> I will build my church; and the gates of hell shall not prevail against it. (Matthew 16:18)

> When the enemy shall come in like a flood, the Spirit of the LORD shall lift up a standard against him. (Isaiah 59:19)

As a result of the persecution, the believers "were scattered abroad throughout the regions of Judaea and Samaria" (v. 1b). The apostles remained in the Jerusalem area. It seemed that Jerusalem remained the headquarters. It seems also that the persecution was more severe against those who were not native to the immediate area, while the apostles were, for the most part, from the Jerusalem area. Luke sidesteps the account of persecution for a moment to tell what happened to Stephen. In verse 2, we read that devout men buried Stephen and made great lamentation over him. There is a sense in which men today should grieve over the abuse of Christ's church!

Saul stepped onto the scene in verse 3: "As for Saul, he made havock of the church." It is here that Saul (Paul) revealed his many qualities, both good and bad. He was devout, energetic, learned, cultured, young, clean, and above all, zealous for the traditions of Israel. Galatians 1:14 and Philippians 3:5–6 list many of his qualities. Saul did not go along with Gamaliel in Acts 5 when he spoke reason to the Sanhedrin in letting the apostles go without recourse. Instead, he "made havock"; laid waste; ravaged the church. This term is used to describe the work of wild beasts! He invaded homes where Christians lived, seizing them, and dragging them away violently. Not only men, but women as well, and he did it all in an official capacity. But Saul's actions speak of more than ecclesiastical zeal; Saul was under conviction. Some observers have commented that it is possible that the persecution would not have been so fierce had it not been for Saul. Saul's guilty conscience was battling with him. This intense persecution was an outward show of the battle in his mind and spirit as Romans 7:23, which Saul (Paul) wrote, so eloquently portrays: "But I see another law in my members, warring against the law of my mind, and bringing me into captivity to the law of sin which is in my members." But the harder Saul tried to crush the church, the more the movement spread.

"Therefore they that were scattered abroad went every where preaching the word" (v. 4). The word "scattered" in the Greek text is an agricultural term; it pictures the act of "sowing" seed. It was the secret of the growth of the church: EVERY BELIEVER A WITNESS! If one believed, he also witnessed and told of his belief. AND THE CHURCH GREW! And the great principle was illustrated, "Except a corn of wheat fall into the ground and die" (John 12:24). Stephen died, and many others identified with him and found LIFE in Jesus.

Philip Preaches in Samaria Acts 8:5-8

Philip is a deacon, as noted in Acts 6:5. If we look ahead to Acts 21:8, we can see that he became a recognized evangelist, which is the emerging fact of this section. Verse 5 of this chapter shows us that with the rejection of the gospel by the Jews, the message is now given to ALL nations. Philip declared the gospel in Samaria. Now, the fact that he went down to Samaria is truly not only in a geographical sense, but also in a psychological sense because the Jews had no dealings with Samaritans. They considered them to be half-breeds, or half-heathen. The separation dates back to the disruption of the kingdom after Solomon's death. They even built a rival temple, but they looked for a Messiah, even as the full-blooded Israelites did. And when Philip went down and preached Christ, they gave heed.

Now, let's look at Philip's ministry a little more closely. Who had prepared the way for Philip? It was Jesus with the woman at the well (John 4:39-42). Jesus had sowed the seed, the woman sowed it in turn, and then Philip reaped the harvest of souls. He preached Christ to them! The heart of his message was Christ; not politics or current events or the newspaper. He preached CHRIST! And that is still the message that is needed today. John 12:21 gives voice to the cry of humanity, "Sir, we would see Jesus." From the pulpit, in the home, in the business world, in the workshop—it is Jesus Christ who is our message!

The response to Philip's preaching was like another wave of Pentecost, as verse 6 records. The miracles and signs sealed and confirmed the authority of Philip's preaching. It was like Jesus's early ministry. The lame and the palsied were healed. Those who had unclean spirits were delivered. "And the people with one accord gave heed unto those things which Philip spake" (verse 6b). This speaks to us of our responsibility to respond to the Word!

If there is a failure in the church today, it is in this respect: A FAILURE TO HEED THE WORD OF GOD. Not only did they give heed, but they were also in ONE ACCORD OVER IT. The phrase "gave heed" in verse 6 means to listen carefully. These people had a healthy introduction to the Spirit-life. They heard the Word of God. They gave heed to it. And in the process of it all, they saw miracles done. And that same response will bring a similar result for any of us. The truth that is set for them here is that the things that draw the response of God on our behalf are not found in an aura of super spiritualism. It is not in a holy ritual of certain things we do, BUT it is the fact that we hear the Word; we give heed to the Word; and we receive the promised return. Again, we see the promise of Mark 16:17 at play, "These signs shall follow them that believe." When we follow God's spiritual order, people are delivered from evil possession, the palsied are healed, and the lame walk again.

Now note the vast difference in the situation in verses 6-8, "And there was great joy in that city," as compared with verse 3, "As for Saul, he made havock of the church." What made the difference? The heeding of the Word of God made the difference. Verse 3 reflected an ignoring of the Word of God, whereas verses 6-8 denote miracles! And this truth is still the same today!

Simon the Sorcerer Acts 8:9-25

In this section of verses, Luke's main objective is to show the outcome of the gospel's first outward encounter with sorcery, or the powers of darkness. Simon was a sorcerer, a user of magic charms and enchantments that ranged from calling upon demons to divination. Sorcerers then, as now, played upon the spiritual gullibility of the people with respect to the unknown. He bewitched the people; literally, they stood out of themselves.

Verse 9 suggests that Simon was well known to the people in Samaria, and they expressed themselves of him as verse 10 records, "This man is the great power of God." And the curious thing about this situation is that not only the ignorant and poor were deceived, but "they all gave heed, from the least to the greatest." There is something diabolically "blinding" about error. Jesus warned about the deception that would try to turn people aside in Matthew 24:4, "Take heed that no man deceive you." Second John 7 also warns us, "For many deceivers are entered into the world, who confess not that Jesus Christ is come in the flesh. This is a deceiver and an antichrist." Satan's chief aim to the Christian is to dispel the truth and power of the Word. Therefore, TAKE HEED!

In verse 11, Luke expresses an attitude that is prevalent even today. Because Simon had bewitched them for a long time, so they had regard for him. They said, in effect, 'We've been this way for so long, why change now?' Simon's hold was strong, but the gospel broke that satanic spell. Jesus said of Himself in Luke 4:18, "The Spirit of the Lord is upon me...to preach deliverance to the captives." The people turned from Simon and gave heed to Philip preaching Christianity and the kingdom. It is significant to note that there were believers upon whom the Holy Spirit had not yet fallen; that came later.

So thorough was this revival that Simon the Sorcerer himself "believed," as verse 13 tells us. Now, the extent and nature of his belief is uncertain. It seemed quite superficial and certainly imperfect. What was the problem? Obviously, he focused his attention upon the oracles rather than the Word. Peter's later rebuke (vv. 20-21) estimates his depth of commitment. He said to Simon, "Thy heart is not right in the sight of God." Jesus Himself took a dim view of belief that rested on miracles alone. John 2:23–24 tells us of this apprehensive response to those who believe conditionally: "But Jesus did not commit himself unto them (those in Jerusalem)."

Simon stayed with Philip and continued to wonder at the miracles. Now, the word "bewitched" (v. 11) and the word "wondered" (v. 13) both have the same root word in Greek, meaning "amazed." Thus, he who had made the people "beside themselves" with witchcraft was now beside himself by God's power. And even though he was baptized in water, it seems that he missed the real meaning of it. RITUAL WILL NEVER REPLACE REALITY!

Verse 14 reports the news of the revival reaching Jerusalem, whereupon they sent Peter and John to encourage the work. Surveying the work of God, they perceived that, though they had received the Word of God, they had not received the Holy Spirit. The next few verses (15-17) are an excellent display of truth. They prayed for them to receive the Holy Spirit, because, though they had received, believed, and been baptized, they had not yet received the Holy Spirit in His fullness. In verse 16, the word "fallen" is in the strongest literal sense: "to press upon." Now, the interval here teaches us the significance of baptism in the Spirit as being subsequent to conversion. In verse 17, it is noteworthy that this is the first time the act of "laying on of hands" is associated with the baptism in the Spirit. This is not always used, as we note in Acts 2:4 and Acts 10:44. But, the significance is that God is a God of variety! There is no formula to "get what we want" from God; He cannot be manipulated.

Now the results of the Samaritan revival were outward and visible, to the extent that Simon was ready to pay money for the power (authority) to do the same. And the word "saw" in verse 18 is evident of the visible demonstration as the Holy Spirit fell upon them, i.e., they spoke in tongues.

And, sadly, Simon shows his true colors in verse 19. We should take note of this: the Holy Spirit, or anything spiritual, is NOT a marketable commodity. Spiritual things are discerned and received by faith. First Corinthians 2:10, 14 give us some straightforward teaching about this:

> But God hath revealed them unto us by his Spirit: for the Spirit searcheth all things, yea, the deep things of God…But the natural man receiveth not the things of the Spirit of God: for they are foolishness unto him: neither can he know them, because they are spiritually discerned.

And Peter's response to Simon's request was one of righteous anger and stern rebuke (v. 20). Simon's action was almost blasphemous; it reminds us of Ananias and Sapphira. This incident is the source of the word "simony," which means the buying and selling of the things of God for gain.

Peter further rebuked Simon the Sorcerer in verse 23, "You have fallen into the bitterest bondage of unrighteousness!" (Weymouth). Apparently, he had not stood with the others to receive the Spirit, but stood back to watch the process. And upon Peter's rebuke and begging for apostolic intercession, Simon's reply showed real fear. However, it is uncertain whether or not he truly repented. Some feel that he repented, and Luke implies this. Tradition says that Simon became the "father of heresy," and the whole matter is uncertain. But WE need not be in uncertainty, rather continue in the Word we have received and believed.

Philip and the Ethiopian Acts 8:26-40

The evangelist Philip was then called from the multitude of a great city to show the way of salvation to one man. God's missionary purpose is not for the masses only, but for the individual. Because of that, the lessons for us here are numerous and applicable. First of all, when the Holy Spirit leads us, circumstances will all fall into place. Perhaps not just the way we want or expect, but certainly in His ways and timing, and many times unexplainable outside of God's design. That is the test of God's leading. Second, when God leads, He deals with every detail. He even told Philip which road to take: one that was deserted and untraveled. There were several roads from Samaria and Jerusalem to Gaza. Verse 27 records that Philip obeyed without question. They were strange instructions, indeed, but this was his response: "And he arose and went (with haste)." Like Abraham, Philip went, when not knowing why except that God had said to GO! And it was there that he found the reason: the Ethiopian man in need of instruction. The third lesson we can pick up in this section is that God usually unfolds His plan as we go. Remember the ten lepers? As they went, they were being cleansed (Luke 17:14). "One step before me is all I need to see" is the walk of faith.

Now, at the appointed place, a high official (the treasurer) of the Queen of Ethiopia was seated in his chariot reading Isaiah 53. Luke reflects Philip's amazement: "Behold, a man of Ethiopia" (v. 27). We are often surprised at the outcome of God's leading. Apparently, this man was already a proselyte of Judaism, and it seems he was in search of more. He was on the right track! The Word is the Source of faith and spiritual life development.

The Spirit spoke to Philip again in verse 29. In what manner He spoke is not so important as the fact that Philip was open to the leading of the Spirit. "Go near, and join thyself to this chariot," was the instruction in this verse. God was using Philip to meet this man's need. And God typically uses man to minister to the needs of man.

Verse 27 reflects the true condition of the Ethiopian man: a man of dignity and yet open to the things of God. Philip's approach to him is direct; which leads to an equally direct response from him to Philip in verse 31. And he said, "How can I, except some man should guide me?" The Moffet's translation puts it this way: "Someone should put me on the right track."

The Ethiopian's searching heart drew him to read from Isaiah 53, and he was truly seeking truth. Few passages could have provided a better text from which to witness, or incited more readiness to hear on his part. This man's problem was not one of critical appraisal, but of honest searching, "Of whom speaketh the prophet this?" (v. 34). Now, before Jesus came on the scene as the Messiah, it was not clear who was meant by this Suffering Servant to whom Isaiah referred. BUT it was no problem for Philip to see because Jesus had settled it when He revealed Himself to His disciples after His resurrection.

> Then opened he their understanding, that they might understand the scriptures. (Luke 24:45)

The man's question was all Philip needed, for there is something to be said here of the timing of our witness. The Word of God is not a club to beat people into submission; it is a sword, and it is the weapon of the Spirit for personal conviction. Philip based his preaching on the passage that was presently on the Ethiopian's mind and preached unto him JESUS. It is the theme of the gospel: JESUS IS THE GOSPEL! Thus learn this, we can often give testimony through the situation at hand.

The Ethiopian's response shows that Philip must have also taught him that faith in Christ is to openly confess with baptism. "What doth hinder me?" he asks Philip (v. 36). His immediate response and obedience is worth observing! Without hesitation, he acted upon his new convictions; matching Philip's immediate obedience earlier in this story!

But Philip tested his faith first, "If thou believest" (v. 37). And he answered in a most convincing and profound manner, "I believe that Jesus Christ is the Son of God" (v. 37). And, folks, it is that kind of confession that is still needed today.

Verse 38 illustrates the immersion mode of baptism, "And they went down both into the water." With his mission completed, God gave Philip a "jet ride" to Azotus! The Ethiopian man went his way rejoicing. God is STILL looking for yielded vessels to lead city-wide revivals or one-man revivals. ARE YOU YIELDED TO HIM?

23

Saul to Paul and Peter's Continuing Ministry

Acts Chapter 9

Paul and Peter: Two of the Bible greats, and pioneers in the early church. Chapter 9 introduces us to Paul as he is transformed from being Saul; and highlights Peter in his role as leading traveling evangelist. Think of how Jesus transformed both of these men. He struck one blind to get his attention; and the other, He never wavered in believing in, even when his faith wavered. God is so faithful to us!

Saul wanted to keep the Jewish faith pure by persecuting the new Christians, but God transformed him into Paul with a new calling to be a Christian apologist. Peter wanted to give up on his calling as a disciple and go back to fishing, but Jesus told him that he wanted to build the church on the revelation the Father had given him, and then fill him with the Holy Spirit! It is this story that Amanda Day, a former student, had to share with me about Dad's teaching:

> I wasn't raised in church, and Acts class was the first time I had heard of the Saul/Paul conversion. It, to this day, is my favorite Bible story, and I remember him teaching it!

Dad had this way about him in teaching, preaching, or just shooting the breeze with you. He could make profound things simple or words on the pages of the Bible come to life! Time with him, pertaining to biblical topics, was always rich. Let's shoot the breeze with him about Saul and tap into that richness.

* * *

The Conversion of Saul Acts 9:1-9

It is at this point in Acts that the attention of the book shifts from Peter to Paul. The significance of Saul's conversion was very evident to Luke. Saul's conversion held the essentials of every Christian conversion: conviction of sin (v. 5), acceptance of Christ (v. 6), and confession. Thus, Saul's conversion from the archenemy of the church, to his appointment as the apostle to the gentiles, was a great turning point. And so important was it in the mind of Luke that he records this story two other times in Acts: before a mob of Jews (Acts 22:6-16) and before Roman rulers (Acts 26:12-18).

Paul himself alludes to his conversion often to attest to his authority as an apostle (see Galatians 1:3-22; Philippians 3:5; 1 Timothy 1:12-13; and 1 Corinthians 15:8-9). One thing that draws our attention very clearly is that, of Saul's conversion, there was no doubt. Now, before we say any more about the text itself, let us look at Paul himself. He was born in Tarsus, and his parents were loyal Orthodox Jews. Thus, he was a Jew by birth, but he also possessed Roman citizenship. In Tarsus, which is a seaport and academic center, Paul had the advantage of a wide range of education. At thirteen, he was sent to Jerusalem to study under the great Hebrew teacher, Gamaliel. Thus, from this background, Saul emerged to meet the world. He was a leader among men, full of knowledge of the Scriptures and well-acquainted with philosophy. He was studious, conscientious, and aggressive. Thus, he became the prime mover of the persecution of Jerusalem. In an effort to keep the Jewish faith "pure," Saul sought to extend the "purge" to the surrounding area. What a contrast to the powerful but unassuming ministry of Philip!

This chapter opens with Saul's turmoil in his own heart, "And Saul, yet breathing out threatenings and slaughter." It suggests the fierce anticipation of a war horse, readying for the battle. The term "slaughter" in verse 1 is significant, for Stephen was not the only martyr of those days: "And many of the saints did I shut up in prison, having received authority from the chief priests; and when they were put to death, I gave my voice against them" (Acts 26:10). Thus, the rage continues, and once again, it pictures the intensity of the inner battle. Now, here is a man who is sincere in his zeal, but sincerely wrong! In Philippians 3:6, Paul indicts himself, "Concerning zeal, persecuting the church." It should speak to us now: there is a lot of zeal today, but for the wrong thing. Verse 2 records that Paul received letters of authority from the high priest, which represented the wishes of the religious leaders of the day, to apprehend Christians. So, he headed for Damascus to hunt them down. Now, the term in this verse, "the way," is the earliest expression of reference to Christianity.

Then, everything changed for Saul/Paul starting in verse 3. On the journey to ravage the Damascus Christians, the Lord made His big play for Saul's soul. A light appeared from heaven, so bright that it arrested him in his way; stunned, he fell to the ground. The arrester was arrested! It indicates the lengths to which God will go to bring men to the Savior. What did He do to win you?

The voice of the Lord expresses the deep concern and emotion of God, "Saul, Saul, why persecutest thou me?" (v. 4). It is not anger, "But that all men should come to repentance" (2 Peter 3:9). This encounter with Jesus in the beginning of this chapter stripped Saul of all his pious pride. HE SAW JESUS! Acts 9:17, 27; 22:14; and 26:16 all give record of this encounter Saul had with Jesus, from his own account, as well as Ananias and Barnabas testifying.

In that gracious moment of divine illumination, Saul recognized the Lord. "Who art thou, Lord?" Saul declares (v. 5). And Jesus responds, leaving no doubt, "I am Jesus, whom thou persecutest." Now, this all came as a climax to the process of Saul's conviction. For some folks, it takes a long time, but not with Saul. Beginning with his inability to answer Stephen's argument, or understand Stephen's testimony, the glory on his face, his prayer, and his death, to the obvious martyrdom of others with similar reactions as Stephen, Saul now sees the truth. It floods over him that HE HAD BEEN PERSECUTING THE LORD!

The next statement of verse 5 is so expressive of the battle within the human heart: "It is hard for thee to kick against the pricks." It illustrates the oxen who react to the driver's "goad," or a tool used to encourage, urge, or stimulate. In like manner, we often rebel against the Holy Spirit. With an enlightened and changed heart, Saul responded in verse 6, "Lord, what wilt thou have me to do?" Saul was beginning to understand, and he fully realized the implication of his statement, "Lord." For the basic Jewish tenet is: "The Lord our God is one Lord." Thus, the theme of Saul's life becomes, "JESUS IS LORD."

The direct dealing of Jesus stopped after the arrest of Saul, as Jesus directed him to go to the city of Damascus with specific instructions. Jesus had revealed Himself to Saul, but He left the privilege of directing Saul's steps in salvation to the unassuming disciple, Ananias. And that responsibility is still the job of faithful disciples today.

Verse 7 records the reactions of Saul's companions to this "Jesus encounter" on the road to Damascus. Saul's deputies were also moved upon, but tied considerably less significance to it than Saul himself did. Then in verse 8, Luke gives us a vivid picture of the humbled Saul. The great persecutor, the would-be destroyer of the church, was led by hand into the city he had come to, Damascus, with the intent to bind the Christians. But instead of Saul binding Christians, God delivered him instead! No one can resist God. The response is either submission or forever damnation! The choice is ours!

The transformation from Saul to Paul happens next, "And he was there three days without sight, and neither did eat nor drink" (v. 9). Old things were passed away; all things were becoming new.

Ananias and Brother Saul Acts 9:10-17

This account presents an encouraging challenge to each one of us: "And there was a certain disciple" (v. 10). No special personality; just a certain disciple. Ananias is an inspiring example to all who are called to live the Christian life amid ordinary everyday circumstances. It is the ordinary that is often the most difficult; fewer outward stimulants require deeper steadfast faith. Christ needs those who will live the ordinary life in an out-of-the-ordinary way! Thus, to every Christian who may feel a sense of ordinariness, Ananias is a bright star of encouragement!

Now, there are some great lessons we may learn from Ananias. He was in the place where God could speak to him. He was ready to obey; and that is the essence of our existence as Christians. Astronomers say that there are stars that appear in the heavens; they are there shining brightly, but soon are gone. Ananias was like that! He appeared for a time, and then faded into obscurity. But he was always ready to heed God's call, "Behold, I am here Lord" (v. 10). What a gracious yieldedness! HE HAD PROVEN HIS LIFE IN DAILY LIVING! Paul testifies of Ananias's character in Acts 22:12, and called him "a devout man according to the law." Such a statement says a lot about a man. He was so honest and upright in his convictions that he could endure the microscope where others would fail. Nothing was morally unimportant to him. The latter part of Acts 22:12 bears his testimony, "Having a good report of all the Jews which dwelt there." It is no small matter to be praised by those who strongly differ from us. Here is a lesson in holy discretion or spiritual diplomacy: a man does not gain such appraisal in a week or so! Think about what a life sermon Ananias is: Mr. Nobody, yet a member of God's hall of stars.

Now, let's turn our attention back to Saul and note the comparison of his before and after. Verse 1 records, "And Saul, yet breathing out threatenings and slaughter" (of Christians). Contrast that with his actions in verse 11, "Behold, he prayeth." What a change! The details with which Ananias is sent to Paul are these: "Arise, and go into the street which is called Straight, and enquire in the house of Judas for one called Saul of Tarsus." And the truth is reinforced here that God does not send where He does not lead. For on the other end, He was preparing Saul with a vision. We find this same miracle again in Acts 10 between Peter and Cornelius. And we can learn this from that pattern; God's way is always deliberate and direct.

Ananias did a good thing; he proceeded with caution. It is not doubt, but caution, 'Are you sure you want me, Lord?' (paraphrase vv. 13-14). But God's encouragement is this, "Go thy way," and then He graciously explains why: "He is a chosen vessel unto me" (v. 15). There is a concept here that applies to every one of us: Saul is not the only chosen vessel here that is of God! We are all chosen vessels of God, "Ye have not chosen me, but I have chosen you, and ordained you, that ye should go and bring forth fruit" (John 15:16). Ananias's ministry to Saul was one of ministry first and THEN teaching (vv. 12-16). Another thing that we can learn from Ananias is his willingness. We would not blame him if he had shrunk away from this mission! By all outward appearances, it was like throwing a lamb to the lions. If Ananias would have told his friends of this direction from God, they would have said, 'Don't go near him!' But the account of Scripture is as expressive on this point as elsewhere with regard to Ananias's character. It simply says, "And Ananias went his way" willingly (v. 17). Then deliberately, and with all authority, he declared the purpose and power of God to be Saul's—to Saul in the flesh. Then Ananias completed his mission, "Brother Saul…receive thy sight and be filled with the Holy Ghost" (v. 17). And Ananias faded off the scene.

Paul's First Steps Acts 9:17-22

With the obedience of Ananias fresh in our minds, we see the excellent and eternal results of such obedience. Saul was healed, filled with the Holy Spirit, and baptized! Let's investigate this small yet impactful encounter between Ananias and Saul. First of all, what a greeting, "Brother Saul" (v. 17). There is a depth of family relationship here. This is no casual acquaintance; this is not forced co-existence. This is a heaven-born relationship: sons of God, heirs of God, joint heirs with Christ. What rich implication that greeting is! Believer, do you know who YOUR Father is? And do you know your brother? Your sister? I'm so glad I'm a part of the family of God! Ananias continued, "The Lord, even Jesus, that appeared unto thee…hath sent me." Ananias was used by God like an apostle, which by definition means "sent one," to reach one who would become one of the greatest apostles. The repeated emphasis throughout Saul's experience, that Jesus of Nazareth is Christ and Lord, was as significant to Saul (Paul) as it is to us today! He is more than a Savior; He is God in the flesh, the Christ, the Messiah.

And He is Lord, "Wherefore God also hath highly exalted him...Jesus Christ is Lord" (Philippians 2:9, 11). With the repeated statement, Paul continually identified the totality of God WITH man. He is indeed IMMANUEL, which is "God with us." And Ananias's part adds to the realization of our privileges as believers: such ministry is the possibility of every believer. Ananias was sent by God.

Now, in verse 18, Luke the physician describes what took place—scales fell from Saul's eyes, and he miraculously received his sight. I think that more important than the scales on his eyes falling away was the spiritual illumination that flooded Saul's heart. Scales also fell from his heart. And THAT is what the church and world needs today! Ephesians 1:18-19 declares this, "The eyes of your understanding being enlightened; that ye may know what is the hope of his calling, and what the riches of the glory of his inheritance in the saints, and what is the exceeding greatness of his power to us-ward who believe."

It seems that Paul spent some time at Damascus, fellowshipping with those whom he had come to bind (v. 19). What a contrast! "And straightway he preached Christ in the synagogues, that he is the Son of God" (v. 20). He went into the synagogues to which the high priest had sent him, but with an entirely different purpose! The persecutor had become the preacher.

And his message was one of deep significance for believers of that day, Jew and gentile alike! His message was this: "Christ, the Son of God." Here is one of the few places in Acts where Christ is specifically called the "Son of God." And it indicates an experience more personal and real than that of other preachers. Jesus Christ is the Son of God. And that personal experience is the catalyst of Christianity.

Verse 21 shows the result of Saul's transformation: confusion and amazement! They could not figure it out! This will always be the reaction of the unspiritual mind; he cannot understand spiritual things. Look at this instruction in 1 Corinthians 2:14, "But the natural man receiveth not the things of the Spirit of God: for they are foolishness unto him: neither can he know them, because they are spiritually discerned."

We read that "Saul increased the more in strength" (v. 22). There is a principle here than can apply to all of us: the more we involve ourselves with the gospel, the mightier we are in God, in ministry, in understanding, in influence, and in results. The word "strength" in verse 22 is not the same as the word in verse 19, which speaks of physical strength after he ate; but verse 22 speaks of inner spiritual strength. May God induce us to a similar might! Take a deeper look into how God strengthened Paul throughout the rest of his life with these verses: Romans 4:20; Ephesians 6:10; Philippians 4:13; 2 Timothy 2:1; 1 Timothy 1:12; and 2 Timothy 4:17. And this is the ultimate result of Paul/Saul increasing in spiritual strength, "Proving that this is very Christ" (v. 22b). The word "proving" in this verse means "put together," and the implication of the verse is in the manner expressing the fact that it was done. That responsibility is still upon us, folks!

Paul the Apostle Acts 9:23-31

Once again, in this context of Scripture, we have emphasis upon the positive change in the life of Saul. The hunter becomes the hunted, "The Jews took counsel to kill him" (v. 23). Saul is an illustration to us of the complete work of God in a yielded vessel: "Old things are passed away; behold all things are become new" (2 Corinthians 5:17). Can YOU say that? Note that Jesus is the great Divider; He divides disciples from dissenters. In His own words, here is that principle, "Think not that I am come to send peace on earth; I came not to send peace, but a sword." (Matthew 10:34)

Verse 24 is the first real identification of Saul as an apostle. It was validation of his appointment by the Lord, which was first noted in verses 15–16: "For he is a chosen vessel unto me, to bear my name before the Gentiles, and kings, and the children of Israel: for I will shew him how great things he must suffer for my name's sake." It speaks to us here, as well, of the care and concern of the Father. As with Jesus, there was a conspiracy to kill Saul. "But their laying await was known of Saul. And they watched the gates day and night to kill him" (v. 24). But as these men conspired, God inspired Saul's disciples to care for him, thus, in the following verse, Saul escapes his enemies for the time being. Now, the gist of this verse suggests the success of his ministry by the anger of the Jews and the loyalty of his disciples. "Then the disciples took him by night, and let him down by the wall in a basket" (v. 25). This is an indication that these were people who were won to Christ through Saul's ministry. Unlike Stephen, Saul's life was spared. Why? One reason could be that God needs workers more than He needs martyrs.

So Saul is on the move, and from Damascus he went to Jerusalem. "But they were all afraid of him, and believed not that he was a disciple" (v. 26). We can hardly blame them! Here is a good lesson in spiritual caution. There are many characters who operate in the name of religion these days, but Barnabas! Barnabas was a friend in Saul's time of need. "But Barnabas took him, and brought him to the apostles" (v. 27). What a fitting name he had: Barnabas means "son of encouragement." He got the full story from

Saul—the Spirit apparently gave witness of its truth—and Barnabas believed Saul. Barnabas speaks to us, always, of the right Christian spirit. In Acts 4, he displays generosity. Here, in Acts 9, he has concern and compassion. Acts 11:24 says this of Barnabas, "He was a good man, and full of the Holy Ghost and of faith."

Barnabas pleads Saul's case; he stood by him on these points: he had seen the Lord, the Lord had spoken to him, and Saul had preached boldly in Damascus in the name of Jesus. This is his plea for Saul's relationship with the Lord, and IT IS THE TEST FOR US AS WELL! Have YOU seen Him? Do YOU speak to Him? Do YOU speak for Him?

The result of Barnabas's testimony is laid out in verse 28; he had won the approval of the fellowship in Jerusalem. But Saul ran into trouble again. He disputed with his former associates, the Hellenistic Jews, and they sought to kill him (v. 29). Now, Saul's situation was not unlike anyone who makes his stand for Christ without reserve. It was the proving of his faith that made him what he was! And it will do the same for us, people! Listen to this encouragement from Jesus, "Blessed are ye, when men shall revile you…for great is your reward in heaven." (Matthew 5:11-12)

To spare his life, once again, Saul's brethren helped him—they sent him to Tarsus, according to verse 30. He went home! Now, Luke takes time to summarize the results in verse 31. It marked a plateau of the preservation of the young church, "Then had the churches rest." But it was not a time of relaxation! The church was edified inwardly and multiplied outwardly. And the two great sources of power and growth were the fear of the Lord (a reverential fear) and the comfort of the Holy Spirit. It seems that with the spiritual growth, there was a companion of numerical growth. THIS IS A PRINCIPLE—healthy things grow.

The Ministry of Peter Acts 9:32-43

Our attention now reverts back to Peter; we left him in Jerusalem in chapter 5. With rapid church growth and the dispersion of many throughout the surrounding areas, it was impossible to report on every happening. Thus, the two miracles are given as examples of what was happening among the apostles.

As we return to the ministry of Peter, consider the Peter of the Gospels and Peter the apostle of Acts. Here we see him boldly explaining the baptism in the Holy Spirit. He is opening the door of the gospel to the Jews. He is supervising the church: administering discipline under the guidance of the Holy Spirit, following up on the work of the evangelists, even traveling to administer some churches. He is healing the sick and raising the dead. He is lashing out at the Sanhedrin, while resisting persecution. WHAT MADE THE DIFFERENCE IN PETER? THE HOLY SPIRIT BAPTISM!

Now, as an itinerant preaching administrator, Lydda was included in his travel plans. Verse 33 tells us that he found Aeneas there. He was a man who had been afflicted with palsy for eight years. Peter responded to meeting this palsied man with a word of faith. There was not prayer specifically offered for that need; just a word of commanding faith, "Jesus Christ maketh thee whole" (v. 34). And he arose immediately!

There are some vital facts about this miracle. It is Jesus Christ who does the work. Psalm 107:20 foretells this power, "He sent His word, and healed them." Sometimes the work of faith is progressive. "Maketh thee whole" suggests a gradual work. Christ does a complete work; He made the man whole again, and even took care of any remainder of his ailment when Peter told him to get up and take his bed. There would be no remnant of his lameness. And Christ is still the same today.

News spread quickly! Verse 35 records this activity, "All that dwelt at Lydda and Saron saw him (Aeneas), and turned to the Lord." These miracles proved a wedge to open the door for evangelism; and miracles are still a valuable tool for evangelism.

Then, another miracle took place, this time in the neighboring town of Joppa. At Joppa, the healed was a woman named Dorcas. She was "women's ministry president of the Joppa A/G." Her name means "gazelle" or "antelope"; an emblem of grace and beauty. She was the prime example of what a Spirit-filled woman ought to be. Her work for and toward others was motivated by her love; she was "full of good works" (v. 36). Now, Dorcas died, and they prepared her for burial. However, with hope in the news they had heard, they sent for Peter. "That he would not delay to come to them" was their earnest request (v. 38). Consider the inspiration she must have been to them; her influence speaks to us! We never fully know who or how we influence others by our lives, attitudes, words, or deeds.

Verse 39 depicts the greatness of their grief; they were almost beside themselves. Amidst their tears, they showed Peter all the things that Dorcas had made. "Peter put them all forth, and kneeled down, and prayed" (v. 40). How like Jesus is Peter's ministry becoming! For this healing parallels the raising of Jairus's daughter in Luke 8:40-56. In the previous miracles, there is no record of prayer, but here he prayed. And the word of faith, once again, produced the miracle! God is a God of infinite variety!

This was not a trial of Peter's faith; Peter had touched God and was simply acting according to His revealed will. Peter declared that will by confession of his own lips. It is confession which activates faith: "With the heart man believeth…and with the mouth confession is made" Romans 10:10. Instantly, Dorcas is restored! Romans 8:11 has an important promise for us that is still ours today: "If the Spirit of him that raised up Jesus from the dead dwell in you, he that raised up Christ from the dead shall also quicken your mortal bodies by his Spirit that dwelleth in you."

Chapter 9 concludes with a testimony of the effects of the miracles and a telling turn of events regarding Jewish law: "Many believed in the Lord" (v. 42). It is through the spiritual ministries that God has provided for the church that men are convicted and convinced. SO BE IT! Verse 43 reveals the encompassing power of the gospel because it records that Peter stayed with Simon, a tanner. For according to Jewish ceremonial law, Simon was unclean because he touched dead bodies as a tanner, yet Peter dwelt there. We need to evaluate our traditions!

Peter's Call and The Roman Outpouring

Acts Chapter 10

Bethel Assembly of God church, Minneapolis, early 1970's—suit and tie inside the church, bell bottoms and bare feet at the church-sponsored coffee shop! Hippies getting free from the bondage of drugs and the weight of carrying their own worth, at said coffee shop—miraculous! But, how to disciple them to walk with Jesus? And, how to bring the church world and the newly saved hippies together so they can learn from each other? There's nothing like newly saved souls for long-time Christians! These are the questions that were on my dad's heart as he navigated this move of God at Bethel.

And then it happened—the first saved hippie made his way into the church on a Sunday morning. The church workers at the coffee shop had been inviting the newly saved to attend church to learn and grow even more, and one brave hippie finally broke the ice.

Approaching the church door on 57th Street in Minneapolis, bell bottoms and bare feet, he didn't hear hymns being sung, but my dad already into his sermon. Eager to learn more about this Jesus that had changed his life, he moved through that unfamiliar territory, singularly focused on hearing the Word of God. Up the center aisle he went, past all the pews, and sat down cross-legged on the floor at the front of the church, just before the pulpit. My dad, not skipping a beat, kept on preaching, but of course, all eyes were on the hippie, and every mind was wondering what would happen next.

A pillar of the church in his suit and tie, feeling the responsibility to respond and feeling the pull of the Holy Spirit, followed the hippie down the aisle. And then, all eyes were on him! How would he respond? Would he politely lead him to a pew to sit properly? Would he pull him aside and talk to him about how to "act" in church? Would he throw him out? No one knew, not even my dad! And, right there my friends, was the gospel in full display. Sorry, Dad, but no sermon from the pulpit was needed that Sunday because what happened next was the sermon.

Suit and tie kicked off his Sunday loafers and joined bell bottoms and bare feet on the ground, cross-legged and singularly focused on the Word of God being preached from the pulpit. And the floodgate was opened at Bethel; more and more and more hippies poured into the church and began establishing roots in their newfound faith, some becoming leaders and even full-time ministers themselves. Oh, Jesus, let my response always be the same!

Let's join "suit and tie" and "bell bottoms" as they, with open ears and open hearts, eat up all the scriptural meat that my dad serves up in this chapter.

* * *

The Roman Outpouring Acts 10:1-8

Luke records for us what we may call the "Roman Outpouring." It is the formal opening of the door to the gentiles. Only cracks had occurred in the wall of prejudice up to this point. We saw one of those cracks at the end of the previous chapter when Peter stayed with Simon the tanner, who was considered unclean according to Jewish ceremonial law. Now the Holy Spirit was reaching out to the gentiles; and He sent a Jewish apostle to a Roman soldier to formally welcome him into the church.

There are key chapters in the book of Acts that portray the succeeding events of development of the worldwide witness of the church. First, we begin with Acts 1:8, the encompassing command of Jesus, "Ye shall be witnesses unto me both in Jerusalem… And unto the uttermost part of the earth." Then, in chapter 2, the gospel touches the Jews. Chapter 8 records the gospel being given to the Samaritans. And in chapter 10, we see the gospel reaching the gentiles.

Our text reveals how God worked to break the walls of prejudice. He dealt first with Peter, and then the whole church was forced to face this issue (we'll dive into that in chapter 11). The big question for Jewish Peter was this, 'Can a gentile come directly into the church through faith in Christ, or must he come through Judaism?' And we are STILL hung up with similar questions in the church today! We still have our walls of sanctimonious prejudice. We hear statements like 'he's a Christian, but he is not a 'real' Christian.' Now, I believe in progressive sanctification; there is room for just about anything in the church of Jesus Christ. First Thessalonians 5:13-14 instructs us, "And be at peace among yourselves. Now, we exhort you, brethren, warn them that are unruly, comfort the feebleminded, support the weak, be patient toward all men." And the Holy Spirit is the great common denominator!

Acts 10 introduces a new character in the unfolding story of the emerging church: Cornelius. Luke describes him at length in verses 1–2. He was an officer of the occupation army in command of 100 men, hence the label, "centurion." Cornelius was a pious, God-fearing man "with all his house" (v. 2). Apparently, he had been greatly influenced by the Jewish religion, or more importantly, the effect of Christ upon the Jew. He met every requirement of Jewish law, except for circumcision. Thus, he was not even a proselyte. He was a giver and a prayer, according to Luke's description in verse 2. Here is a picture of a religious man who was not a Christian. He was pious, liberal, reverent, prayerful, receptive, obedient, etc. He may have known the essential facts of Christ, but he did not know the way of the cross. On the basis of his seeking heart, God revealed Himself in a vision. An angel of God appeared to him and addressed him directly. Remember this, folks, it is the seeking heart to which God responds most readily!

God drew aside the veil of another world, and Cornelius saw things that he had never seen before. And God wants to do the same for us today! God opened up the spiritual world to Cornelius; and seeking after God will bring a similar response today. First Corinthians 2:9 tells us, "Eye hath not seen, nor ear heard, neither have entered into the heart of man, the things which God hath prepared for them that love him." And Isaiah 64:4 in the Amplified Bible encourages us in this holy unveiling: "Nor has the eye seen a God besides You, Who works *and* acts in behalf of the one who [gladly] waits for Him." Are you gladly, or earnestly, waiting in God's presence?

In verse 4, the angel reassured Cornelius that his giving and praying were remembered by God. In essence, the angel was saying, 'Your prayers and charities have not gone unnoticed by God.' God was responding to both the heart-seeking and spiritual ignorance of this man. The angel gave instruction for Cornelius to send for Peter; he did not preach to him. For, the ministry of reconciliation is given to men, not angels. Second Corinthians gives us this theological foundation of reconciliation in chapter 5, verses 18-21, "And God has given us this task of reconciling people to Him...And He gave us this wonderful message of reconciliation." (NLT)

Verse 6 of chapter 10 expresses the exactness in the leading of God, even to the point of what Peter would be able to do. GOD CARES! He cares about the seeking and searching heart. Later in this chapter, we see that Cornelius acts promptly. May it speak to us of the necessity of acting with speed at the direct leading of God!

Peter's Vision Acts 10:9-16

This chapter is a study in the way that God will work His will out in our lives, preparing every step for His ultimate purpose. We saw this previously in chapter 9 as He prepared Ananias and Saul for one another. What assurance this is of the faithful care of God in dealing with us as to our individual needs. And He did just that with Peter! Peter had some long-standing prejudices that had to be dealt with, and the precise timing and orderliness is a factor to be observed. God is a God of logic and a God of order. Romans 5:6 reminds us that God works out His plan "in due time."

So, let's watch this God-ordained meeting play out. Verse 9 opens with this: "As they went on their journey, and drew nigh unto the city, Peter went up…to pray." It was about noon, this hour of prayer; it was the middle prayer time. According to their custom, the Jews prayed at the third hour, the sixth hour, and the ninth hour of the day, which would have made it about noon. This tradition speaks to us of consistency in prayer—a specific time set aside for uninterrupted communion with God. How beautiful! Now, at this time, being noon, he became hungry. While lunch was being prepared, he fell into "a trance," as verse 10 tells us. Trance means "ecstasy" or "standing out of one's self." This special form of the vision corresponded with his physical condition, but it was a spiritual experience because Peter needed to be rid of his deep prejudice. And that DID happen in the next chapter.

Now, this is always the test of valid spiritual experience:

1. Does it change my character for the better?
2. Does it glorify Jesus?

In light of the spiritual activity of our day, we must reckon with this!

The rest of this section describes the vision; in it, Peter "beheld" what seemed like a great "sheet" tied at the corners being let down toward him (v. 11). The implication here is that it was from God. James 1:17 tells us, "Every good gift and every perfect gift is from above, and cometh down from the Father of lights, with whom is no variableness, neither shadow of turning." Verse 12 opens the "sheet" for us, and within it were all kinds of four-footed beasts (bugs and birds, etc.), both clean and unclean. Now, in one authoritative act, God abolished the law of the clean and unclean! For reference to the law, see Leviticus 11:20, 25-26 and Deuteronomy 14:3-31. But the vision had a far greater significance; the unclean represented the gentiles. Thus, in encouraging Peter to eat food that was regarded as unclean, He was preparing him for ministry among the gentiles. And the lesson for us is this: we may self-righteously set standards of things we do and don't do, and yet, the very attitude of our heart may be more of a sin than the object of our prohibition or temperance. Be careful!

The Lord instructed Peter to "kill and eat," and the voice is obviously familiar to Peter (v. 14). However, he answered, "Not so, Lord." This reaction reveals the firm hold that the old regulations had and what would be required to break it. UNCLEAN! Not so, Lord! Shades of "old Peter" showed up. It is a study in the spiritual vs. the carnal man. Peter saw the vision with carnal eyes, not spiritual eyes—much like in John 13:8 when Jesus began to wash his feet, and Peter refused. Jesus rebuked him there. Too often, we interpret the spiritual from a carnal point of view. And, in verse 15 of Acts chapter 10, Jesus rebuked him again, "What God hath cleansed, that call not common." Peter was contradicting God! The old covenant was void. Galatians 3:28 reminds us that after Jesus's death and resurrection, there was neither Jew nor Greek. Jesus instituted a new order upon the higher "cleanliness of the heart."

Verse 16 records that Peter saw this vision three times, and then "the vessel was received up again into heaven." That being the case, it could hardly be considered unclean anymore. This is the third time that Peter is dealt with in threes. And that fact speaks to us that we are not perfect. Our sanctification is progressive. We shall BE like Him when we SEE Him. Until then, we must grow in grace; burying the old man with all his quirks, while feeding the spiritual man as much as we can!

Peter Meets Cornelius Acts 10:17-23

Continuing with the Roman Outpouring, we have seen Cornelius and his situation. Remember, in verse 2 we learned that Cornelius is "a devout man and one that feared God." He was benevolent, and even a man who prayed much, but still desperately in need of a revelation of Jesus Christ. There are a lot of people like this today. We have seen the example of Peter, a prejudiced Jew, desperately in need of a deeper work of the Spirit in his own life. How much more for anyone else that is alive on this earth today?

Back to Peter's vision—in verse 17 we see that Peter remained on the roof following his vision. Luke said that Peter doubted himself; in other words, he was thoroughly perplexed as to what all of this meant. Here is a demonstration of how God works with us today. He works with us one degree, one step, at a time. And often times, we become very perplexed, but when we look back, we see how, indeed, all things work together. It's like a work of embroidery, and we only see the back side; or as 1 Corinthians 13:12 tells us, "Now we see through a glass, darkly; but then face to face." "Then" we will see the beauty of His work embroidered on our lives. Now, this doubting of Peter's does not necessarily indicate a lack of faith, but rather suggests that he gave much thought to what was implied by it all. Luke's terms in verses 19-20 indicate that he thought through and through in an honest effort to understand its meaning. And, fellow saints, there is a place for this kind of doubting! Too many of us do not think deep enough on matters that are vital. Christians can be some of the most gullible people on God's earth! I don't want to complicate things here, but simply point out the need for more depth in our relationship with God!

Now, while Peter was trying to figure it all out, God already had the "Let not that man think he shall receive anything from the Lord" (James 1:7) truth in mind. However, Peter's was not a questioning or doubting spirit, but one of seeking or looking for the truth in the matter, and God knew that. Here then is a good word for positive, clear-cut convictions as a born-again child of God. We see in verse 20, after a very positive command to meet the men at the door, that God uncomplicates it for Peter with this word of assurance, "For I have sent them." The Spirit graciously provides for Peter. He was to act, even if he did not fully understand.

So many times, we see this faith walk repeated in Scripture! For instance, Joshua had the commands of God laid out before him, and then God added the token of His everlasting grace: "Have I not commanded thee? Be strong and of a good courage; be not afraid, neither be thou dismayed. For the LORD thy God is with thee withersoever thou goest" (Joshua 1:9). Now Peter seemed to take it all as a matter of course and obeyed. And to all of this, we say, simply answer the door and do the Lord's bidding. Hallelujah! Fellow followers of Jesus, it is to such an obedient heart that God speaks!

The Spirit said to him (perhaps it was an inner voice this time), "Behold, three men seek thee. Arise therefore, and get thee down, and go with them, doubting nothing" (vv. 19–20). The one thing that is foremost in this command is "doubting nothing." If we are to follow Christ, there can be no room for doubting. The literal translation here is: "making no distinction, no dividing or wavering in his mind." Here is what James 1:6 has to say on the subject, "But let him ask in faith, nothing wavering. For he that wavereth is like a wave of the sea driven with the wind and tossed." How good it is to see men get together at the leading of the Holy Spirit, as we see happening here between Peter and Cornelius!

With the assurance given Peter in verse 20, we see him move forward in confidence in verse 21. Peter acted in full assurance, introducing himself and in quoting as to their mission. Peter was to be entertained in a gentile's house. The meaning of the vision was becoming clear.

God is No Respecter of Persons Acts 10:24-34

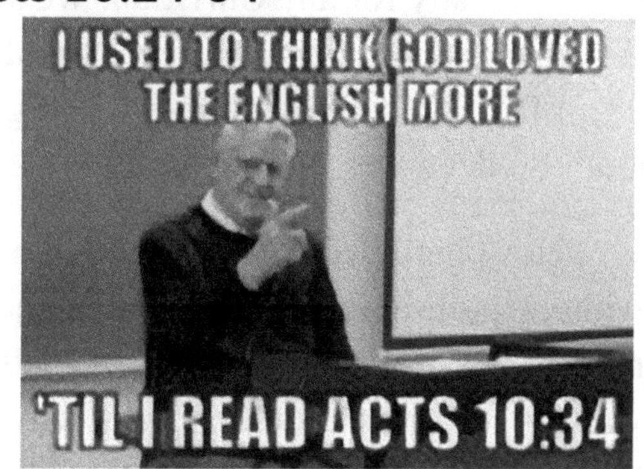

Always loving his British heritage, but never treating people differently! Dad loved people, believed in people, and wanted them to know truth, period. But, somehow, he always made truth understandable with a joke inserted!

As events progressed in chapter 10, we see the determined moving of God in the lives of men. This is a vital need in our lives: a sense of God's moving, and to realize our part in God's plan! It should be as keen as any of the other five senses. God was leading the men, Peter and Cornelius, to a momentous meeting; a meeting at which the tides of history would be turned. And there is a sense that our relationship with God will determine the turn of events for us.

Verse 24 brings us to Peter making his way to Caesarea. He found Cornelius waiting for them; not alone, but with his relatives, friends, and associates as well. There is a word to be said here about our influence upon those close to us; is it good or bad? Is it toward God or away from God? Cornelius apparently had a good influence, and those with him sought the same thing he did.

Upon seeing Peter, Cornelius's first reaction was to fall down and worship him (v. 25). He did not need to do that, but it reflected a humility of spirit on the part of Cornelius—a necessary ingredient in all our lives! Philippians 2:3 exhorts us, "Let each esteem other better than themselves." Pride is such a destroyer! Peter responded in like humility, "Stand up; I myself also am a man" (v. 26). Beware the danger of exalting the man instead of the Master! Now, Peter lifted him up; illustrating for us the work of the Savior. Psalm 40:2, "He brought me up also out of an horrible pit."

The plan further unfolds as verse 27 reveals he "found many that were come together." There were many there in Cornelius's house to hear the full gospel. So Peter began laying it out for them. He first clarified his presence there in view of Jewish attitudes toward the gentiles (see Mark 7:17-23; John 18:28; Acts 11:2-17; Galatians 2:12-14). While the law did not specifically forbid such association, the whole attitude of Jewish law dictated it. In the Jewish mind, the gentile was unclean; but Peter's testimony was one of revelation, "God hath shewed me" (v. 28). What an important experience that was! And the revelation of truth is still a vital necessity for any Christian. We see here that Peter grasped a principle of life that changed him completely, "I should not call any man common or unclean" (v. 28). LISTEN, he would never have gone there were it not for that revelation of God! So deep was that prejudice!

Peter continued to explain his change of heart, "Therefore came I unto you without gainsaying (hesitation, objection, or misgivings)" (v. 29). When God reveals His truth to our heart, it ends all controversy. What a gift! In the same verse, Peter then asks them why they had sent for him. Though he was aware of the circumstances, he asked Cornelius to repeat his story. Cornelius then referred to his vision, recounting his experience: the command of the angel and his obedience. And in his obedience, Cornelius opened the door for the ministry of Peter. Verse 31 reflects on the condition of this man's heart. He was upright and sincere. He gave, prayed, and had a desire for God, etc. Remembrance by God, promised to Cornelius as he recounts the story in verse 31, was important to the Jew and gentile alike.

Cornelius commended Peter for coming and then opened the door wide for Peter to minister the gospel to his household. "Now therefore are we all here present before God, to hear all things that are commanded thee of God" (v. 33). What a congregation! They are a classic illustration of the proper attitude toward God, His Word, and His minister! And this open door to minister is the fertile environment for Peter to share the beautiful gift of salvation. He started his ministry to the gentiles with this statement, "Of a truth I perceive that God is no respecter of persons" (v. 34). For Peter, and the gentiles gathered in Cornelius's house, there is no hint of hesitation but full obedience to the Holy Spirit. Folks, let that be so of us today! They responded, so let's take their lead! May we sense the leading of God. May we influence others for Him. May we maintain a spirit of humility. May we lift up the Lord Jesus Christ. May we recognize and pray for God's leading.

May we obey without question. May we cultivate a spiritual attitude toward God, His Word, and His minister.

Salvation Comes to the Gentiles Acts 10:34-48

Immediately upon Cornelius's introduction, Peter began to preach. He had no gimmicks; they were there for spiritual business! And WE CAN LEARN FROM THIS! What a difference it makes when there is preparation of the heart. Peter began his sermon with two monumental statements: "Of a truth I perceive" and "God is no respecter of persons" (v. 34). The term "perceive" means to grasp or seize. He came to understand the conviction that God has no favorites. All that had happened to Peter up to that moment, and all that was going to happen, hinged upon this revelation of truth. The term "respecter of persons" means literally "acceptor of face" or "to judge according to the face of a man (or outward appearance)." Deuteronomy 10:17 lays out this truth for us like this: "For the LORD your God is God of gods, and Lord of lords, a great God, a mighty, and a terrible, which regardeth not persons, nor taketh reward." In other words, He is bigger than anything or anyone we can imagine, and cannot be manipulated by us. Romans 2:11 and James 2:1-9 further uphold this view of God to not think of one people group as better than another.

However, the Jews were a proud people; they had come to feel that they were favorites of God. Peter's attitude in verse 14 of this chapter shows this spiritual pride when he "reminds" God that he had never "eaten anything common or unclean." And we, folks, are not exempt from such spiritual pride. As 1 John 2:16b admonishes us, "The pride of life, is not of the Father, but is of the world." But Peter had had an insight into the relationship of God and people, and also the gospel; and he declares it here in verse 34, "God is no respecter of persons."

The next great statement he made is this, "He that feareth him, and worketh righteousness, is accepted." In other words, God will take any man who will honor Him and His Word; that man "is accepted with Him" (v. 35). Peter's sermon was not a lengthy one, but brief and to the point concerning Jesus Christ: "He is Lord of all" (v. 36).

In verses 36-38, Peter spoke to them of matters that were common knowledge to those of Judea and Galilee. He informed them of what was already published, but he did so in the power and conviction of the Holy Spirit, which brought them to a place where Christ met their need! After introducing them to common truth, he said, "And we are witnesses of all things which he did" (v. 39). NOW, that is convincing! It is the best form of testimony: 'I was there when it happened, and I ought to know.'

Peter continued with his salvation presentation, "Him (Jesus) God raised up the third day" (v. 40). Peter is faithful to the message he preached: Jesus, incarnation, crucifixion, resurrection, ascension, judgment. And the culmination is, "To him give all the prophets witness, that through his name whosoever believeth in him shall receive remission of sins" (v. 43). Thus, with the term "whosoever," Peter firmly and effectively opened the door to the gentiles.

The last five verses of this chapter record the response of the people gathered in Cornelius's house. With a message of such truth and love, it is not difficult to understand why the crowd responded as they did. GOD GRANT THAT SAME RESPONSIVE HEART TO US GENTILES TODAY! There are some figures of speech here with respect to the Holy Spirit's ministry: "The Holy Ghost fell on all them which heard the word" (v. 44); "Poured out the gift of the Holy Ghost" (v. 45); "Speak with tongues, and magnify God" (v. 46); "Have received the Holy Ghost" (v. 47); "Tarry" (they continued in that atmosphere) (v. 48). Note the balance!

"They heard them speak with tongues, and magnify God" (v. 46). May we never compromise that experience. We compromise by allowing it to become passé. In the beginning of the Holy Spirit's outpouring, Acts 2:17 defines the reach as "all flesh." This prophecy is becoming reality here to Peter. Now, the thought that runs through the whole chapter will keep it from becoming passé: a yielded, unprejudiced vessel in the plan and purpose of God. Oh, let it be said of me!

Divine Guidance Uncomplicated and the Gospel Spreading

Acts Chapter 11

Guidance and encouragement: my dad was called to both. He made a difference in people's lives by guiding and encouraging them. But he wasn't sugary sweet about it; he was a practical Brit with a shepherd's heart. In one breath, he could give a little kick-in-the-pants one-liner, and in the next moment, ask you about your current struggle.

Along the lines of divine guidance broken down by Peter's actions and testimony in the beginning of this chapter, Dad had a great one-liner about how to know God's will as you consider your next practical step in life. He would say, "Follow the peace of God." Plain and simple, folks! The key to following the peace of God is spending time WITH Him. Solitude breeds clarity!

The spotlight shines on Barnabas in this chapter, as he investigates the happenings in Antioch with the gospel spreading there. He was known for being an encourager, and he does not disappoint the believers in Antioch. Encouragers notice things that others don't, and voice them. Barnabas did that, and my dad did that for so many people. He cared. Plain and simple. As one student, who was from a town where my dad had previously pastored, said of him:

> He always asked me how things were in North Platte. No one ever asked me how things were in North Platte. And that made me feel special. (Sapphire Goins)

Encouragers have a way of doing that.

I think Dad is just starting his lunch in the cafeteria. Let's go grab a seat next to him and be ministered to by that signature guidance and encouragement mixed with British wit!

* * *

Principles of Divine Guidance Acts 11:1-18

In the continuing ministry of the Holy Spirit, with regard to the Roman Outpouring, Peter had to answer to the charges of "the brethren" over the fact that he had eaten with the ceremonially unclean gentiles. News of the events at Caesarea had travelled fast: "The Gentiles had also received the word of God" (v. 1). It meant that they had been brought into the church. This was indeed news, but it so aroused the indignation of the righteous, legalistic Jews, that Peter had to defend his actions. Verse 2 introduces us to a new group in the Jewish system, and so were born the Judaizers. They mixed legalism with the gospel. This group made much trouble in the early church. Paul's letter to the Galatians was written to correct this matter in the church in Galatia. Consider this: Satan's attack from without had failed when Saul was converted (Acts 9:27). Thus, Satan's attempt is now from within. Religious conflict is the devil's work and his grandest achievement. But here is the answer, folks: we need to simply take God's Word for what it says, rather than trying to make it say what we want it to say (like the Judaizers did!)

The Judaizers charge Peter, in verse 3, with the violation of eating with gentiles. This was unforgivable by Jewish tradition because of the law of clean and unclean. But, in verse 4, Peter begins his defense with a careful recounting of his time with the gentiles. He sets about to show them how God had led him. And in so doing, he sets for us ten definite principles of divine guidance: prayer, consideration, the voice of God, caution, providential circumstances, the prompting of the Spirit, confirmation, memory, comparison, and united testimony. Allow me to unpack each of these for you.

Prayer is a good point to start with, and Peter did—in action and in his defense. He begins his account with the fact that he was praying (v. 5). And here is where "divine guidance" begins—in the closet of prayer! It is the basis of trust in God. "Those that seek me early shall find me" (Proverbs 8:17). It is a law of God that governs His responsiveness to His people. "Ask, and it shall be given you; seek, and ye shall find; knock, and it shall be opened unto you" (Matthew 7:7). It all begins with prayer because prayer puts us in a proper perspective, which is: GOD IS IN CHARGE! "Our Father which art in heaven." (Matthew 6:9)

After we pray, consideration, or the weighing on one's mind, is crucial to this process. Peter continued, "I considered" (v. 6). He thought it over. He weighed the whole matter in his mind. Remember this, fellow saints: divine guidance is not blind ignorance or holy guesswork. It is carefully considered in the atmosphere of prayer.

The time invested in prayer and consideration will lead us to hear from God. In verse 7, Peter tells them, "And I heard a voice." This was not a human voice; this was the voice of God! A good companion of this point of divine guidance is the next principle, which is caution. Caution, for Peter, looked like him referring to what he knew of God's commands for him as a Jew, "But I said, Not so, Lord" (v. 8). This is not doubt or disobedience, but good common-sense caution. With regard to matters of the supernatural, it is essential to determine their source! In this case, Peter recalls in verse 9, "But the voice answered me again from heaven," and the same answer was repeated. God's call will be clearer and more authoritative as we respond to it. But it is good to approach it with caution.

Then follows the next principle in determining divine guidance: providential circumstances. Verse 11 continues with Peter's recount of his new call. He tells us that the men sent from God, through Cornelius, further attested to the divine nature of Peter's present experience. Circumstances are a valid test of God's guidance. The voice of the Spirit is an essential part of this process and can be a prompting of the Spirit. Peter gives this evidence in verse 12, "And the Spirit bade me go with them, nothing doubting." People, we need a divine sensitivity! We are too self-sensitive and not God-sensitive!

Peter proved his God-sensitivity was accurate with the next principle: confirmation. "And he shewed us how he had seen an angel in his house, which stood and said unto him, 'send men to Joppa and call for Simon (Peter)'" (v. 13). Now, in the succession of events, Peter discovered that the Word of God was truth for guidance. The next principle in determining divine guidance is a plug for scripture memorization and Bible study. Peter introduced memory as the next principle, "Then remembered I the word of the Lord" (v. 16). Perhaps he had committed it to memory, or certainly the revelation of truth had been indelibly implanted in his heart.

Verses 16-17 reveal the next principle: comparison; specifically comparison of God's promises to reality, past or present. In this case, it was Jesus's promise to them of being baptized with the Holy Ghost: "Forasmuch then as God gave them the like gift as he did unto us, who believed on the Lord Jesus Christ; what was I, that I could withstand God?" (v. 17). As he compared the truth of God's Word, he found it to be just as it said.

Unity in testimony is an undeniable sign of God's guidance, and it is stated here in verse 18, "When they heard these things, they held their peace, and glorified God." The NIV puts it this way: "When they heard this, they had no further objections and praised God." God's guidance was vindicated for Peter, and it always will be for us if we follow these simple guidelines.

The Gospel in Antioch Acts 11:19-24

Following the positive vindication, or proof, of Peter's ministry, we move into another area. The gospel had spread as a result of "the persecution that arose about Stephen" (Acts 11:19). It had spread to areas north of Galilee, namely Phoenicia, Cyprus, and Antioch. And again, we see the problem of discrimination manifest itself: for they preached to the Jews only.

Now, it is here that Antioch (Syria) comes into focus as a city of importance. Antioch was to become the great missionary center: the Roman capital of Syria. It was the center of Greek culture, half a million in population, and the third ranking city of the world behind Rome and Alexandria. It was strategically located on the routes of commerce. Thus, a city of power. Interesting to note that Nicolas, one of the first seven deacons named in Acts 6:5, was from Antioch. But Antioch was a vile and immoral city. Their worship included immorality in the name of religion.

Some of the group that went to Antioch were men from Cyprus and Cyrene (v. 20). They had no doubt heard of Peter's experience in Caesarea; and they came to preach the gospel to these pagan Greeks. They were thoroughly convinced of the power of the Lord Jesus to accomplish what He had promised in Acts 4:28-30. Verse 21 gives the confidence, "And the hand of the Lord was with them." This was an answer to the prayer, "Grant unto thy servants, that with all boldness they may speak thy word, by stretching forth thine hand to heal; and that signs and wonders may be done by the name of thy holy child Jesus." (Acts 4:29-30)

Oh, that we might be conscious of the hand of the Lord as He upholds all things by the word of His power! (Hebrews 1:3). Conscious of His creative hand, the one that slides the world into place. Aware of His sustaining hand, as 2 Corinthians 5:17 reminds us, "If any man be in Christ." Attentive to His restoring and guiding hand at work in our lives, "As many as received him, to them gave he power to become the sons of God" (John 1:12). Thankful for His chastening hand, as Hebrews 12:6 helps us see, "Whom the Lord loveth he chasteneth." Familiar with His loving and willing hand, as displayed for us in His prayer in the garden of Gethsemane, "Nevertheless not my will" (Luke 22:42). Responsive to His beckoning hand, as He promises us in Revelation 3:20, "Behold, I stand at the door, and knock." He healed them all with His healing hand. Receiving from His healing hand according to Acts 11:21, "And the hand of the Lord was with them." Oh, for the distinct evidence of His sacred hand among us! May it be so with us, that great numbers may believe and turn to the Lord!

Now, when news of the happenings in Antioch reached Jerusalem, they sent Barnabas to investigate, verse 22 informs us. We remember Barnabas from Acts 4:36-37 and Acts 9:27. The spirit of Barnabas had not changed, for he is the son of encouragement. It was his name AND his nature. Barnabas was a Cypriot Jew; thus he was close to the situation during their evangelistic activity.

When Barnabas came upon the situation at Antioch, "He had seen the grace of God" (v. 23). It is wonderful when you can see the grace of God! Think about this: what do you see in the workings of God amongst His people? Some folks see imperfections, insincerity, and inconsistency, etc., but Barnabas saw the grace of God. And it made him glad. He "exhorted them all, that with purpose of heart they would cleave unto the Lord" (v.23). Barnabas lived up to his name, as verse 23 points out, "He exhorted them all." Incidentally, is this not the work of all of us, that of exhorting one another? Hebrews 10:25 instructs us, "Not forsaking the assembling of ourselves together, as the manner of some is; but exhorting one another: and so much the more, as ye see the day approaching." I have an exhortation for you, fellow Christians, "Cleave unto the Lord with purpose of heart!" Conversion must be followed by continuance. Matthew 10:22 encourages us, "He that endureth to the end shall be saved."

Now, to further enhance the message, Luke gives the credentials of this Barnabas: "He was a good man, and full of the Holy Ghost and of faith" (v. 24). Such a spirit will always bring the same result: "much people was added unto the Lord." (Acts 11:24)

Could Dad have been named Barnabas? Somehow, I don't picture Barnabas with the wit and sass of my dad, however, he did encourage so many people, often individually. Let me tell you of one such person: Jeff Turner, a student at Trinity Bible College in the '90s, answering God's call on his life to preach the Word. Listen to Jeff tell it:

> Here's a story not many people know. My first semester of preaching, I preached a horrible sermon in front of the class. In fact, when it was over, I said, If any of you got anything out of this, well, God bless you." I went to Dave's office and told him I was quitting school and going back to Olympia, WA to my old job and life. He simply said okay. Then he asked me if I could be satisfied doing anything else other than what I'd been called to do? He and I both knew the answer to the question the minute he said it. I obviously stayed.

Christians in Antioch Acts 11:25-28

We take off from the wonder pronouncement of "much people was added unto the Lord" from verse 24. WE NEED THAT TODAY! With the obvious growth in the church, Barnabas sought assistance. Thus, he went to Tarsus, personally, to seek Saul/Paul. It is immaterial what Saul had been doing in the years since chapter 9. The point of verse 25 seems to be in the cooperative attitude of Barnabas. As before, his bigness of heart is evident. There is no fear of rivalry; the only concern seemed to be the nurturing of the Antioch believers. May such an attitude be ours today! Saul, the persecutor, is now put into circulation; and this time, FOR Christ. At this time, the church was at rest, having been given a golden opportunity for growth and development.

Thus, when Barnabas found Saul, he brought him back to Antioch (v. 26). This was the headquarters of missionary activity. While in Antioch, they spent a year preparing. They enrolled everyone in Bible school and taught them a systematic way to study the Word of God. This is vital to every assembly—a systematic digestion of truth. The strength of any church is in the grasp of the Word that its people have in them. GET A HOLD OF IT!

Now, there is a significant 'first' mentioned here: "The disciples were called Christians first in Antioch" (v. 26). This was a term used by others in reference to them. It speaks highly of their actions and their attitudes. Ponder this: Do YOU merit the name Christian? It is not used here in a derogatory manner. Not until later, during the Roman persecution, did the name Christian take on a derisive note. Then, the very name associated with a man was enough to condemn him. But there is no indication of hostility on the part of those at Antioch toward the believers. Rather, it reflected their devotion; these people are just like Jesus Christ! May God grant such an accusation of my life: "Mr. Christian!"

Prophets also came from Jerusalem to Antioch. This is the first mention of the term "prophets" in the book of Acts (v. 27). Paul recognized the vitality of this ministry in Ephesians 4:11, "And he gave some, apostles; and some, prophets; and some, evangelists; and some, pastors and teachers." In 1 Corinthians 14:39, the gift of prophecy is exemplified, "Wherefore, brethren, covet to prophesy." Generally, the prophet was a "forth teller," but in this case, he is "foretelling" in dynamic, divinely inspired speech. It is instantaneous revelation—a sudden inspiration.

By the Spirit, Agabus told of a coming dearth, or famine, upon a great part of the world, which was to take place during the reign of Claudius Caesar (41-54 AD), according to verse 28. Secular history does record a famine during the period of 44-48 AD. Thus, by inspiration, the church was encouraged to help their brethren. Judea was apparently the hardest hit by the famine. Thus, the Christians determined to send relief, "Every man according to his ability" (v. 29). In their comparative plenty, they shared with those who had need. So let's learn this from the Antioch church: they manifested a spirit of grace that must be in all our lives if we are to grow. Our attitudes and concerns are a demonstration of the reality of Christ's work in our hearts. Thus is reflected a true Christian spirit.

MAY WE BE CHRISTIANS INDEED!

Herod's Aggression and End; Peter's Submission and Escape

Acts Chapter 12

Studying Acts 12 is taking a close look at the great irony of God's plans, for we have an assailant's deeds met with an innocent man's submission and then miraculous escape. The end of this chapter puts an exclamation point on God's great irony as Herod all but declares himself a god, but then meets his own destructive end. Praise God that His plans, when followed, always lead us to freedom, and the promise of justice being served on the ungodly.

Dad would walk into class today shouting, "Hallelujah," at the chance to teach about God's glory manifested in these ironic happenings of Acts 12. Who else can turn the tides like God? Dad loved focusing on the glory of God! But, in a way only David L. Jones can do, he marries reverence with wit and delivers a unique way to see Peter in his sleepy state. Reaching the second section of this chapter, and Peter's crazy escape from jail with an angel's help, Dad would say with a smirk, "And the angel said, 'Get up, Peter!' And Peter said, 'Ugh, leave me alone, I'm sleeping.'" And then, the chuckle, as he enjoys his own joke. Undoubtedly, someone in class would be jerked back into paying attention because of this little joke. And that, my friends, was my dad's secret weapon.

I think today's class is just beginning, so let's join them and wait for that joke to make its appearance.

* * *

Herod's Persecution Acts 12:1-5

We come now to the church under persecution, once again. There is one good thing to be said about persecution: it divides the "sheep" from the "goats." This account marks the fifth persecution that affected the church as a whole. In order, they are found in Acts 4 with the priests and the Sadducees, Acts 5:17 with the priests and the Sadducees when the prison doors are miraculously opened, Acts 6:12 when Stephen is brought to the counsel, and Acts 8 with Saul as the chief persecutor.

Now, the fifth persecution finds Herod as its chief agent. This Herod is one of four Herods mentioned in the New Testament, Herod Agrippa I. He instigated a persecution, not on the basis of religious difference between the Jews, but with the civil and state authorities. It was a persecution that was to gradually increase until the time of Constantine in 313 AD. Beware the infringement of civil governments. In our world today, by its very nature, we are feeling the mighty hand of the state take more and more control of our lives: taxation, registration, or legislation.

Now, James and Peter, and other disciples, had no voice in the civil affairs of their day, but we still do. Christians ought to be informed and vocal in national, state, and local affairs.

It seems that Herod selected as his victims certain prominent Christians "and set forth his hand to abuse, afflict, torment, and oppress them" (v. 1). As the text reads, he apparently did not kill them all, but James became his first victim. Verse 2 records, "And he killed James…with the sword." James, the brother of John, was known as one of the sons of thunder, and he was close to Jesus. He was beheaded and disgraced before the Jews. In the "Hall of Faith," it is recorded in Hebrews 11:37, "They were stoned, they were sawn asunder, were tempted, were slain with the sword." And while James was beheaded, Peter was miraculously spared.

Thus, while the Jews were not the prime movers of the persecution, they were enjoying every moment of it, as verse 3 indicates, "And because he saw it pleased the Jews." They delighted in the sufferings of the Christians. It demonstrated the awful results of religious hatred! There are many examples of this throughout history: the Crusades during medieval times, the Thirty Years' War in the 17th century, the religious turmoil in Ireland known as "The Troubles" in the latter part of the 20th century, etc. Within the realm of religion, the devil seems to revel in such attitudes. NEVER let it be so in our hearts! Now, this is all that Herod needed to lay hold of the prize: Peter himself. It was Passover time, so Herod determined to wait until it was over. He showed some favoritism toward the Jews and posed as a devout adherent of their religion.

According to verse 4, Herod imprisoned Peter and intended, after Passover, to bring Peter forth to the people. Herod did not want to spill blood during the feast. They had their religion all neatly wrapped and brought it out at the proper moments; when those people were religious, they were really religious. When it was convenient, they forgot about the Law and, in the name of tradition, wrought havoc against the emerging church of Jesus Christ. There is a striking similarity with the plans of the Sanhedrin with respect to Jesus in Mark 14:1, "After two days was the feast of the Passover… and the chief priests and the scribes sought how they might take him." Now, because of Peter's record in Acts 5:19, Herod secured him with every precaution taken: four guards of soldiers, which is sixteen in all! It was a mockery against the delivering power of God.

Luke pauses in verse 5 to prove a positive truth to every reader: PRAYER DOES CHANGE THINGS! Allow me to unfold the proof with a vivid picture of the imprisonment: "Peter therefore was kept in prison" (v. 5). There seemed to be little hope for Peter. On the one side, the power of Roman civil authority: sixteen soldiers, prison walls, three sets of gates, and chains. However, verse 5 continues, "But prayer was made." This is direct opposition to all the alien powers of God's wonderful purpose. And the whole church was united in prayer. It is worthy to note that the CHURCH PRAYED! "But prayer was made without ceasing of the church unto God for him." The Greek word for "without ceasing" is the same word used in 1 Thessalonians 5:17, "Pray without ceasing." It means "to stretch out," and in this sense is literally translated as "reverent." Thus, the praying, united, intense, fervent church is pitted against the evil plot of Herod. What value in such praying! And guess who won, folks?

THAT SAME KIND OF PRAYER IS NEEDED TODAY!

What Happens When the Church Prays Acts 12:6-11

We must consider the verses in this section in the full light of the events before they occurred: "But prayer was made without ceasing of the church onto God for him" (v. 5). It was intense prayer. The original meaning, "to stretch out," expresses the intensity with which the whole church prayed. PRAYER LIKE THAT GETS THINGS DONE! GOD MAKES US INTERCESSORS!

Now, with this picture of the praying church before us, we come face to face with seeming impossibility. Verse 6 tells us of Herod's plan to execute Peter in just a few hours. Picture this impossibility: Peter was sleeping between two soldiers, bound with two chains, and keepers were outside Peter's cell. Let's take a few moments to appreciate such a beautiful picture of a sleeping Peter in the midst of his bondage and impending death. He had Christ's promise, "Lo, I am with you always" (Matthew 28:20). Peter applies this truth even in prison! AND THAT IS OUR PROMISE TOO! No wonder Peter writes in his letter, "Casting all your care upon him; for he careth for you" (1 Peter 5:7). Peter had found a place of confidence in God, and so may we! Here are a few scriptural promises you can hold onto:

> Peace I leave with you, my peace I give unto you: not as the world giveth, give I unto you. Let not your heart be troubled, neither let it be afraid. (John 14:27)
>
> Be careful for nothing; but in every thing by prayer and supplication with thanksgiving let your requests be made known unto God. And the peace of God, which passeth all understanding, shall keep your hearts and minds through Christ Jesus. (Philippians 4:6-7)
>
> It is vain for you to rise up early, to sit up late, to eat the bread of sorrows; for so he giveth his beloved sleep. (Psalm 127:2)
>
> I will bless the LORD at all times. (Psalm 34:1)

Herod was taking no chances with Peter, remembering his previous escape! But, what a mockery to the power of God! God did the very thing that Herod tried to prevent.

Speaking of Peter's calmness and confidence in God, I never remember my dad panicking about anything. Did worrisome things concern him? Of course! Did he get miffed, or even angry about some things? Yes, indeed! But I never remember a moment of panic in my growing up years or in my adult years when I shared ministry arenas with him. Now, some of this was certainly due to his British reservedness, but not all of it. It was not just a dismissive attitude, rather, a confident foundation in the sovereignty and grace of God that held him in those human moments. What an example of trust in God!

Luke tells us, in detail, in verse 7, about the angel who appeared and a light filled the prison. Peter was sleeping, to the extent that the angel had to shake him to wake him! It seems that Peter was like one in a trance, with evidence of that in verses 9 and 11. He needed to be ordered at every step and, obediently, he followed the angel's direction. It is divine intervention, and while there is haste indicated, there seems to be an air of calculated leisure. God waited until the last watch of the last night before Peter's planned death, to free him. And against this fact, Peter's trust in God stands out more than ever! Oh, God, give us that same faith!

Now, Luke notes the last gate in verse 10 with special interest. It is an impressive barrier. Had God led him this far to just leave him there alone? It is a study in the careful purpose of God for us. Ephesians 1:11 encourages us: He "worketh all things after the counsel of his own will." Note that "counsel" here is that the leading of God is often in calculated steps, unknown to us until we take them. For example, Israel crossing the Red Sea and then the Jordan River on dry land! And there are times when, in the purpose of God for us, we come upon impressive barriers, things that seem to nullify all that has happened in the past. But note what happened! The iron gate, that impressive barrier, "Opened to them of his own accord," and they went out (v. 10). Listen, folks! "In shady green pastures so rich and so sweet, God leads his dear children along" (God Leads us Along). And when God leads the way, ALL obstacles are removed.

Verse 11, with that evidence of Peter being in a trance, says, "And when Peter was come to himself." It seems that up until this time, he was in a trance and he "came to." He rejoiced, "Now I know of a surety, that the LORD hath sent his angel, and hath delivered me."

Peter's Believe-it-or-Not Acts 12:12-18

We could call it "The Great Escape" or "Peter's Believe-it-or-Not," but whatever we call it, before us is the amazing and miraculous deliverance of Peter from death row! To what do we attribute this miraculous deliverance? Was it just the volition of God that delivered Peter? If this is so, then why pray at all? The truth is that Peter was delivered by the same power of God through intercessory prayer. And prayer does change things on our behalf! Let's look at the story about prayer in Exodus 32:11-14. Moses is pleading with God to have mercy on His people, whom He wanted to smite because of their waywardness. But prayer changed things for the Israelites through Moses, "And the LORD repented of the evil which he thought to do unto His people."

It seems that God worked in such a way that Peter was not fully aware of what was happening to him, as verse 12 suggests. Thus, upon considering the whole situation, he went to tell of his deliverance. Now, it is in just such a manner that God bears with us at times...we may not fully realize what has developed until we "consider the thing" (v. 12). We need to revive the art of considering God's dealings with us! Some people never have any idea about why things happen as they do—LET US CONSIDER!

Upon coming to John Mark's house, we see that they are still praying. Apparently, they had been praying all night; it is near morning at this point in the story. Peter knocks on the door, and the scene relayed in verses 13 and following is both comical and illustrative of the basic nature of unbelief that is in all of us. But it also emphasizes a valuable spiritual truth: God's faithfulness to us (sometimes) feeble humans. Verse 14 records the comical; Rhoda, a damsel in the house of John Mark, came to the door, and upon recognizing Peter's voice, became so excited that she forgot to open the door! Now, here is a young lady with the right kind of faith: she had not seen him; she had only heard his voice. Remember the words of Jesus, "Blessed are they that have not seen, and yet have believed" (John 20:29). Peter must have reflected upon this scene when later he wrote of Jesus, "Whom having not seen, ye love; in whom, though now ye see him not, yet believing, ye rejoice with joy unspeakable and full of glory." (1 Peter 1:8)

Now, the rest of the household did not accept her testimony, "Thou art mad," they said (v. 15). And these were the same people who had just been praying! The trouble with them was that they did not know when to stop praying and start praising. This may be some of our trouble in prayer, to be sure! Rhoda stood by her testimony, and they weakened a little in their unbelief. "It is his angel," they said (v. 15). How feeble our faith is at times! Here they were, Spirit-filled prayer warriors, but they just couldn't seem to believe that God had actually done this thing. And here is the illustrative part of the story; their waffling faith gives us hope (but not an example) that God is still working ON us and IN us. They had not "arrived" in their spiritual walk, but God kept working. The same is true for us; praise God!

When they finally responded to Peter's continued knocking, their reaction was astonishment (v. 16). Now, while we may look with censure upon their lack of faith, there is a truth here that comes home to all of us. It is not our eloquence of words or great faith alone that moves God to act on our behalf; it is His GREAT FAITHFULNESS that hears the feeblest plea!

Peter relays his deliverance story, and then instructs them to relay the story to others, but especially to James. James, the Lord's brother, was an unbeliever until after the resurrection. He was a leader in Jerusalem, as we shall see in Acts chapter 15. Now with that instruction, Peter exercises some common sense in "departing to another place" (v. 17). Not presuming upon the protection of God, Peter made provision to move on; times were crucial, and common sense was vital! Verses 18-19 show us that from this moment, persecution ceased again for a while—ALL BECAUSE THE CHURCH PRAYED!

The End of Herod and Persecution Acts 12:19-25

It is suggested strongly in this section of Scripture that the persecution by Herod stopped at this point. It is also verified by history that this was so. Luke opens this chapter with Herod's attempt to destroy the church, and closes it with an account of Herod's destruction. There is something significant in the accounts with regard to God's concern for us today (and those believers of all ages). The church suffered much under Herod's torment; perhaps sometimes wondering if this "way" was really worth it. But they rejoiced to see God deal with their tormentor. And the cause of Christ PREVAILS in victory once again! Likewise, the Christian today, faced with the trial and tribulation of a scoffing world, may sometimes be tempted to ask, 'Is it worth it?' But someday, Christ will come and set us free from the bonds of this earth! He'll shout the victory, and Satan will be stopped!

At this point in the class, Dad would break out in song with his smooth baritone voice, "It will be worth it all when we see Jesus." GOD'S RECKONING DAY WILL COME!

Thus, Herod's days were numbered. In controversy with Tyre and Sidon over some trivial matters (something had displeased him), Herod came under fire from these two cities. They were part of Syria but separated by rugged mountains. Thus, they were dependent upon Herod's territory for food. So, through Blastus, they sought to settle the matter immediately, all according to verse 20.

The historian Josephus tells us that a special festival was held at this time to give thanks for the emperor's safety. It was the second day of a feast commemorating Claudius's return from victory in Britain. Those poor Brits! Thus, on this day, Herod, arrayed in royal apparel, gave a great speech, verse 21 tells us. Now, as Herod gave his oration, the pagan people, used to defying conquering emperors, poured the same "honor" upon Herod. "It is the voice of a god, and not a man" (v. 22). And instead of rebuking them, he accepted and enjoyed their flatteries. But Solomon warns, "Pride goeth before destruction" (Proverbs 16:18). In effect, Herod was making himself like God. "I am a jealous God," is His warning! It was one thing for those pagan idolaters to offer such honor to a mortal, but quite another for Herod, a nominal Jew and professed protector of Judaism, to accept it.

Verse 23 denotes his downfall, and because of his pride and dishonor of God, an angel of the Lord smote him before ALL. What a contrast between the other "smiting" of an angel, concerning Peter, earlier in chapter 12. One resulted in liberty, the other in death. One glorified his Lord, the other made himself as lord. It reminds us of a previous event in Acts; when God smote Ananias and Sapphira. Thus, we are reminded again that our God is a God of righteousness. He demands holiness! And what a violent death: to be smote and then eaten by worms! It is in itself a picture of hell. In Mark 9:44, 46, 48, Jesus gives a solemn warning of hell, "Where their worm dieth not, and the fire is not quenched." And here in Acts, Herod is getting a foretaste of what his eternity will be like. Thus, Herod died as he lived, and he "gave up the ghost" (v. 23).

Now, verse 24 is a bright contrast to the death of Herod: "But the word of God grew and multiplied." It seems this is always so. Each new wave of opposition serves to spread the gospel further (see Acts 6:1; 6:7; 9:31; 16:5; 19:20). And the impression of the Word is that it kept growing and multiplying. Oh God, grant that it may be so for us!

First Missionary Journey, with Fruitful Ministry

Acts Chapter 13

We come now to the last part of the recorded Acts of the apostles. We have thus far observed them in Jerusalem, in Judea and Samaria, and now, according to the command of the Lord, the gospel must be preached to the uttermost part. The portion of Acts that follows this chapter covers three missionary journeys of Paul, and traces a fourth journey. The outpouring of the Holy Spirit on the day of Pentecost was evangelical in purpose. And wherever and whenever the church has truly aligned herself with the life and message of Jesus Christ, she has experienced a world missions outreach. Likewise, in an individual! We need a little rekindling of that life and message for greater outreach today!

Let me tell you a story about when Dad prepared for a greater outreach. Dad pastored Bethel Assembly of God church in Minneapolis in the '70s, amongst the hippies and drug addicts of the city. He was in search of a way to reach out to this lost group of people and knew the story of David Wilkerson and his success with Teen Challenge, which started in New York City. So he had a parishioner, Tom Hennessy, who just happened to be a pilot, fly him out to New York to attend a helpful teaching that would get them started. David Wilkerson's mom was leading a workshop on how to start a coffeehouse as an outreach. She came at it from a very common-sense approach, and that was right up Dad's alley!

When he shared this story with Dan and I, he said that he got more and more excited as she taught, and feeling the Holy Spirit's nudge, said to himself, "This is us!" This idea, this ministry, this approach fits Bethel and Minneapolis. "It is for us," is what the

Holy Spirit was conveying to Dad. So Dad and Tom flew home to Minneapolis, and he shared this Holy Spirit idea with his congregation; they agreed, "This is us!"

They followed Dad's lead and created a drop-in coffeehouse, more like a hangout than a restaurant, that sold coffee in downtown Minneapolis. They named it *His Place*. Bathed in prayer and preparation, planning and staffing, *His Place* became a safe and comfortable place to come, be yourself, share your life, and be introduced to the power of the gospel. Consequently, many drug-addicted hippies came to know Jesus through *His Place*!

Let's listen in on some conversations that Dad may have had with some of these newly saved, as he shared words of life.

Preparation for Greater Outreach Acts 13:1-3

Now, the first missionary journey lasted about two years and covered about 1,300 miles. Antioch, Syria was the headquarters for this outreach. It was the third great metropolis of the world. All three journeys were launched from there. We pause here to reflect that the missionary movement could not have effectively issued from Jerusalem. There was too much racial and spiritual prejudice there. A good approach to such attitudes today should be that when I think of my ministry, I think of the world, and when I think of my sufficiency, I think of Christ. This chapter is the "watershed" of Acts. A watershed event is a turning point for a group, movement, person, etc. A watershed moment for me was moving from England to America when I was just ten years old; there was no going back; my life took a drastic turn at that point. And sadly, because I was teased in a Minneapolis grade school, I had to hide my charming British accent. However, I can free the hidden lilt like a jolly ol' chap whenever the need arises or the mood suits. Back to this watershed of the book of Acts; it is in this chapter that the missionary journey begins, and the world has never been the same. It is our missionary manual declaring divine principles to guide in missionary service. Chapters 13 & 14 recount the first missionary enterprise by the church to the gentile world. And the first thing that is done is the ordaining of workers.

Special mention is made in verse 1 of the prophets of Antioch: Barnabas, Simeon called Niger, Lucias of Cyrene, and Manaen, a foster brother of Herod the Tetrarch (he was raised with Herod). Note the contrast in this list: Manaen is a prophet of God, while Herod was a murderer and an adulterer. Needless to say, with these prophets before us, the Holy Spirit points out the need for prophetic ministry within the church today. First Corinthians 12:28 lists prophets as a need, "In the church, first apostles, secondarily prophets." Also needed is the gift of prophecy itself. First Corinthians 14:1 instructs us to "follow after charity, but rather that ye may prophesy."

So what is the purpose of prophecy? First Corinthians 14:3 here tells us it is for edification, exhortation, and comfort. But Acts 13 verse 2 tells us another purpose, "They ministered to the Lord." Literally, it means "to do service to." It is the word from which we get the word "liturgy." This is what our life for God is to be: a ministry. The Amplified version of the Bible states verse 2 this way, "They were serving the Lord." Jesus is our example here. He came not to be ministered to, but to minister. And that is our lot in life as believers. The sad thing is that we often have it turned around. We want to be ministered to, but Isaiah 40:31 says, "They that wait upon the LORD shall renew their strength." The source and supply of our service is in serving Him.

This ministry to the Lord was then coupled with a more determined sacrifice of fasting. The tone of the church that continued to grow and develop was prayer and fasting. It is in this kind of atmosphere that the Holy Spirit does His grandest work. He reveals the mind of almighty God to mere men. And God must reveal Himself today, or we die! Through fasting and prayer, the plan of God was made clearer, with regard to means by which the world was to be evangelized, as unveiled in verses 2-3. Specific men were called by God and sent forth by the church. Barnabas and Saul (Paul) are "separated" to the work to which they had been called. Through fasting and prayer, the Holy Ghost confirmed to the whole company what He had called these men to do.

In verse 2, the directive of God was "separate me Barnabas and Saul for the work." "Separate me" in this passage literally means to "mark off as with a ribbon." Numbers 15:38-40 is an awakening of God to the Israelites to do just that; He wanted the Israelites to literally separate themselves and make a distinction between them and those that cut themselves off from God and His ways. "That ye may remember, and do all my commandments, and be holy unto your God" (Numbers 15:40). God wants separated people for His highest work. And His work is committed to all of us to one degree or another. Note the consciousness of the mind of God in this matter concerning these men. Oh Lord, make us sensitive to the leading of the Holy Spirit in our lives today.

First Missionary Journey Acts 13:4-15

This begins the first missionary journey of Paul. It begins on the Isle of Cyprus; landing at Salamis, they journey across the Island of Paphos: from Antioch to Seleucia, to Cyprus, to Salamis, to Paphos. Now, Cyprus was the center of the worship of Venus and Aphrodite, the mythical goddesses of love. As a result of this, the area was greatly influenced by immorality and pagan rituals. Verse 6 tells us that, in Paphos, they came across an evident result of paganism: a sorcerer named Barjesus. He was a magician—a fortune teller and dabbler in black magic. A rise in such activity on a vast scale should stir us to seek God for a full measure of the Holy Spirit's anointing TODAY!

Verse 7 tells us of this sorcerer's influence and power, "Which was with the deputy of the country, Sergius Paulus." So, Barjesus was apparently an advisor to him. Sergius Paulus was a prudent man, according to verse 7; apparently this deputy sought the sorcerer's advice in the affairs of the government. The Weymouth translation uses these words of description: "Sergius Paulus was on keen intelligence," and his desire proves it. Again in the Weymouth, Acts 13:7, "He sent for Barnabas and Paul and asked to be told God's message."

There is more of this that goes on today than we realize! It is damnable, from the pit of hell itself! "Blessed is the nation whose God is the LORD" (Psalm 33:12). He, alone, should be the Source of our guidance! What a contrast: Satan's delusion vs. the Word of God. And there is still a movement to pervert the truth. Inwardly, those who will not receive truth (2 Thessalonians 2:10); outwardly, those who peddle half-truth (Acts 13:8).

Let's talk about that half-truth peddling in verse 8. Elymas was a sorcerer and withstood, resisted, and opposed Saul and Barnabas. No doubt, this was done by means of some curse or incantation, or, perhaps, some half-truth concerning his sorcery. This would result in perverting the gospel in the mind of this man who was not yet a believer. And Satan's messengers do the same today! One of the classic perversions of that is, "A God of love would never send anyone to hell."

But Paul, through the anointing of the Holy Ghost, produced a triumph for the gospel. Verse 9 tells us that, "Paul filled with the Holy Ghost, set his eyes on him (Elymas)." Remember this: the best defense to satanism is a positive offensive of God's Holy Spirit. Under the unction of the Spirit, Paul rebuked him and the foul spirit that inspired him. Paul calls the spirit out, "O full of all subtilty and all mischief, thou child of the devil, thou enemy of all righteousness" (v. 10). We need to isolate the works of Satan and call them for what they are! Too often, we try to tip toe around the devil; we play a detente. LISTEN, there is no peaceful co-existence with the devil, folks!

The curse of God upon his physical being, displayed in verse 11, only matched the darkness of his soul. Such a rebuke against satanic activity toward the work of God needs to be more prevalent in these days of "mounting darkness," as 2 Thessalonians 2:11-12 and 2 Peter 2:17 warn us. But HALLELUJAH! there is an opposition to the darkness of this world, and His name is Jesus! (See 2 Corinthians 4:4-6; John 9:39-41; 1 Thessalonians 5:4-5).

The result of the demonstration of God's displayed authority, as stated in verse 12, was that the consul BELIEVED! The Living Bible comments in this way on this verse: "When the governor saw what happened, he believed and was astonished at the power of God's message." Now, this demonstration had a two-fold influence. It removed a hindrance: the sorcerer; and it convinced the consul of God's power. He was astonished at the gospel message. He had never seen power like this; it was more than just mere amazement or fascination. And people, let us never lose the astonishment of the gospel effect. It is God's best! It is the world's only hope! It is life's surest way!

The remaining verses of this section list their travel plans. From Paphos, the company sailed to Perga, and it was there that John Mark deserted the group and returned to Jerusalem. From Perga, they went to Antioch Pisidia. And there they had their first invitation to preach in a synagogue.

Paul's Sermons Acts 13:16-43

Paul's message here recounts God's ancient deliverances and mercies leading to the coming of Christ. First, Paul recognized who his audience was (v. 16). Then, in verses 17-25, he refreshed them with a breakdown of Jewish history: from the Exodus all the way up to John the Baptist preparing the way for Jesus.

Paul reminds them where they came from, after that Jewish history lesson, "Children of the stock of Abraham" (v. 26). He said, "To you is the word of this salvation sent," relating the whole matter to the coming of Christ. As he continued his message, Paul set up a comparison in verse 36 between Jesus and the well-known Jewish hero, David. "For David, after he had served his own generation by the will of God, fell on sleep." The epitaph of David's life is most striking, "He served his own generation by the will of God." Now, set with this comparative ministry of Christ is an example in David. Is that not the matter that lays upon all of us? To serve our generation by the will of God? Oh Lord, let it be so with me.

In verses 38–39, Paul clearly shows the practical application of God's dealings through the years. It is Christ that makes the difference for us with forgiveness of our sins. What a glorious alternative to the gnawing sense of guilt that sin creates. Ephesians 1:7 shouts His praises with this, "In whom we have redemption through his blood, the forgiveness of sins, according to the riches of his grace." Colossians 1:14 echoes, "In whom we have redemption through his blood, even the forgiveness of sins." Paul boasts of the justification and forgiveness through Jesus in verse 39. Justification means complete pardon by simply believing in Him. Nothing else could wipe the slate clean, but His provision! So, we are not only forgiven, but also justified. That's like frosting on the cake! He not only cancels our sins; He imputes His righteousness to us. GLORY TO GOD!

Paul ends his sermon with a solemn warning to all of us as to our responsibility to the gospel of Christ (vv. 40–41). And what was the result of his sermon? Verse 43 tells us that he "persuaded them to continue in the grace of God." Such persuasion is necessary today to come against the drawing power of Satan and the lure of the world. What does it mean to continue in the grace of God? The same thing that drew us to God must be cultivated to help us continue. For example, the desire for the knowledge of God, conviction of truth, and obedience to the Spirit must all be cultivated and continued. The tendency of all mankind is to degenerate. Therefore, continue in the grace of God.

Allow me to illustrate this. My husband and I had the great privilege of serving in pastoral ministry with my dad and mom for six years in North Platte, Nebraska. We were a great team, and Dad was a great leader. We believed in our heart for souls to find freedom in Jesus, and he allowed us free rein in our youth ministry there. Some of our best memories of ministry, so far, are tied to that church and what became our second home: The Rock House (the church annex, a block away from the church, where the youth met).

Along with 'enough rope to hang ourselves,' my dad also had great practical wisdom about ministry that has stood the test of time. One of those jewels of wisdom was this: "What you do to get them in the door, you'll have to keep doing to keep them there." In other words, if you put on a flashy show to get youth in the door of your ministry, you're gonna have to keep up the flashiness to keep them there. In other, other words: Jesus doesn't need help marketing himself; His Spirit is enough!

Let me tell you how that played out in our youth ministry in North Platte, which had substantial growth of teenagers being introduced to Jesus. Praise the Lord! My husband, Dan, had an evangelistic philosophy of training the youth that were already in the youth group, to grow in their relationship with Jesus and then share THAT with their friends. Then we would give them the opportunity, several Wednesday nights a year, to bring their friends to youth group to meet Jesus and other adults and teens that loved Him already. We called them "Friend Nights." Here is where the genius wisdom of my dad comes in: we didn't do anything flashy on our Friend Nights. We had normal youth group, with a focused salvation message. The flashiest thing we did on Friend Nights was celebrate at the end with free pizza. Free pizza is a given in youth ministry; it's not flashy. So, we didn't have to keep doing flashy things to keep the teens coming; we just introduced them to the love of Jesus, and He would grab their hearts like only He does. And because of Jesus, we couldn't keep the teens away. "Just give 'em Jesus," my dad would say.

The Gentiles Believe Acts 13:44-52

Paul and Barnabas are yet in Antioch, and the response to the message is an encouraging one. Verse 44 celebrates, "Almost the whole city" came to hear the Word of God. There were no doubt many that came out of curiosity, and this scripture implies that they came to HEAR the Word of God! That's a good attitude to come to church with today! And, by the way, if I come to your church and you're not preaching the Word of God, I'll burn your house down!

But, with this move toward the things of God, the enemy began his attack. This time, it was through the Jews; as verse 45 discloses, "They were filled with envy." The church's greatest opposition often comes from within. This is true from Acts all the way through history, until now! Even back to the Israelites, who murmured and complained. Listen, there must be a unifying factor within the church today, or it cannot survive. That involves the whole body of Christ, in general, and YOUR church in particular. Christ is building a church today, and it will survive to the degree that the Word of God is positioned in our spiritual priorities. The prevailing need today is for unity—Spirit-anointed, Word-oriented unity!

It is indeed strange that opposition often stems from the so-called leadership, but God calls for unity. Paul admonishes us:

> Now therefore ye are no more strangers and foreigners, but fellowcitizens with the saints, and of the household of God; And are built upon the foundation of the apostles and prophets, Jesus Christ himself being the chief corner stone; In whom all the building fitly framed together groweth unto an holy temple in the Lord: In whom ye also are builded together for an habitation of God through the Spirit. (Ephesians 2:19-22)

And this is the whole purpose of God in the gospel of Jesus Christ. But the Jewish leaders were filled with envy, doing everything they could to belittle the gospel: contradicting, blaspheming, speaking profanely about sacred things. Such a response from the Jewish leaders points us to a need today: it is vital that we maintain an open mind and a teachable spirit. They knew the Word of God; they were the religious leaders! But did they follow it?

With that response from the Jewish leaders, Paul and Barnabas waxed bold! When enemies of the gospel begin their daring opposition, our attitude should be like that of Peter in Acts 4:29, "Grant unto thy servants…boldness." They declared their position without reservation! They basically told them, 'You have rejected the gospel after God brought it to you first. You have judged yourself unworthy by your actions' (v. 46). The biggest excuse of mankind today falls into this category of judging self: "God can't save me" or "I'm too wicked." Willful actions become the judge of life; but Christ is our righteousness, and that is what those leaders could not accept.

Paul recognizes God's will for the gospel in verse 47, "I have set thee to be a light of the Gentiles." It reminds us of Matthew's admonition:

> Ye are the light of the world. A city that is set on a hill cannot be hid. Neither do men light a candle, and put it under a bushel, but on a candlestick; and it giveth light unto all that are in the house. Let your light so shine before men. (Matthew 5:14-16)

There is such a need for that light! And the response from the gentiles in verse 48 is this, "They were glad, and glorified the word of the Lord." So, the Jews were mad, but the gentiles were glad. How we treat the Word of God is really what we think of Jesus. Are you mad? Sad? Glad?

Verse 48 continues with this proclamation, "As many as were ordained to eternal life believed." We touch upon the sovereign grace of God and the free will of man, and the answer is: God neither ordains the act of believing or unbelieving. It is our choice. "As many as were disposed to (ready to settle the matter of) eternal life, believed (aimed to make sure of it)" (v. 48, Mace). Also, Romans 8:29 tells us this, "For whom he did foreknow, he also did predestinate."

The first publishing house is mentioned in verse 49, with the news that "the word of the Lord was published." And the Jews aroused so much feeling and contempt in the city at this point, in verse 50, that Paul and Barnabas had to leave. So, they responded with a brush-off, "They shook off the dust of their feet against them," and went to another city. The result of this whole scene was that "the disciples were filled with joy, and with the Holy Ghost" (v. 52). What a testimony!

First Missionary Cities and Paul is Stoned

Acts Chapter 14

From Antioch, this first missionary journey continues to share the gospel in several other cities: Iconium, Lystra, Derbe, and then back to Antioch. In some of these cities there was a favorable response, some not so much, and there were also mixed reviews. Lystra had the most diverse reactions, from much spiritual fruit, to Paul being stoned. However, seeds of the gospel were always spread! And even in Lystra, the good outweighed the bad because Paul getting into trouble with the religious leaders was balanced by the spiritual success taking place in that town.

Sometimes you need to incite a little trouble to make a difference. My dad didn't set out to do that, and yet, sometimes it happened. As one student of his, Kelly Gafkjen, recalled:

> I remember a ministerial class where he did nothing but tell stories about situations that happened in churches. We had about three or four class periods where I had absolutely no notes, but he wanted to prepare us for situations we might deal with. I remember laughing at so many of his stories to the point where we were disturbing other classes, and one of the other teachers came in thinking that Brother Jones wasn't there. He opened the door and said, 'All right guys, you need to…' and then realized Brother Jones was there. He said, 'Sorry,' and walked back out. That made us all laugh even more. I love your dad and am so grateful for his investment in all of our lives.

Why don't we sneak into this class with Kelly and hear more biblical and ministry wisdom from my dad?

* * *

First Missionary Journey Continues Acts 14:1-18

The first missionary journey of Paul continues to the city of Iconium. There they followed the same procedure as in Antioch Pisidia. They visited the Jewish synagogue and began proclaiming the gospel. Many of the hearers believed the good news, both Jew and gentile alike; but, as before, active opposition from the religious hierarchy created a division among the people. The gospel will always bring a similar response. Compromise is not allowed concerning the gospel; commitment is required. Jesus said in Mathew 10:34, "Think not that I am come to send peace on earth: I came not to send peace, but a sword." Verse 2 of this chapter tells us what happened in Iconium, "The unbelieving Jews…made their minds evil affected against the brethren."

But God continued to work the gospel amongst them, "Speaking boldly in the Lord, which gave testimony unto the word of his grace, and granted signs and wonders to be done by their hands" (v. 3). Two things are evident here in this verse. First of all, the signs and wonders of the gospel are an integral part of its ministry. For example, if we speak, God will honor His Word. And the promise is that "these signs shall follow them that believe" (Mark 16:17). Second, the ministry of signs and wonders to attest the gospel is a sovereign act of God. Remember from this verse, "The LORD which gave testimony…and granted signs and wonders." He gave the signs. The word "granted" indicates the volition of God behind the miracles, but they had to respond in faith! First Corinthians 12:11 encourages us, "But all these worketh that one and the selfsame Spirit, dividing to every man severally as he will."

The longer the work of evangelization went on, the more decisively did the population take sides. Eventually, a riot broke out and a mob was incited to stone the apostles. By some means, Barnabas and Paul got wind of the mob's intention and fled the city.

Now, the reception of the next city was quite the opposite! It began with a miracle! "And there sat a certain man at Lystra, impotent in his feet, being a cripple from his mother's womb, who never had walked" (v. 8). There are four things which are essential ingredients of every miracle that play out here: hearing the Word of God, faith, a word of knowledge to implement healing, and obedience. Verse 9 shows us the first ingredient on the part of the crippled man, "The same heard Paul speak." Romans 10:17 echoes this truth, "Faith cometh by hearing, and hearing by the word of God." Verse 9 also shows us evidence of the faith ingredient, "He (the crippled man) had faith to be healed." If you don't have faith to be made whole, don't bother! Some people come to God in the same way they take aspirin; there is nothing of the Spirit involved. The following verse shows us the last two ingredients in action. A word of knowledge to implement healing is displayed in the words, "Stand upright on thy feet." Paul employed the word of knowledge to initiate the healing. He didn't even anoint him with oil or pray for him. It was a command of faith, "Stand upright on thy feet!" Then, we see obedience by this crippled man. "And he leaped and walked" (v. 10). Obedience in faith is a vital factor in the matter of the miraculous.

Things take a different turn at Lystra, and the people immediately begin to revere them as gods. One of the great dangers with the miraculous is in revering the man instead of the message or Master. Such a path will always lead to ultimate failure! The apostles' disdain for their reverence, and their rebuttal, are recorded for us in verses 14-15. "We also are men of like passions with you and preach, unto you that ye should turn from these vanities unto the living God" (v. 15). Then Paul and Barnabas begin to exalt the Lord, where reverence belongs. "Nevertheless he left not himself without witness, in that he did good, and gave us rain from heaven, and fruitful seasons, filling our hearts with food and gladness" (v. 17). To persuade these people of Lystra of the real Source of the healing power, they point out their humanity and God's omnipotence. IT IS GOD, not man, who holds the power to heal!

Paul is Stoned and Returns to Antioch Acts 14:19-28

The continuation of their first missionary journey drew the antagonism of the enemy more violently than before. The strength of their hatred for them is obvious from the way these unbelieving Jews followed after these early missionaries. In the case of those from Antioch, they had come from over 100 miles. They stirred up the local people and proceeded to stone Paul, casting him out of the city (v. 19). Paul relayed this later in 2 Corinthians 11, "Howbeit as the disciples stood round about him, he rose up, and came into the city" (v. 20). Much spiritual fruit came from Lystra: the lame man, Timothy, Lois, and Eunice (see 1 Timothy 1:2; 2 Timothy 1:5; 2 Timothy 3:11). So it's not surprising when Paul miraculously rises up from his death bed, with the sympathizers looking on.

Let's imagine for a moment this group of onlooking believers. Paul was stoned in the city and dragged out of town by the stoning Jews, who thought he was dead. The believers were probably stunned, scared, and uncertain of what to do next, when, lo and behold, Paul comes to and gets up. I'm sure they were still stunned, and possibly still scared, but no longer uncertain of what to do. Paul recovers so completely that the NEXT DAY they journey to Derbe.

They apparently had little or no opposition at Derbe, for they "preached the gospel…and had taught many" (v 21). From Derbe, they retraced their steps in order to revisit the Galatian converts. In so doing, they did three things that are vital to any new Christian: confirmation, exhortation, and warning. The apostles confirmed, or strengthened, the faith of those new Christians. This is a vital matter at any age, in view of the temptations to backslide that are strong and numerous. They also exhorted them to continue in the faith. The cause for failure and spiritual anemia is failure to continue. Lastly, they warned them that there would be tribulations in serving God. Now, understand that this word does not refer to the seven-year period of judgment, wrath, and Antichrist rule. It is a word frequently used in the writings of Paul and is also translated as "afflictions." Consider the simple exhortation toward Christian maturity by Paul to the Colossian Christians: "You have finished with the old man and all he did and have begun life as the new man, who is out to learn what he ought to be, according to the plan of God" (Colossians 3:9b-10, Phillips). Such a learning experience will lead us to a maturity of life in the Spirit. The Jewish opposition continued throughout the Galatian cities, and the new Christians were in danger of becoming disheartened.

To help support the individual churches, in the wisdom of God, they chose (appointed by stretching forth their hand) spiritually mature men, who would be leaders within the churches, to carry out what they had done. The term "elder" or "presbyter" is the minister who is responsible for the spiritual welfare of the congregation and conduct of public worship. They were also termed "bishops" or "overseers" in Acts 20:28. They prepared them spiritually as they "prayed with fasting" (v.23).

Thus, Paul set a propagation order in the early church, which is still good for us today. Verse 22 speaks of the confirmation and exhortation of the new Christians, with ordination and commendation of the appointed elders laid out for us in verse 23.

After traveling to several cities to preach, they arrived back in Antioch, the headquarters. There, they "rehearsed all that God had done with them" (v. 27), especially drawing attention to how God "had opened the door of faith unto the Gentiles" (v.27). What a great thing to celebrate—the gospel being shared with people who hadn't yet heard about the saving grace of Jesus! They had a testimony night! And who doesn't love some good, God-glorifying testimonies!

Dissension and Decision, and Paul's Second Missionary Journey

Acts Chapter 15

Here we are in the middle of Acts: the Holy Spirit descended, the church age exploded on the scene, Paul was converted—all amazing moves of God! And now we have what naturally follows: dissension. This chapter gives us hope though, for two reasons. First, it shows us that even though these men were being used by God in big ways, they were still human. Second, we see how the disciples dealt with dissension in a practical way. Let me tell you a story of how Dad handled, in a practical way, a situation that could have possibly broken apart a work of God.

As referenced earlier in this book, the church that Dad pastored in Minneapolis in the early '70s saw an influx of converts that came out of the city's drug scene. It all started at *His Place*, the coffeehouse downtown. It was more of a safe place to hang out than it was a place to get coffee; and it just happened to be run by people that loved Jesus. So, as hippies and people on the street were drawn in by the relaxed environment AND the Holy Spirit, they were introduced to Jesus through relationships with the workers.

After some of the "coffeehouse kids," as one of the workers affectionately called them, got saved and *His Place* became a regular hangout for them, a certain man started hanging out there too. He had a smooth way of talking and began sharing some of his exquisite wisdom with the eager converts. He had them eating out of his hand, so to speak. My Uncle Norm, who was on staff at Bethel at the time and served many hours at the coffee shop, shared with Dad his concern about the situation. In his wisdom, Dad said, "Let's wait on it and see what the Lord does." Well, the scenario continued, and Dad looked into that man's past, only to find out that he had a dangerous pattern. He was not accountable to any church, any pastor, any leader, or anyone. He would win over a new group with his charisma, lead them toward him rather than to Jesus, and then when confronted, he would leave and find the next unsuspecting group. So, after some time in prayer about it, Dad told Norm, "Give him an application to work at the coffeehouse, and see how he responds."

So Norm did just that, and the man's character was revealed. He became indignant about answering to anyone and left the building, and the group, creating a bit of a scene right in front of some of the new converts. Therefore, their blinders were taken off, and they saw that he was not in submission to authority; and they learned a big lesson. This was all done without confrontation. The charlatan was revealed by his own crooked ways. What a great testimony of seeking the wisdom of God in tough situations where dissension is possible.

So, let's join my dad and Uncle Norm as they minister to the "coffeehouse kids" with the words of life.

* * *

The First Dissension in the Church Acts 15:1-21

Here we have the first real internal problem of the church. The problem was conveyed in verse 1, concerning the Mosaic ritual of circumcision. There were some that said, in effect, unless you do "such and such," you are not saved (unless they observed the whole ceremonial law). There is a strange proneness in us to make our own opinion and practice a rule, and ascribe a law to everyone else. They actually reduced the miracle of salvation for some ecclesiastical ritual. What a discouraging doctrine! In verse 2, Paul and Barnabas share their disagreement and do not go along with it. They had seen the power of God work, not as a result of ceremony, but simply as a result of the people's response to the grace of God. Because of this disagreement, they called a general council at Jerusalem to work out the problem and settle the dissension. This was by revelation of God, as shown in Galatians 2:1-10.

On their way to Jerusalem, they discussed the conversion of the gentiles (v. 3). There was no question in their minds as to the sufficiency of God's grace ALONE to save from sin. Paul portrays this tenet in Ephesians 2:8, "For by grace are ye saved through faith; and that not of yourselves: it is the gift of God." Upon arrival in Jerusalem, they aired their feelings and told what God had done with regard to the gentiles who did not follow ceremonial law (v. 4). Romans 12:3 conveys this inclusivity, "God hath dealt to every man the measure of faith." "But there rose up certain of the sect of the Pharisees which believed…it was needful to circumcise them" (v. 5). As Dad would say, and as we have seen, if Satan cannot hinder from without, he will try to wreck from within. The prayer of the church must be for unity. However, they harped on the outward man and his actions alone, forgetting that God looks on the heart. Also, the keeping of the law MUST be motivated from within, not from without. What about this attitude now? Does the church face problems like this today?

Verse 6 opens with a reach for unity, as they consider the problem together. That is a good solution—considering together! Peter was the first spokesman for Christian liberty, with a word of wisdom in verse 7-8. He summed it up well, "And God, which knoweth the hearts, bare them witness, giving them the Holy Ghost, even as he did unto us." Inward purity, not outward ceremony, is the source of true religion. Also, the issue with the blood of Christ purifying the conscience from the guilt of sin superseded the ceremony. The latter was only a type of the former. In verse 10, Paul likens our man-made interpretations to "a yoke about the neck," and verse 11 affirms this, "We believe that through the grace of the LORD Jesus Christ we shall be saved, even as they." There is only one way, folks!

Now in verse 12, we hear from both Paul and Barnabas. They simply testified of what God had done among the gentiles. There is nothing that silences dissension faster than personal testimony! Greater is he that hath an experience than he that hath an argument. In a sense, they had divine credentials: signs and wonders.

Now the reply of James in the remainder of this section, verses 13-21, is an important one. It is significant in that it gives the divine purpose for this age: the taking out from among the gentiles a people for His name. This is the distinctive work of their present, the beginning of the church age. The church is the "ecclesia," meaning the "called-out assembly" or the spiritual Israel. And this is the spiritual implication of circumcision: a separated, called-out, holy people. In verse 19, James comes up with a compromise to not trouble the gentiles who have turned to God already, while giving them some instruction of how to keep pure, "That they abstain from pollutions of idols, and from fornication, and from things strangled, and from blood" (vv. 20–21).

The Apostles' Decision Acts 15:22-35

The apostles had a conflict to resolve about enforcing the demands of the law upon the gentiles as against the grace of God. The council of leaders met in Jerusalem, under the direction of the Holy Spirit, to resolve the problem. Galatians 2:2 gives us some insight here, "And I went up by revelation, and communicated unto them that gospel which I preach among the Gentiles, but privately to them which were of reputation, lest by any means I should run, or had run, in vain." So, with a solution in hand, the leaders sent out men with letters to declare the decision of the council. It is part of the rich heritage of God's people that we can be so guided by Him! "It seemed good unto us, being assembled with one accord, to send chosen men unto you" (v. 25). And there is the final outcome of that situation—that great doctrinal study, and new territory for the Jews! To fully appreciate the conflict, read Galatians 2:1-10.

Verse 28 spells out the solution for us, "For it seemed good to the Holy Ghost, and to us." The injection of the Holy Ghost into verse 28 clarifies how they came to unity in verse 25, "It seemed good unto us." When each of us finds what is good to the Holy Ghost, we will find that there is undisputed agreement. The mind of God will always be compatible; it will not cause inner conflict or outer disagreement. Thus, we need to cultivate an open mind toward the things of God. Not an empty mind, but an open mind! How can we accomplish this? We do that by reading God's Word, prayer, and thinking spiritually! Follow that protocol, and it will always be good to the Holy Ghost and to us. It exemplifies a oneness with God instead of an opinion of self.

Let me tell you about an instance in my marriage when "it seemed good to the Holy Spirit and to us." Dan and I have always been a team in full-time ministry. Sometimes I joined him on staff at a church; sometimes I was an active volunteer. Whatever the case, though, we've always approached ministry as a team. This one particular time, I was on staff as Assistant Pastor in Mechanicsburg, PA. We had just hired a part-time worship leader at our church who was looking for housing because he was going to be graduating college soon. At our staff meeting one mid-Spring Tuesday, said worship leader asked for prayer for his housing need. I felt the Holy Spirit so strongly impress on me to invite him to live with us that I almost just blurted it out. I caught myself, thinking, *I'd better talk to my husband about this first!*

Later that afternoon, we were sitting in our respective offices, working. The secretary had left for the day, the almost college graduate worship leader was busy on campus, and it was just Dan and me in the church. Almost without thinking, I yelled over to Dan's office, "Hey babe, do you think Martin should just live with us?" He answered,

"Yes." And that was it! That was all the conversation that decision needed because "it seemed good to the Holy Spirit and to us."

Paul's Second Missionary Journey Acts 15:36-41

This section marks the beginning of Paul's second missionary journey. After the harmony that ensued from the Jerusalem Council, one would think that there would never be another problem. But, in verse 37, we come across a problem that arose between Paul and Barnabas. Barnabas was determined to take John Mark with them on this missionary journey. The word "determined," in this verse, is also used in Acts 5:33 in reference to the slaying of the apostles. Its literal translation is, "was minded." With that, the word indicates that Barnabas persisted in his wish to take John Mark. "But Paul thought not good to take him with them, who departed from them" (v. 38). The result of their opposing views? The contention was so sharp between them, that they separated (v.39).

Thus, after the harmony of the Jerusalem Council, we have this trouble between two of God's great men! Who was right? Paul or Barnabas? From this contention, there is something for us to learn: the devil will cause contention any way and anywhere he can. Paul and Barnabas, for all their great work, were still very much human. Now there are some important practical truths here: they did not allow disagreements to breed personal resentment. In 1 Corinthians 9:6, we see that they worked together again. God even used their discontent for His own glory. Because of their disagreement, there were then two teams of missionaries. As a result, more people were reached!

Paul chose Silas and departed, being recommended by the brethren. Note the recognized rightness of Paul's decision seems to be expressed here. "No man, having put his hand to the plow" (Luke 9:62). Paul was not against John Mark as a person, but he could not tolerate an unsatisfactory worker. Also, Barnabas was like an uncle to Mark, and thus his judgment may have been biased. But Paul later recognized Mark's value as a fellow laborer (2 Timothy 4:11).

Paul's ministry continues! His ministry was found confirming and strengthening the churches. Thank God for the ministry of the Holy Spirit!

Paul's Second Missionary Journey Continues and Midnight Jailbreak

Acts Chapter 16

What an inspiring and encouraging chapter this is, filled with strong, spiritual lineage and character with the introduction of Timothy to the missionary journey scene. And, then there is also joy in the midst of darkness with a worship concert breaking out in the wee hours of the morning in prison.

The combination of strong spiritual lineage and real joy in the midst of darkness makes me think of my Grandma Jones. Doris Catherine (Lancaster) Jones: mother to five British boys and wife to preacher T.J. Jones. This woman raised those five British boys, of which my dad was the youngest, in England during WWII—by herself. My grandpa had come to America to preach some camp meetings one summer in the early 1940s, which is when England joined the war and all domestic travel over the Atlantic Ocean halted. I often marvel at the strength and faith of my Grandma Jones, to have accomplished such a feat with her faith not only intact, but strengthened! Which brings me to a great little conversation between my dad and my grandma that I want to share here to highlight the foundation of my spiritual heritage.

In her later years, my grandma lived in a cute little house with the steepest driveway I've ever been on, overlooking Prior Lake in the Minneapolis suburbs. We visited her there every so often, sometimes fishing or swimming in the lake, but always enjoying a grandma's love and her British accent. Her boys, my dad and uncles, always gave her such a hard time with their endless teasing or goofiness, but she always took it in stride, like the proper British woman that she was, often matching them with her own wit. One time, when we were visiting her, my dad saw her stack of devotional items on her kitchen counter: Bible, prayer notepad, and some Christian books or magazines. Looking over the prayer list, he needlingly said, "Mom, I don't see my name on your prayer list." She matched his wit, somewhat enjoying his jab, with this direct statement in her sweet British lilt: "Oh David, I don't need your name on a list." Praise God for praying mothers and grandmothers!

* * *

Paul's Second Missionary Journey Continues Acts 16:1-24

Paul's second missionary journey is the setting of this chapter. At Lystra, Paul came into contact with a certain young Christian named Timotheus (Timothy), the "son of a certain woman" (v. 1). He gives more detail in 2 Timothy 1:5 concerning this family: "When I call to remembrance the unfeigned (sincere and unqualified) faith that is in thee, which dwelt first in thy grandmother Lois, and thy mother Eunice; and I am persuaded that in thee also." What a tribute to a mother with regard to the raising of her boy! Faith like that is taught by word *and* example. Timothy was probably saved during Paul's first trip to Lystra.

Verse 2 of Acts 16 adds to the tribute in 2 Timothy. According to the reports, even other people said, in essence, 'What a grand fellow young Timothy is.' And so highly did they speak of Timothy that Paul wanted him to go along with him; so Timothy joined Paul. It is a good testimony when we are "well reported of" (having a good reputation) by our brethren. This seemed to be a very important qualification of leaders in the early church (see Acts 6:3; 1 Timothy; Titus).

Verse 3 brings up something that, on the surface, seems to be a contradiction. "(Paul) took and circumcised him (Timothy) because of the Jews which were in those quarters: for they knew all that his father was a Greek" (v. 3). Why would Paul insist on circumcision for Timothy? Didn't they JUST come to a decision on freeing new believers from this rule of ceremonial law? But, oh how this shows the love that Paul has for people and the drive to connect with them so they can understand the gospel! Paul's heart cry is displayed in 1 Corinthians 9:20: "And unto the Jews I became as a Jew, that I might gain the Jews; to them that are under the law, as under the law, that I might gain them that are under the law." And here he is, mentoring Timothy in how to do just that! What amazing devotion to the call of God that Timothy shows us by being obedient, to the extent of going "under the knife!"

Verse 5 reveals the result of the labors of Paul, Silas, and Timothy. Those they ministered to were established in the faith. This is the prime requirement for progress. There can be no growth unless there is planting, firming, and nurturing. The natural outcome of such churches is that they increase in number daily (Acts 2:47). In that church, not a day passed that someone did not respond to the gospel message in some way! Here, as in Acts 6:7; 9:31; and 12:24, Luke concludes another period of missionary work.

The next section, verses 6-11, is a study in the leading of the Holy Spirit. The question arises: why did the Holy Spirit keep the gospel from Asia? Verse 6 says it directly, "And were forbidden of the Holy Ghost to preach the word in Asia." It serves to remind us of the need for God's leading and the keenness with which we must listen to the Holy Spirit. Paul retained an openness toward God; he did not become bull-headed. Even with his strong personality, Paul still submitted to God and His leading.

God had appointments for Paul with people in Macedonia. The first was Lydia at the river, the second was a slave girl, and the third was a jailer and his family. Getting Paul to these appointments was no easy task, but the Holy Spirit got him there. To do this, He closed some doors of opportunity and opened others. We do not have to try to get the Holy Spirit to guide us; that is what He does! But, like Paul, we need to seek that guidance as we are faithful to what we already know to be God's will, and as we trust God, even when we cannot explain what He is doing.

There have been occasions in history of similar guidance—closed doors. David Livingstone tried to go to China, but God sent him to Africa instead. William Carey planned to go to Polynesia in the South Seas, but God guided him to India. Adoniram Judson went to India first, but was driven to go to Burma. In like manner, we need to trust God for guidance and rejoice equally in His restraints and constraints. God still leads us today in a plain path!

Do you remember that in chapter 11 we learned that God has various ways of leading and confirming us in His will? A way by which God leads, as listed in chapter 11, is brought out in this passage: God giving a vision. Paul had a vision, in this chapter of Acts, of a man in Macedonia who said, "Come over into Macedonia, and help us!" (v. 9). It is significant that there was a man in that vision asking for help. For when Paul got to Macedonia, all he found that seemed to be inclined to seek God were women. It is so often true that the things of the Spirit are left to the women. GOD BLESS THE WOMEN! My dad looked to my mom for her wisdom and fairness; even saying about her, "I don't need to consult the Holy Spirit, I just ask my wife." Oh dad!

One of those women in Macedonia was a wealthy cloth merchant named Lydia. She was the first European convert, as recorded in verses 14-15. It was a validation of God's leading, indeed!

But Satan is always at the heels of God's servant. The woman they encountered in verse 16, after Lydia's conversion, was a fortune teller. Through her, a demon proclaimed, "These men are servants of the most high God, which shew unto us the way of salvation" (v. 17). What a contradiction indeed! What is wrong with that kind of testimony? Why did Paul put a stop to it in verse 18? The spirit and the testimony of that girl did not coincide with the message of the gospel. God doesn't need that contradiction! It is the saint's duty to "shew forth the praises of him who hath called you out of darkness into his marvellous light" (1 Peter 2:9). The woman was a hindrance, not a testimony, because her knowledge did not come from God, but Satan. Those who had made money from her powers became enraged (v. 19). They took Paul and Silas to court, and they were accused, stripped, beaten, and cast in prison, as recorded in verses 20-24. But, in prison, they prayed and sang praises to God. And the prisoners heard their praise to God! You can have a song in your heart in the night, folks! Our disappointments are often God's appointments, for Paul led the jailer to Christ!

Dad had much success in pastoral ministry in his 50 plus years as an ordained minister. He packed a punch with his sermons, related to his church members as a loving and wise shepherd, and was beloved by many students who darkened the door of his classroom or office at Trinity Bible College. And yet, he had disappointments in ministry. To him, the redemption of those disappointments is something that the Lord shared with him in a prayer time. He told my dad that if he hadn't gone through disappointments in ministry, then he would come across as a know-it-all and not have the same scope of influence for those preparing for ministry at a Bible college.

What does God want to do through your disappointments?

Imprisoned and Delivered at Philippi Acts 16:25-40

The double discomfort of a beating and the stocks was not calculated to fill Paul and Silas with joy. But, at about midnight, the other prisoners heard sounds coming from the inner prison, not of groaning or cursing, but of praising and singing! This is the correct idea here—a continuous activity of praise. The early Christian apologist, Tertullian, captured what was happening here, "The legs feel nothing in the stocks when the heart is in heaven." The response of the other prisoners was equally unusual: they listened attentively. So impressionable was their singing, and so attentive was their listening, that it put Paul and Silas in complete command of the situation. Think of it! In complete command! And the miraculous display here goes far beyond earthquakes and deliverance from prison. The revelation of supreme value to us is that the power of Christ enabled them to overcome the bitterness of very difficult circumstances. It was not a song of deliverance that they were singing, but a song of perfect contentment in bondage. And that is the supreme miracle of the gospel! Any man can sing when the prison doors are open, but only the soul set free can sing in the prison (or sorrow, or trial, or difficulty, or trouble). And that is the supreme triumph of the Christian experience: You cannot shut a Christian out from fellowship with God! HALLELUJAH!

Thus, when Paul, soon again, is imprisoned in Rome, it is not self-pity, but joy that he exudes! "Rejoice in the Lord always" (Philippians 4:4). And he regards himself not a prisoner of Rome or Nero, but always "the prisoner of Jesus Christ" (Ephesians 3:1). Now, this account not only reveals the power of Christ to overcome bitterness, but also the POWER OF CHRIST TO DELIVER. And whether the earthquake be coincidental, or the touch of His hand to shake the earth, He sets them free.

Now, consider what an absolute turn-about that takes place with respect to the jailer and his prisoners. Verse 24 shows us that he is brutal and unemotional. He thrusts them into the inner prison, in stocks, and leaves them without concern. And then, he goes to sleep! He sleeps so soundly that it takes an earthquake to awaken him. Now, at the sight of the open doors, the jailer prepares to kill himself (v. 27). But a voice sounds out from the darkness, "Do thyself no harm: for we (Paul and the other prisoners) are all here" (v. 28).

His humbled response, while trembling, is, "Lords, what must I do to be saved?" (v. 30, Wycliffe). He uses the word "lords" instead of "sirs" here. It is the same term as that which refers to Christ. It was a term of supreme respect regarding the prisoners (Paul and Silas) as superiors; they were in command. Whether or not the jailer fully understood the implication of his question concerning salvation is unsure. He was panic-stricken. But one thing is sure: Paul seized upon the opportunity to present to him salvation through the Lord Jesus Christ (Acts 4:12). Thus, Paul pointed to the Lord as the answer, not to momentary deliverance from punishment, but for eternal salvation. It is offered to all who would believe; and the jailer and his whole family got saved (v. 34)!

The jailer showed immense compassion in verses 33-34 when he washed their beaten backs and fed them a filet mignon, medium well! There's another commercial for ya, folks...just to see if you're awake! You can write that one down and use it someday; it won't even cost you anything. (Laughter ensues in the classroom from the attentive students, bewildered looks from the less attentive, and a dry chuckle from Brother Jones.) Thus, he washed them from their stripes, and he himself was washed from his sins.

Verses 35-40 give us another look at Paul's humanity. They were set free, but Paul's response was, 'We've got our rights! You guys, come and get us!' Perhaps we are seeing the reaction of a tired and battered Paul. We may also be seeing an unsanctified part of Paul's strong and rule-following personality coming to the surface. Is it possible this is an example of what Paul could have been thinking about when he penned the following words? "When I want to do what is right, I inevitably do what is wrong" (Romans 7:21, NLT). The point being, Paul was human just like you and me. Was he right in his attitude? I'll leave that for you to ponder for yourself.

Paul's Journey: Thessalonica, Berea, and Athens

Acts Chapter 17

We return to a scene in chapter 16 where the magistrates ordered the release of Paul and Silas from jail in Philippi. Not to be humiliated or punished without a cause, Paul proceeded to expose their injustice. Their treatment of him was illegal: beaten, condemned, no trial (he was a Roman citizen). "And now do they thrust us out privily? nay verily; but let them come themselves and fetch us out" (Acts 16:37). Was Paul right in his reaction? He need not retreat because he was a Christian, but he also saw this as a good opportunity to draw attention to the gospel witness. That he did, and we will see many different results in this chapter.

Enter the office of Pastor Jones in North Platte, Nebraska, where my husband and I served with my dad in ministry as the youth pastors of the church he pastored. What a privilege and adventure that was! So, in the office sat Dad at his desk, and me, frustrated, with the wind knocked out of my sails, so to speak. Ministry is hard sometimes, and I was despondent because of some of our teens' reactions to the gospel. When you're pouring all you have into trying to set someone free with the words of life, and they push you away…ugh, that is hard to handle, between the feelings of failure and feelings of compassion. I poured out my heart to this patient man, who understood my woes and had walked that same path himself, many times. With empathy and wisdom, he leaned over his desk and delivered a classic Jones one-liner, "Jen, you can't make people good." Thank you, Dad! I have reminded myself of that many times over our years of ministry; it has taken the pressure off of me, and the people we have served.

Would you like to come into his office with me, pour out your heart about a current frustration, and await one of his wise one-liners? Let's go.

* * *

Responses to the Gospel Acts 17:1-18

Free from prison now, they went to Lydia's house to encourage the new believers. Such is the duty of every Christian yet today; encourage one another! "Bear ye one another's burdens." (Galatians 6:2)

Now we find them in Thessalonica, and we see a variety of reactions to the gospel. First, at the synagogue itself, in Thessalonica, they "reasoned with them out of the scriptures" (v.2). In our confrontation with the wisdom of men, this is our only ground of reasoning. It is not what I think, or what "so and so" says, but what the Word of God says! The authoritative WORD alone will stand against the arguments of men.

> All scripture is given by inspiration of God, and is profitable for doctrine, for reproof, for correction, for instruction in righteousness: that the man of God may be perfect, thoroughly furnished unto all good works. (2 Timothy 3:16-17)

> The law of the LORD is perfect, converting the soul: the testimony of the LORD is sure, making wise the simple. The statutes of the LORD are right, rejoicing the heart: the commandment of the LORD is pure, enlightening the eyes. The fear of the LORD is clean, enduring for ever: the judgments of the LORD are true and righteous altogether. (Psalm 19:7-9)

Moving on to the next reaction, in verse 3, the theme of his witness was JESUS IS CHRIST! Their reactions unfold in verse 4, "And some of them believed," meaning some of the Jews, many of the Greeks, and many of the leading women of Thessalonica. What a wonderful response to the ministry of the WORD. They received and believed, but from that reaction, we go to the complete opposite in verse 5; the Jews which believed not! This verse tattles on those jealous Jews by telling us that they gathered "certain lewd fellows of the baser sort." The Amplified Version says it this way: "Ruffians, rascals, bums, rabble-rousers." Their effort was to turn the whole town against Paul and to bring him before the people. But they could not find Paul, and instead brought Jason and other Christians to the rulers of the city. Now, those rabble-rousers made an interesting observation: "These that have turned the world upside down are come hither also" (v. 6). What a dynamic influence upon their world. God grant a like effect upon our world! Again, their response is plainly evident, "They believed not." There will always be those who will not believe.

But there will also be those like the Bereans at Paul's next destination. Verse 11 gives a wonderful description of their response to the message of Christ, "These were more noble than those in Thessalonica, in that they received the word with all readiness of mind, and searched the scriptures daily, whether those things were so." The Amplified Version says it like this: "They were entirely ready, accepted, and welcomed the message of the gospel." These Bereans were Jews, not gentiles. We have seen, in two situations here, the effects of the Word when properly received: at Thessalonica and Berea. Let it be so in our lives! Listen, we never get beyond the working of the Word in our hearts:

> Wherefore lay apart all filthiness and superfluity of naughtiness, and receive with meekness the engrafted word, which is able to save your souls. (James 1:21)

> Husbands, love your wives, even as Christ also loved the church, and gave himself for it; that he might *sanctify and cleanse it with the washing of water by the word.* (Ephesians 5:25-26)

Those Bereans accepted it with "all readiness of mind" (v. 11). Now, understand they did not accept it blindly; "they searched the scriptures daily" (v. 11).

Troublemakers followed them from Thessalonica (v. 13), and so Paul goes to Athens, as recorded in verses 15-16, where he finds a different response. We read that, "his (Paul's) spirit was stirred" (v. 16). Their reaction was not of genuine interest, but of curiosity. They only wanted to dispute and discuss. Then, they went as far as mocking him with the insult "babbler" (v. 18). Let's review the responses to the Word in this section. First, in Thessalonica, some Jews accepted the Word but others were jealous and did not believe the Word. Then, the Jews in Berea received the Word with open-mindedness. Lastly, the philosophers in Athens mocked the Word. In light of all these responses to the Word: acceptance, jealousy, receptive, or mocking, what is YOUR response to the gospel?

Paul at Athens Acts 17:19-34

In spite of the general cynicism at Athens, there were a few who DID believe. In fact, there were three responses in this city: mocking, the desire to hear more, and conversion. The study in this section of verses is of those "wise, curious" Athenians. When Paul brought them the gospel in his disputing in the Synagogue, they did not receive it as truth but as just a new point of discussion. "For all the Athenians and strangers which were there spent their time in nothing else, but either to tell, or to hear some new thing" (v. 21). This verse somewhat reflects the typical temperament of the Athenians who were influenced greatly by the Epicureans and the Stoics. The Epicureans were lovers of comfort and pleasure, dictated by an elaborate philosophy. Their chief aim was "freedom from care." The Stoics were in harmony with nature and obedience to natural law. As the rational element in the universe, enduring hardship uncomplainingly only suggests one aspect of their philosophy. Such philosophy without Christ, most naturally from its unfulfilled reasoning, will be searching for some new thing. And we see this today, don't we? Many people abandon one philosophy for a higher or better sounding one. Unfortunately, we see it in the church as well: those whose lives are not directed by the Word, and those to whom Christ is not Lord, those who are always looking for some new thing, revelation, or truth. Like 2 Timothy 3:6–7 warns us, "For of this sort are they which creep into houses, and lead captive silly women laden with sins, led away with divers lusts, ever learning, and never able to come to the knowledge of the truth." The answer is that THERE IS NO NEW THING!

To those who look for a revelation today, Paul has an answer, "Ye men of Athens, I perceive that in all things ye are too superstitious" (v. 22). He then proceeds with the famous sermon on Mars Hill. This sermon is unlike any other in Acts, in that he makes use of ideas and quotations from the very common understanding. Paul begins from an altar ascribed "TO THE UNKNOWN GOD" (v. 23), and goes on to denounce idolatry. He shows, in verse 29, that in all men there is something implanted by God, which is intended to lead men back to Him. Paul goes on to say that God has overlooked "the times of this ignorance" (v. 30) during which man gives himself to idols. But now God calls "all men to repent" (v. 30) in preparation for the final judgment, which has been committed to a risen Christ. It is interesting to see that Paul's sermon was not high sounding or philosophical, but direct and practical. It stressed the resurrection of Jesus as proof of God's choice, and the future judgment which is committed to Him. This then declares the fact that no matter who you are or what you think you are, the simple gospel is sufficient! Hallelujah to God!

Some read the account in verse 33, "Paul departed from among them," and assume that Paul's ministry in Athens was a failure. And later references of Paul to "the wisdom of this world" in 1 Corinthians chapters 1 & 2 are intended to reinforce that fact. But there is a lesson to be learned here in appreciating the insignificance of the smallness of some things. The result of Paul's preaching was the salvation of one member of the supreme council of Athens, Dionysius (a prominent woman of the city), and others as well. Those are pretty good results in any century, 1st or 21st! This measure is sure—faith in Christ is partnering with the one, living, eternal God!

Paul's Journey: Corinth and Many Other Cities

Acts Chapter 18

Still in the midst of his second missionary journey, we find Paul in many cities to whom he later writes letters of instruction, correction, and encouragement: Corinth, Ephesus, Caesarea, Antioch, Galatia, and Phrygia. In these cities, we see evidence of Paul's encouragement and his desire to strengthen the young churches. He truly was an apostle with a pastor's heart!

The infamous city of Corinth was wide open in its religions and morals. Modern day "sin cities" have nothing on this place! There was a time in our family travels, in the '80s, when we visited Las Vegas: the modern "sin city." We were on our way to the Assemblies of God General Council in Anaheim, California, and made a stop to see the beautiful lights of that city. I was an innocent eleven-year-old Midwesterner, and in that innocence, driving down the Las Vegas strip, I said in delight, "Imagine if all these lights were for Jesus!" I don't specifically remember anyone's response to that declaration, but I know there was a general smile of agreement. And I'm sure there was some parental delight in passing down their love for Jesus.

So, why don't you jump in the car with us on our journey and either hear some 8-track Andre Crouch, some goofiness, the proverbial 'are we there yet' question, or possibly some great spiritual discussion.

* * *

Paul at Corinth Acts 18:1-8

At the time of the Roman conquest of Greece in 146 BC, Corinth was destroyed and lay in ruins for 100 years until it was restored by Julius Caesar as a Roman colony. In

27 BC, it became the capital of the province of Achaea. The temple of Aphrodite had as part of its worship 1,000 consecrated prostitutes. The new Corinth was like the old, a great commercial center and also noted for sexual immorality. That specific sin was the target of Paul's insistent warnings in the epistles to the Corinthians. Their whole lives were influenced by it: their religion, their commerce, their art, their everyday lives. It is against this backdrop that Paul brings the gospel, the straight and narrow gospel, the purifying gospel. What a contrast! And, by the grace of the Lord Jesus, through the ministry of the apostles, many were delivered out of the corruption which is in the world through lust. That need is no less today, in a society where immorality is as common as the air we breathe! The church will inevitably fall victim unless we keep in mind 1 Corinthians 6:11, "But ye are washed, but ye are sanctified, but ye are justified."

In Corinth, the apostle Paul found himself acquainted with an exiled Jewish couple named Aquila and Priscilla, as recorded in verse 2. They were his hosts at Corinth; they shared his work at Ephesus where they also "laid down their necks" for him. They illustrate somewhat the migratory character of many of the Jews under the Roman rule. Both names are distinctly Roman. Of the two, Priscilla seems to have been the predominant personality, for in four places out of the six they are mentioned in the Word, her name comes first. Some suggest that she was a Roman lady of higher rank than her husband, but whatever the case, they were vital to Paul in this gospel ministry.

Verse 3 reveals that they were "of the same craft," which was perhaps a factor in their meeting. It was not unusual for men of high standing to begin in the humblest of vocations. Paul was one such case, from tentmaker to PhD, that he might more ably preach the gospel to educated and uneducated alike. And thus we see him here, "And he reasoned in the synagogue every sabbath, and persuaded the Jews and the Greeks" (v. 4). The tense of the phrase "he reasoned" in verse 4 marks continuance, or another translation is, "Brought their attention to." The word "persuaded" in this verse is in the perfect tense, which expresses that he sought to persuade them of Christ: "Laying upon them the name of the Lord Jesus." (Wycliffe)

Apparently, the arrival of Timothy and Silas encouraged Paul with the news of the steadfastness of both the Thessalonian and Philippian converts (v. 5). The text says that Paul "was pressed in the spirit." But the word is the same word that Luke used in Luke 12:50, of the constraining force of the Father's will, "But I have a baptism to be baptized with; and how am I *straitened* till it be accomplished!" Also, in 2 Corinthians 5:14, we see it in the stimulus of the Savior's love: "For the love of Christ *constraineth* us; because we thus judge, that if one died for all, then were all dead." Another example is found in Philippians 1:23, showing the longing desire for the spiritual good of men, "For I am in a *strait* betwixt two, having a desire to depart, and to be with Christ; which is far better." With this evidence, the literal translation declares, "Paul was constrained by the word." Above all else, we must feel the constraint of the Word in our spirit. Other translations read, "He was wholly absorbed in preaching."

It is obvious that his persuading was not completely fruitful. They rallied upon him and blasphemed. Paul responded to them, "Your blood be upon your own heads" (v. 6). Was Paul right in this action? How much time should we spend persuading? The answer: until there are some who respond, like Justus and Crispus (vv. 7–8).

Finalizing the Second Missionary Journey Acts 18:9-28

Paul's ministry at Corinth was a ministry of the Spirit's preaching. The Lord in a night vision commanded him (Paul) to speak and not to hold his peace (v. 9). Go back to Corinth in a few years, and you will find a great church there, which is a literal fulfillment of the prophetic words, "I have much people in this city" (v. 10). In fact, before Paul left, the church at Corinth existed as an efficient and growing church. So, Paul continued there for a year and six months, but that still was not the end. "When Gallio was deputy of Achaia, the Jews made insurrection with one accord against Paul" (v. 12). Paul had received a divine promise that no harm would come to him through any attack in Corinth. However, he had not been promised that no attack would be made. The significance of the accusation in verse 12 was that if Gallio, as the Roman pro-Consul, had not rejected the Jews' case against Paul, it would have had repercussions toward Christianity throughout every Roman province. But Gallio rejected the Jews' accusation that Paul was preaching an illegal religion, and that is the summation of his attitude, even in the face of further religious treachery.

More action takes place when the Greeks beat up the chief of the synagogue. "Then all the Greeks took Sosthenes, the chief ruler of the synagogue, and beat him before the judgment seat. And Gallio cared for none of those things" (v. 17). Paul stayed at Corinth for some time after this incident. Then, he left Corinth and sailed to Ephesus with Priscilla and Aquila (note the sequence of names in verse 18). He then set sail for Syria and Palestine.

At Cenchrea, he cut his hair, "For he had a vow" (v. 18), for some unnamed reason. Perhaps the reason was connected with his missionary work at Corinth, where he had undertaken a temporary Nazarite vow for the duration of which he allowed his hair to grow long. The cutting of his hair indicates that the period of his vow would have come to an end. Now, do not confuse Nazarene with a Nazarite vow. You can find the particulars of the Nazarite vow in Numbers 6:1-21. Jesus never took a Nazarite vow, but He was a Nazarene. What about vows today? Are they foolish? In the Old Testament, vows were made for numerous reasons: consecration, preparation for offering sacrifices, personal commitment or devotion, as collateral to get something from God, etc. With Jesus fulfilling the Law and changing our relationship with God, making a vow to get something from God is foolish. However, sincere consecration and devotion are commendable.

It seems that although Paul was an advocate of gentile liberty, he did conform himself, at various times, to the laws and customs of his own people. Thus, he undertook a temporary Nazarite vow, perhaps because of delivery from some great danger at Corinth. The function of the vow was not just a religious charm, but indicated a deep, purposeful commitment of some thing or some situation to the Lord. Numbers 6:2 enlightens us, "When either man or woman shall separate themselves to vow a vow of a Nazarite, to separate themselves unto the LORD." Thus, the criteria of a vow must be in our separation unto the Lord.

At Ephesus, verses 19-21 tell us that Paul leaves Priscilla and Aquila after he stayed a while. Then he goes on to Caesarea, Antioch, Galatia, and Phrygia. He traveled to these places to strengthen all the disciples. Apollos appears on the scene in verse 24, and there was some discrepancy in his knowledge of the gospel with respect to baptism. He knew only of John's baptism. But Priscilla and Aquila helped him by explaining the total gospel to him. Let's allow these facts to encourage us simple folk. Priscilla and Aquila traveled with Paul and others, doing the work of spreading the gospel, but they are only mentioned in these few chapters of Acts. Apollos, however, was a traveling preacher of his time, leaving a trail of believers in his path. We hear of him later as Paul considers him a preaching contemporary. Here's the encouraging part: Priscilla and Aquila took him (Apollos) aside and explained the way of God even more accurately (v. 26). And from this encounter with the couple, Apollos effected the Jews in Achaia, "mightily convincing" them and "shewing by the scriptures that Jesus was Christ" (v.28). One couple took the time with one man to help him better understand the gospel, and God then multiplied their discussion with an influential man to effect many more for the gospel. What if Priscilla and Aquila had not talked to Apollos? Every single person is important to God, and we never know what God will do with our simple acts of obedience.

Apollos combined great biblical learning and accurate knowledge of the story of Jesus with spiritual enthusiasm. He was regarded by the Corinthians as equal with Peter and Paul, as 1 Corinthians 3:6 suggests, "I have planted, Apollos watered; but God gave the increase." First Corinthians 4:6 & 16:12 also mention Apollos. His ministry was a mighty one.

Paul's Third Missionary Journey, Miracles, and an Uproar

Acts Chapter 19

Nearing the end of the book of Acts, chapter 19 would have definitely been covered in the classroom after Fall Break. So, sometime around the end of October, Dad would walk into class and try to liven things up with some of his well-known British, dry humor. About this chapter, he would say, "Well, folks, get ready for some prime time, soap opera drama today as we see some of the Ephesians respond to the gospel in crazy ways."

I remember one time when I was sitting in his Isaiah class, and it being the first class of the day, some students were not fully functional yet. I went to Trinity two separate times, about 10 years apart. This particular story happened during my second stint there; I was finishing my bachelor's degree, while my husband worked in college administration.

The best part about this particular class, besides the teaching, was the three Jones generations present: my dad, me, and my niece, Mindi. Of course, Mindi and I sat by each other in class and always behaved! One of the first mornings of class, Dad made some witty comment early on in the period, to which Mindi and I responded with a chuckle. But we noticed something odd—I don't think anyone else in the classroom laughed. Mindi and I looked at each other with a 'that was funny guys, you can laugh' smirk. Either they were too sleepy to catch the humor, or they weren't sure if they could laugh at his somewhat sarcastic comment. Either way, it was all entertaining for Mindi and me.

So, join Mindi and me as we await more of his humor and the words of life that he doled out every class period.

* * *

Paul's Third Missionary Journey Acts 19:1-8

Paul has found disciples in Ephesus. "He said unto them, Have ye received the Holy Ghost since ye believed?" (v. 2). Literally, "having believed, did ye receive the Holy Ghost?" This is a question that confronts every born-again believer. The truth of its message is that there is, for the believer, an unlimited supply of spiritual power (Acts 1:8), of blessing, and glory to be discovered and enjoyed! God's promise to every seeking heart is that there is a plane of spiritual living that far exceeds the run-of-the-mill Christian experience. For a Christian, life empowered by the Spirit is a plush life. Such living took an impetuous Peter from a life of mediocrity into a life of victory and power. It took Saul of Tarsus from the dust of the Damascus road to evangelizing the world. And it takes ordinary church members and motivates them, even beyond themselves, to evangelize their generation.

And the question still necessitates an answer today, "Have YE received?" It is a question to those in ignorance of God's precious promise of, "Ye shall receive." It is a question to those in a world of spiritual anemia, and of shallowness and insincerity. It is a question to any who are hung-up in religious pride. Beloved, there is more! And by vivid example, here are twelve men who put their ignorance and everything on God's altar and became "receivers" of the Holy Ghost. It is ironic but understandable that in any society, a man will live below his potential because he can get by. As it is in a materialistic sense, it is in a spiritual sense too! We are prone to live like spiritual paupers because we are getting by, but the question challenges us again, "Have ye received the Holy Ghost since ye believed?" For "Ye shall receive power after that the Holy Ghost is come upon you." (Acts 1:8)

May God challenge us with that spiritual crisis, that we might be receivers, empowered by God's Spirit! For Pentecost begins with a spiritual crisis; every event of life begins with a crisis experience; a turning point. Life itself begins with a crisis: birth. Our formal education begins with a crisis: that FIRST big day of school. Our spiritual life begins with a crisis: new birth. And the Spirit-filled life begins with a crisis, as illustrated in our text: the baptism in the Holy Spirit.

Let me tell you about a crisis of my own, folks. I was a young lad growing up in jolly ol' England, and every young British lad should learn to swim in the Thames. At least, that's what my four older brothers thought. One summer day, as the five of us ventured down to the river, as destiny would have it, it was young David Jones's day to learn how to swim. And learn, I did, very quickly, thanks to Pete, Steve, John, and Phil.

We speak of this crisis experienced by the Jesus-followers in Ephesus, as the baptism in the Holy Spirit. And like all other crises, it brings us to a turning point. It is the beginning of a new level of spiritual life. Scripture gives ample evidence of such crises in people's lives: Peter, the other disciples, Saul/Paul. It is life in the Spirit!

Pentecost added a new dimension to the lives of weak, fearful believers. Consider that these pre-Pentecost believers were saved; so, salvation and Holy Spirit baptism are two separate experiences. The disciples were not of this world even as Christ was not of this world (John 17:14). Luke 10:20 tells us that their names were written in heaven. "Now ye are clean through the word" (John 15:3). The proceeding verses tell us that they were united to Christ as a branch is to the vine (vv. 4–5).

In the condition of being cleansed from sin, He commanded them to tarry until they were endued with power from on high (Luke 24:49). They needed a crisis of heaven's power and glory to enrich their spiritual lives. They needed a divine experience in their lives. And so do we.

The Old Testament gives an excellent illustration of this crisis experience, which the New Testament portrays in reality. In the Meal Offering of Leviticus, fine flour mingled with oil pictured the work of the Holy Spirit at the birth of Christ. Mary was overshadowed by the Spirit, and so were we at our new birth. Then, in the offering, the fine flour was anointed with oil. Note here the "ministry" of the oil. It was typical of the anointing of Christ by the Spirit that was to come at the River Jordan, and shows the second work of the Spirit in the life of the believer—anointing.

Another illustration from the Old Testament is the cleansing of the leper. The ministering Levite first applied the sacrificial blood to the right ear, the right thumb, and the right big toe. This was followed by the applying of oil in the same manner. It is illustrative of the work of the Holy Spirit in salvation (born of the Spirit, as explained to Nicodemus in John 3), but there was more! The remaining oil was poured over the head of the leper. HALLELUJAH! And if it had been today, I believe that leper would have burst forth in tongues!

Thus, as we search the Scriptures, we discover that this Pentecostal crisis opens up a world of experience before unknown, even as a born-again Christian. For example, 1 Corinthians 2:9-10 gives us this promise, "Eye hath not seen, nor ear heard, neither have entered into the heart of man, the things which God hath prepared for them that love him, but God hath revealed them unto us by his Spirit." Now, understand that Paul was writing here to Christians who had experienced the outpouring of the Holy Spirit, not to the unconverted. And the exhortation is for believers to enter into the realm of the Spirit—to live in the Spirit. Oh, how much we miss of God's blessing because we are content to stand on the periphery instead of plunging into the center of things.

Israel did that. God led them right to the door of the promised land. All they had to do was cross the Jordan River and begin to avail themselves of Canaan's milk and honey. BUT doubt and fear kept them out, and they wandered for forty years! Now, understand that God was still their God. He still met their needs. He still spoke to them and led them. BUT all they did was roam for forty years! When feeding on manna, they could have been IN Canaan feeding on the corn of the land. They lived in mediocrity when they had God's best within their grasp! The message is clear: If you have been born again of the Holy Spirit, then tarry until ye be endued with power from on high. If you are a believer, then be a receiver!

Let me take a moment to share a reprimanding encouragement that my dad said to me at times when I would whine like the Israelites. Much like the Israelite experience, God met my needs, spoke to me, and led me, but sometimes justice didn't seem proper to me in life and/or ministry. So, I would call my dad, who always answered my phone call—always. And listened to my complaints—always. And then, always he would say, "Jen, take another lap around Mt. Sinai." It would make me so mad when he would say that! I wanted justice; I wanted an answer! But my dad understood the sovereignty of God and the fact that God would bring justice in His time; and resting in that is not only how we worship God, but how we live victoriously among the injustices of our world today.

Herein lies the value of the "plus life." For if my spiritual experience does not last beyond the crisis, it is of little value. If salvation ends with a confession of sin, it has accomplished little. If your education ends with kindergarten, it is grossly inadequate. If Israel had camped just on the other side of the Jordan, they might as well have stayed in the wilderness! What I am saying is that being a receiver is more than a momentary crisis. It is not IN tongues; that is simply an evidence. The importance of being a receiver is that we are filled (present perfect tense) with the Holy Ghost, which means continuously. And in this strife-torn, trouble-laden world, God verily pleads through His Word, "Have YE received?" Do you know His presence? Are you filled with His love? Are you conscious of His compassion? Do you discover Him in His Word? Do you feel His power? Do you know the joyful labor of intercessory prayer?

If your answer is yes, then you know the truth of what Paul speaks of in 1 Corinthians 2:9-10. If your answer is no, then your solution is graciously prescribed, "Tarry until ye be endued with power from on high." In a world so troubled and filled with man-made hang-ups, it is vital that every believer follow the pattern of those twelve receivers in our text who definitely were not "hung up."

HAVE YE RECEIVED THE HOLY GHOST SINCE YE BELIEVED?

Special Miracles by the Hand of Paul Acts 19:9-20

For two years, Paul stayed in Ephesus, teaching in the lecture hall of a man named Tyrannus. It constituted the basis of a strong church in Ephesus and, no doubt, was the chief influence in the establishment of other churches in Asia (the churches of Revelation). Now, to add credence to the teaching of Paul concerning Christ, "God wrought special miracles by the hands of Paul" (v. 11). It seems that God used Paul to work miracles by the power of the Holy Spirit. And in the "workings" of miracles, a phenomenon arose to draw attention to the particular Source of the miracles.

One phenomenon was healing by a handkerchief. Now, such phenomena were not new, and are not unknown today. Mark 5:27 and Mark 6:56 give examples of people who were healed by touching the hem of Jesus's garment. In Acts 5:15, many were healed by Peter's shadow. Phenomena are not unusual in spiritual ministry, but we must be careful to separate such workings from specific signs, for example: wind, tongues of fire, and ecstatic utterance were present on the day of Pentecost. Wind and flame were phenomena peculiar to that event, but speaking in tongues was a sign of a new era—a visitation of God such as the world had never known.

> For with stammering lips and another tongue will he speak to this people. To whom he said, This is the rest wherewith ye may cause the weary to rest; and this is the refreshing: yet they would not hear. (Isaiah 28:11-12)

> And these signs shall follow them that believe…they shall speak with new tongues. (Mark 16:17)

We need to be careful that we do not make doctrine out of phenomena! We must stick to the message: Christ! Such care will produce the ultimate, as stated in verse 20, "So mightily grew the word of God and prevailed."

However, we have what I like to call "the professional faker" in verses 13-16. In no other arena of life is there more fakery than in the realm of religion! As in Paul's day, there are those today who are ready to jump on the bandwagon of the latest spiritual gimmick. Let me list some special marks that always characterize the faker, or the pretender. He takes advantage of present interest. It was when Paul was working real miracles that these "shysters" appeared. Another example of shysters trying to copy the miracles of God are the magicians in Pharaoh's court trying to replicate the miracles that Moses displayed with his rod (Exodus 7-8). There is a marked absence of concern over sin, but rather a concern of proselytizing. This is true with regard to various cults. They make superficial use of sacred phrases. Verse 13 displays this misstep in action: they "took upon them to call over them which had evil spirits the name of the LORD Jesus." The multiplicity of holy phrases is no thermometer of spiritual quality. It may be impressive, but it does not prove anything! We need to be careful, folks, how we employ God's name—to what use we submit the holy name of Jesus. The exorcists in these verses were not praying, but blaspheming! And their end was justified.

Truth was revealed, and the fear of the Lord gripped their hearts (vv. 15-17)! The result of true authority is shown in verse 17 with the knowledge of the gospel spreading; the people were in awe, and Jesus was magnified! Many confessed their sins and made manifest their evil deeds. Verse 19 shows proof of these new converts separating themselves from their old life of witchcraft with the burning of their incantation books. The truth is attested to by the prevailing power of the Word of God! The Weymouth Version puts it this way, "Thus mightily did the Lord's message spread and triumph" (v. 20). Here is the Amplified Version of that same verse: "The word of the Lord [concerning eternal salvation through faith in Christ] was growing greatly and prevailing" (v. 20). The word "prevailed" here means to go on continually, as it is in the imperfect tense. And, lastly, the Living Bible enlightens us this way: "This indicates how deeply the whole area was stirred by God's message" (v. 20). God's message is supported by God's Word alone (see Acts 6:7; 9:31; 11:24-26; 12:24; 13:49; 16:5), not by phenomena or gimmicks.

Uproar at Ephesus Acts 19:21-41

Verse 21 actually summarizes the remainder of Acts 19 with Paul's ministry travel plans. Though Luke only once hints at Paul's purpose in visiting Jerusalem, in Acts 24:17, it becomes clear that his final visit to Macedonia and Achaia has its objective of taking a collection from the European churches. His personal intention of conveying the collection from the younger gentile churches to the mother Jewish/Christian church at Jerusalem had a threefold significance. First, it indicated the continual poverty of the Jerusalem church, made evident soon after Pentecost. Then, it reflected the Christian gratitude and generosity of those gentile Christians for their brethren from whom they had received the gospel. Lastly, it evidenced Paul's purpose to maintain the spirit of unity and goodwill between the Jewish and gentile elements of the Christian church. Such was also the purpose of the general council in Acts 15.

"Paul purposed in the spirit…I must also see Rome" (v. 21). There seems almost a Spirit-inspired obsession to visit Rome. Thus, he sent two of his helpers to prepare the way for a far-reaching ministry in Europe. They were advanced men for the coming ministry. The period of Paul's ministry drew to an end in Ephesus. He had made it his headquarters, and Christianity had a secure foothold on both shores of the Aegean Sea.

But, before they left Ephesus, there was a BIG STIR. "There arose no small stir about that way" (v. 23). Paul's message had incited a revolt amongst the people. The main objector was Demetrius, a leader of the guild of silversmiths. It was May, a time of religious celebration in Ephesus, and he had a complaint. Demetrius led a demonstration to refute the effects of the gospel. He said, "This Paul hath persuaded and turned away much people, saying that they be no gods, which are made with hands" (v. 26). Praise God for THAT kind of holy disturbance! There are some people who never disturb anything. Listen, we need to be the sort of Christians whose lives make a difference!

Verse 28 displays the response of the Ephesians listening to him, "And when they heard these sayings, they were full of wrath, and cried out, saying, Great is Diana of the Ephesians." "And the whole city was filled with confusion" (v. 29), and a revolt-led mob broke out. They seized upon Paul's companions, Gaius and Aristarchus, and "rushed with one accord into the theatre" (v. 29). This was a meeting place for the town forum, seating 20,000-30,000 people. "Some therefore cried one thing and some another: for the assembly was confused" (v. 32). They did finally come together in nonsensical unity, "All with one voice about the space of two hours cried out, Great is Diana of the Ephesians" (v. 34). Imagine for a moment, full-grown men with brains in their heads bleating out a sentence like that for 120 successive minutes! Such is the meaningless gibberish of a mob; they always end as they did there—with nothing!

Finally, someone stopped the ranting, "And when the town clerk had appeased the people" (v. 35). He is a true politician! That man was taking both sides of a controversial subject. Accomplishing his purpose, though, he dismissed the crowd. For all his politics, one thing can be said of him that we can all learn from: he was a peacemaker. And blessed are the peacemakers! But his actions perhaps became the source of the Ephesian church indictment in Revelation, "Thou hast left thy first love" (Revelation 2:4). And the loss of first love in the history of the church is followed by protection and patronage from outside the church, which causes complacency inside the church.

Eutychus's Untimely Death and the Ephesian Elders

Acts Chapter 20

Paul's journeys from Europe back toward Jerusalem encompassed a number of stop-overs: Greece, Syria, back through Macedonia, Troas, Philippi, Assos, Samos, Trogyllium, and Miletus.

Preachers, let's learn something from Paul here in this chapter: the art of not needing to depend on the spiritual gift of divine healing, and keep our messages concise. Dad, the original Ted Talk speaker, as my husband called him in reference to the length of a sermon, had a few things to say about getting to your point behind the pulpit. "If you can't say it in twenty to thirty minutes, you'll never get it said." "A sermon doesn't have to be everlasting to be eternal." And my personal favorite, "Preaching is like drilling for oil, if you don't strike in thirty minutes, quit drilling."

Another one of Dad's one-liners, especially in the classroom was, "I have twenty-nine minutes, but I'll quit when I'm done." It was his way of saying, "I know the parameters exist, but what I have to share with you is just so good, I'm not going to want to stop!" He always ended on time, but of course, with this dry British humor, he got his classroom's attention. A very ironic, but amazing, thing happened at his funeral. He had asked my husband to preach his funeral several years prior to his death, which he was honored to do! In the opening line to the funeral message, my husband paid homage to this quip of Dad's, quoting it as his parameter of time for the funeral message. I happened to look down at the time when he said those words, and sure enough, twenty-nine minutes later, my husband was closing out the message. I just laughed and thought to myself, *of course*!

So, let's join a class of his to hear some dry British wit mixed with biblical wisdom, but make sure and look at your watch as you walk in. Let's test him to see if he actually does finish in twenty-nine minutes.

* * *

Paul and Eutychus Acts 20:1-16

While in Troas, a very interesting thing happened in the ministry of Paul. As to its purpose in the account of Paul's ministry, it is questionable. But the fact is that Paul preached at length, to the death of Eutychus. The young man was sitting in a window while Paul preached. Due to the late hour, he fell into a deep sleep and fell "down from the third loft, and was taken up dead" (v. 9). "And Paul went down, and fell on him, and embracing him said, Trouble not yourselves; for his life is in him." Church meetings were not regulated by the clock in those days, and the opportunity of listening to Paul was not one to be cut short! It did not matter if he went on until midnight and beyond.

Verse 7 indicates the earliest reference to the meeting day of the early believers, upon which we base our meeting day: the first day of the week.

Thus far in Acts, Luke has recorded three of Paul's public addresses: his message to the Jews in the synagogue of Antioch Pisidia (Acts 13:16-41), an address based upon natural religion to the pagan Lycaonians at Lystra (Acts 14:14-17), and an address based upon natural religion to the intelligent Athenians (Acts 17:22-31).

Now, this account of Paul's final charge to the Ephesian elders is Luke's first and only record of a message by Paul, delivered specifically and exclusively to Christian believers. It contained many striking parallels to his epistles. His message dealt with four basic areas: Christian character, devotion to duty, remembering where we came from, and the Word of God is vital. Paul related to his personal example and ministry in verses 17-21. What an example of Christian character in verse 19, "Serving the LORD with all humility of mind, and with many tears, and temptations, which befell me by the lying in wait of the Jews." He had been faithful to the message of the gospel, no matter what happened. It is the kind of reaction to life's "blows" that produces Christian character. Every one of us has experiences in life that are difficult, but the difference that produces character is that some build on their difficulties and rise above them, and some wallow in them and become bogged in the mind of self-pity. The apostle James wrote, "My brethren, count it all joy when ye fall into divers temptations; knowing this, that the trying of your faith worketh patience. But let patience have her perfect work, that ye may be perfect and entire, wanting nothing" (James 1:2-4). This is Paul's example in Acts: Christian character instead of self-pity.

Paul's character is equaled by his devotion to duty, as evidenced in verses 22-27. If the church lacks anything today, it is in this area: not devotion to Christ, but devotion to duty. But Paul is totally committed to his task, "Bound in the spirit" (v. 22). Paul is committed to the leading and direction of the Holy Spirit, even though it became increasingly evident that he would face much trial and affliction (v. 23). And the capstone of Paul's devotion is summed up in this verse, "None of these things move me" (v. 24). How like his last words to Timothy these words are, "I have fought a good fight, I have finished my course, I have kept the faith" (2 Timothy 4:7). His consuming passion was to fulfill the claim of the gospel upon his life to God's glory: "All the counsel of God" (v. 27).

Paul's Charge to the Ephesian Elders Acts 20:17-38

It is at Miletus, a stop on their journey, that Paul calls for a meeting of the elders from Ephesus. The apostle Paul's final charge to the Ephesian elders is a study in the total Christian ethic. We Christians are great for flaunting our strengths and ignoring or excusing our weaknesses, but here Paul deals with four basic areas of Christian response.

Christian character is the first area to look at, in verses 17-21. Verse 19 specifically upholds the idea of "Serving the Lord with all humility of mind, and with many tears, and temptations, which befell me by the lying in wait of the Jews." Devotion to duty is discussed in verses 22-27 as the next area. "None of these things move me, neither count I my life dear unto myself, so that I might finish my course with joy, and the ministry, which I have received of the Lord Jesus, to testify the gospel of the grace of God" (v. 24).

Verses 28-31 wrap up a final charge to those Ephesian leaders with a truth that is basic to everyone. It is a common denominator which runs through every Christian experience; remember from whence we are come! Paul said to those elders, "Feed the church of God, which he hath purchased with his own blood" (v. 28). The tendency of our heart is to forget from whence we came; from where we draw our life; from where is the Source that "continually cleanses us from all sin" (1 John 1:7, TPT). Let this verse be another reminder to you of whence we came:

> Giving thanks unto the Father, which hath made us meet to be partakers of the inheritance of the saints in light: who hath delivered us from the power of darkness, and hath translated us into the kingdom of his dear Son: in whom we have redemption through his blood, even the forgiveness of sins. (Colossians 1:12-14)

We tend to drift from that knowledge and experience, but God declared its fundamental principle centuries before Christ became "the one sacrifice for sins forever." Leviticus 17:11 sets this up, "For it is the blood that maketh an atonement for the soul." And it is demonstrated in Exodus 12:13, "And the blood shall be to you for a token upon the house where ye are: and when I see the blood, I will pass over you, and the plague shall not be upon you to destroy." It is the great common bond; no matter how great or small, young or old, talented or ordinary, beautiful or common, WE HAVE ALL, as Christians, been purchased by His own blood. "In whom we have redemption through his blood, the forgiveness of sins, according to the riches of his grace" (Ephesians 1:7). This is basic; and Paul exhorts us to never forget it!

The fourth, and last, area of the Christian response is that the Word of God is vital to continuing life and development. Verse 32 lays it out for us here, "And now, brethren, I commend you to God, and to the word of his grace, which is able to build you up, and to give you an inheritance among all them which are sanctified." Positionally, we are sons of God, heirs of God and joint heirs with Jesus Christ. But we are what we become experientially through our relationship with the Word of His grace.

Listen, you cannot blame your heredity or your environment or your circumstances forever! These things affect our lives; indeed they are powerful influences, but "The word of God is alive and powerful, and sharper than any two-edged sword, for the purpose of dividing the fleshly from the spiritual, even to the point of revealing the thoughts and intents of the heart" (Hebrews 4:12). And that translation is the "Jones Translation," folks. You won't find it on any bookshelf, but it's a good one.

This is the only means by which we are sanctified in preparation for His return! Ephesians 5:25b-27 upholds this: "Christ also loved the church, and gave himself for it; that he might sanctify and cleanse it with the washing of water by the word, that he might present it to himself a glorious church, not having spot, or wrinkle, or any such thing; but that it should be holy and without blemish."

There is another thought added here which is primarily a personal vindication of the apostle Paul's life and ministry. But there is a law of life, which is all but buried in our affluent society, "It is more blessed to give than to receive" (v. 35). The usual attitude today, with regard to investment of our life in others, is 'what's in it for me?' But Paul reminds us of the law of giving and receiving declared by Jesus, "Give and it shall be given unto you; good measure, pressed down, and shaken together, and running over, shall men give into your bosom" (Luke 6:38). Now, we continue that truth to the offerings in church, but it is a principle that works in all of life's experience!

Agabus's Prophecy and Paul in Jerusalem

Acts Chapter 21

As Paul wraps up his last missionary journey, tragedy befalls him; he is arrested to be brought to Jerusalem. Someone tries to warn him not to go, but he must follow God's call. Once in Jerusalem, he stirred things up because he brought with him the presence and the truth of Jesus. It is hard to think of that being unwelcomed by some, but if people are not ready to submit, trouble ensues. But Paul stays committed to his witness for Christ.

Some of Dad's best advice for those going into ministry was this, "If there is anything else you can do but preach or pastor, then you need to do that." In other words, if you are dissatisfied and miserable doing a secular job, and the passion for God's Word is bursting out of you, then prepare yourself for ministry. It is a consuming fire! And when you are called to proclaim it, you can do nothing else.

Let's step into his office—his office with all the books, British memorabilia, and a pile of papers needing to be graded—and hear more of his helpful ministry advice.

* * *

The Prophet Agabus Acts 21:1-13

We come, in the first verses of this chapter, to the final part of Paul's third missionary journey. Destiny seems to drive him to Jerusalem where he is ultimately seized, and from where he is eventually sent to Rome; there to give his life. But, in these verses, there is an interesting display of the ministry of prophecy. This is the first reference of prophesying in Tyre, "And finding disciples, we tarried there seven days: who said to

Paul, through the Spirit, that he should not go up to Jerusalem" (v. 4). The Weymouth translation puts it this way: "And taught by the Holy Spirit, they repeatedly urged Paul not to proceed to Jerusalem." The obvious truth here is that Paul was clearly warned of the dangers that awaited him in Jerusalem. But Paul seemed destined to go to Jerusalem, according to verse 5, and there seemed to be a premonition that they would never see him again. On the way, they spent many days with Philip and his family. And although there is no direct reference to any prophetic utterance from them, it is significant that Philip had four daughters who prophesied.

Verses 8-9 introduce us to Agabus as he arrives at Philip's house; and verse 10 describes him as "a certain prophet." When Agabus came to them, he took Paul's belt and "bound his own hands and feet, and said, Thus saith the Holy Ghost, So shall the Jews at Jerusalem bind the man that owneth this girdle, and shall deliver him into the hands of the Gentiles" (v. 11).

Now, there is somewhat of a surface contradiction there, with regard to Paul going to Jerusalem. There was a prophetic utterance that declared that Paul should not go to Jerusalem. And if indeed Philip's daughters prophesied the same thing (v. 9), we have no record that they did. The prophet Agabus, with visual aid, declared the inevitable capture of Paul at Jerusalem.

There are some things worthy of consideration here: was Paul disobedient to God by proceeding to go to Jerusalem? There are two aspects of prophetic ministry here, in verses 4 and 9. They refer to the gifts of the Spirit, which province is limited to edification, exhortation, and comfort. But verse 10 refers to the office of the prophet. The difference being that the office of the prophet is inseparable from the person (Ephesians 4:11). The GIFT of prophecy, however, is only an instrument (1 Corinthians 12:10), and this instrument does not qualify for prophetic office. The office of the prophet deals with revelation of things outside of the Word of God. An example is Acts 2:30, "Therefore being a prophet, and knowing that God had sworn an oath to him, that of the fruit of his loins, according to the flesh, he would raise up Christ to sit on his throne." The test of the prophet is this personal and exclusive revelation, "If there be a prophet among you, I the LORD will make myself known unto him in a vision, and will speak unto him in a dream." (Numbers 12:6)

Why the seeming contradiction? Consider the ministry of the prophetic office superseding all other apparent instruction. The utterance by the Spirit in verse 4 was more exhortation than forbidding. Perhaps it was a preparation for Paul for the coming storms. Certainly the response of the people in verse 11, which is like that of verse 4, only serves to fill Paul with indignation for their desire to pamper the flesh rather than be willing to die for the gospel.

There is a phrase in verse 13 which should stir all our hearts concerning the gospel, "I am ready." Now, there is a curious but very revealing conclusion to this whole matter of Paul's determination to get to Jerusalem. When all their persuading was unfruitful concerning what they thought God's will was, they declared, concerning his apparent stubbornness, "The will of the Lord be done" (v. 14).

Paul in Jerusalem Acts 21:14-36

The last part of this chapter declares a curious array of circumstances in the life of the apostle. He was welcomed in Jerusalem by Christian leaders, James being the head of the group. No doubt the welcome was due, in part, to the offerings he bore, though there is no mention of the offering to the Jerusalem church. It is significant to note that the first thing Paul did after he was welcomed was tell all about what God had done among the gentiles through his ministry. Another testimony night! The time of Paul's arrival was the Feast of Pentecost, therefore, two million Jews crowded Jerusalem. Roman oppression was still the chief enemy of the Hebrew people. Rebellion was not far below the surface on the part of the Jews, but Rome was ready. These facts will help us understand the attitude of the elders toward Paul.

Unfortunately, Paul becomes a victim of the zealots of the law. Verses 20-21 tell us that the Jewish people of Jerusalem were mindful of Paul's history; and his presence made for hostility. And to add to the problem, the believing Jews were not friendly toward him. Thus, Paul became a victim of that volatile atmosphere. There was a segment of the church, Jewish believers, who still observed rites and ceremonies, and were diametrically opposed to Paul's view that a man in Christ has been set free from every other yoke of bondage. No doubt Galatians, and 1 & 2 Corinthians, had already been publicized. It was a sad day for Paul; he would think of the days of Stephen, twenty years prior, and of the four previous visits to Jerusalem. He had never been welcomed there. The elders seemed to have no conviction that the zealots of the law were wrong.

Then, in verses 23-25, the elders advised Paul to give his consent to the legalists in the church by associating with the ceremonial Nazarite vow. They asked Paul to deny the rumor that he had abandoned rites and ceremonies, by observing them. Now, the heresy of this move was that the Jerusalem Council had won liberty from the Jewish law for all in Acts 15:21-25. But such liberty was never afforded the Christians in

Judea. And the thousands of Jewish believers of Judea were extremely zealous for the law of Moses.

Now, the truth for us here today is that LEGALISM IS A KILLER! The effect of legalism in the early church is evidenced by the fact that Palestinian Jewish Christianity never outlived the first century. It was at this point in his ministry that Paul seemed to make a grave mistake. In verse 26, he identified with the ceremonial law by taking the vow. Yes, the reason for his consent was not one of expediency (necessity), or of policy, but one of DEVOTION. Let's take a look at 1 Corinthians 9:20, "And unto the Jews I became as a Jew, that I might gain the Jews; to them that are under the law, as under the law, that I might gain them that are under the law." It is perfectly declared in Romans 9:1, "I say the truth in Christ, I lie not, my conscience also bearing me witness in the Holy Ghost." And win his brethren he did in Romans 10. But the question here is: does the end justify the means? Paul, by the prompting of the elders, sought to accommodate his brethren, contrary to his own convictions, in order to gain an opportunity of testimony. However, he lost his opportunity. His brethren were not won, in fact, they turned on him.

Paul, of pure heart, truly just wanted people, Jew or gentile, to experience the love and freedom that is offered through Jesus. But, the Jerusalem Jews, holding tight to what was comfortable to them—the law—manipulated Paul to come back over to their side by setting him up. It was all a show to them. Why couldn't they just have a discussion with Paul about their differences, their questions, and their troubled hearts? Instead, they covered up their own filthy-rag righteousness and used Paul.

There is a great teaching for us here: LOVE MUST EVER BE LOYAL TO TRUTH. To sacrifice a principle for a moment, in the hope of gaining an opportunity to establish it later, is always destined to fail. We do it in our churches, families, and in our secular connections. C.C. Morgan upholds this principle, "It is in our moment of highest spiritual purpose that we must be most watchful against the possibility of compromise." We never establish a principle by compromise; we always lose it.

And now we see Paul's fate unfold in verses 26-31, for he is attacked by a Jewish mob. Thus, Paul's well-intentioned conduct did not accomplish its desired end. He was even IN the temple, following through with what the Jewish leaders had set him up to do, when Jews from Asia incited a riot and took Paul out of the city to kill him. The threat of murder from a mob was based on an accusation and an assumption (vv. 28-29). How quickly things got out of hand!

Paul is then saved from the crowd-killing by a Roman army, but arrested, once again. However, they continued their uproar, and in true mob-like fashion, all began shouting "away with him (kill him)" (v. 36, Amplified). You have to wonder if some of them even knew why they were yelling this. It reminds me of the angry throng yelling, "Crucify Him, crucify Him." (Luke 23:21)

But it is at this point that the Lord, through the Roman guard, of all people, delivered Paul from premature death. Allowed by the guard to speak to the crowd, Paul hushes them and proceeds to talk to them in their own language: Hebrew. Rome is Paul's destiny; and he will fulfill it.

Paul's Defense Argument

Acts Chapter 22

We can see in this chapter the passion and true heart for people—any person that God put in front of him—that Paul had! It truly did drive him to be able to accomplish, and also endure, all that transpired for him in ministry. I believe that my dad had the same kind of drive that Paul had for people to see the lifesaving truth of the gospel. It truly is a calling!

My dad was in full-time ministry for over fifty years, spanning the decades of "free love," the Jesus Movement, the Decade of Harvest, seeker sensitive churches, etc., small town churches to big churches, and bulletins being typed on a typewriter to being mass produced on a computer. He saw many changes throughout his years of ministry, but one thing was always true: he delivered the Word of God with authority and passion, mixed with humor. Aleena Morgan, a former student of his, summed him up well: "When he would say something that made people laugh when he spoke about the Word of God, and when he talked about a life being transformed by Jesus, his face lit up, and he had a light from his eyes that was exciting and comforting at the same time."

I think he's in his office right now. Let's peek our head in and ask him to tell a story about growing up in England during the war, or an entertaining faux pas he may have had delivering a message, or a breakthrough he saw in a new convert. And let's watch his face light up!

* * *

Paul's Defense Argument Acts 22:1-30

Chapter 22 is Paul's defense argument, not so much for himself, but he was defending the method of his ministry, which had stirred up the situation at hand. That was the hour of his final and decisive break with Judaism. The defense was a vindication of the WAYS OF GOD.

Arrested in the Jerusalem temple, Paul addressed the mob. He first gets their attention by speaking in their native tongue, Hebrew. Here we have Paul, in chains and not knowing how much time he has left to live, yet he is concerned with the best way to connect with his listeners to make Jesus known! He is literally living out the verse he penned, "I am made all things to all men, that I might by all means save some. And this I do for the sake of the gospel" (1 Corinthians 9:22b-23a). If he were to speak to the Greek captain, he would use the Greek tongue. If he spoke to the mob, he spoke in the Hebrew tongue. If his captain ordered Paul's examination by scourging, he appealed to his own Roman citizenship. All of his wonderful personality is exerted for one purpose: that the gospel would be preached!

In verse 3, the essence of his words to them was 'I am a Jew; I belong to your nation, and the God whom you worship has given me the vision of the Lord—of the One for whom you wait and for whom you hope. I have seen the Righteous One.' Verses 6-16 show us that his line of appeal is flawless. We witness here his claim of sincerity. There was no turning away from the God of their fathers. Thus, he gave to those listening men his most powerful argument: his own personal experience! There is no better appeal to the hearts of men than that of a personal experience with Christ. He proceeded to give his salvation testimony; what a powerful story of God's redemptive power! Recounting the story of his conversion experience, recorded in chapter 9, Paul gives us a few more details to the story. He shares with these Jews more of what Ananias had encouraged him with in his first moments with Jesus, and revelation through personal prayer time. Why this added information to the angry crowd? To substantiate his work with the gentiles, with the words of God spoken to him by Ananias and by the Lord Himself.

Now, they could tolerate the testimony of salvation, but the spark of their frenzy was set off by the fact that the God of their nation had sent him to the gentiles (v. 21). And all this time, his desire and passion were that his own brethren might be saved, as his heart shows in Romans 10:1, "Dear brothers and sisters, the longing of my heart and my prayer to God is for the people of Israel to be saved" (NLT). His method of approach to this defense was for the gospel. His central loyalty is to the salvation of his brethren after the flesh and the appointment of God. He argued not for his apostleship, but for the gospel!

Observe the process of his defense; there are some vital applications for us to make in this chapter. First, by observing the mob—the furious mob, at that! We learn first the danger of prejudice, and in this case, ecclesiastical prejudice. The test of conviction is the temper it produces. Frenzy in defense is always a condemnation of the thing being defended. Test it by all the New Testament pictures, and it will be found that those who were set for the defense of the gospel were always quiet, calm, sure, and never panicked. Now, observe Paul. In this account of his reaction, we are brought face-to-face with the true motive and method of ministry for God. The one motive must be that of a passion for the accomplishment of the divine purpose. For Paul, what else could have sustained him through all his experiences? He was convinced of God's will, and that must be the true motive of all Christian work! The method is the use of all our powers consecrated to that one purpose. For Paul, that looked like speaking Greek to the Greeks, speaking Hebrew to the Hebrews, and using his Roman citizenship for the purpose of the establishment of the kingdom of God. And let us do the same, folks! Let our "powers" be consecrated to His kingdom's growth and development today!

The last thing we learn, and the most significant, is that more powerful than all the argument is the experience of one man arrested by Christ and changed by that experience! That is more vital than our powers or talents or education or heredity; the witness of a life changed by the living Christ!

A Plot to Kill vs. the Encouragement of the Lord

Acts Chapter 23

This chapter showcasing some of Paul's tumultuous events reminds me of God's providence in our lives, especially during tough or seemingly hopeless times. He is always among us, encouraging us. Lift up your eyes, and see! Let me share with you a story that my dad did not share with a lot of people regarding his first time behind the pulpit as pastor. This story was re-told by one of his students, Rick Applegate, who listened as my dad shared in class, where he not only taught scriptural truths but practical life application as well.

> The story was about the first church he pastored (I believe). When he got up to preach the first sermon, he was terrified. He said that he told the Lord he couldn't do it (pastor) if He wasn't with him. As he began to address the congregation, he said the Lord lifted him out of his body and sat him on the clock in the back of the auditorium. There, he watched the Lord preach his entire message through him. He then had the confidence that he would never do this job alone. It encourages me and challenges me all at the same time. The longer I'm in ministry, and the more familiar I become with "how things work," the easier it is to depend upon what I know. However, this keeps me trusting in God, knowing that if He isn't the One working through me, nothing of eternal value will ever happen.

Let's peek our head into class to hear more Scripture revelation mixed with practical application.

* * *

The Encouragement of the Lord Acts 23:1-11

In this passage of Scripture, Paul's defense becomes a very critical situation. There are two things to note here in this first section of chapter 23: Paul and his circumstances and Paul and his Lord. His circumstances involved a day of strange and perplexing emotions. He was beaten and misunderstood, but protected. His Lord showed up for him that night, following his time before the council. Physically, mentally, and spiritually, Paul was wounded and bruised.

His day unfolded by first being arraigned before his accusers. Their attitude was inevitable, and their findings a foregone conclusion. That was no court of justice! The only possible friend Paul had was the Roman captain who had him rescued in order to investigate a situation that perplexed him; for, as Paul disclosed in Acts 22:25-28, he was a Roman citizen. The shadow of failure in Paul's spirit is revealed in his very first words here in verse 1, "Brethren, I have lived before God in all good conscience until this day." Listen, have you ever felt like Paul did in the face of overwhelming trouble? Beyond this, Paul is upright in his venture to "have always a conscience void of offence" (Acts 24:16). He was able to say at the end of his life, "I have fought a good fight" (2 Timothy 4:7). What a marvelous witness of a man's life!

Now upon that witness, the high priest immediately commanded the guard standing next to Paul to "smite him on the mouth" (v. 2). And in a moment, Paul's dejection turns to flaming anger. Paul's response was not one of emotional anger, but of righteous anger against injustice and unrighteousness. His anger was merited according to Leviticus 19:35 and Deuteronomy 25:1-2. The principle of God's righteousness had been insulted; justice had been violated.

> Ye shall do no unrighteousness in judgment, in meteyard, in weight, or in measure. (Leviticus 19:35)
>
> If there be a controversy between men, and they come unto judgment, that the judges may judge them; then they shall justify the righteous, and condemn the wicked. And it shall be, if the wicked man be worthy to be beaten, that the judge shall cause him to lie down, and to be beaten before his face, according to his fault, by a certain number. (Deuteronomy 25:1-2)

However, Paul did not realize that he was speaking to the high priest. Thus, he used his own hasty response to reveal the greater injustice done him, by apologizing with reference to the position of divine order. Even though the high priest was wrong, he was the appointed ruler in the divine economy, therefore, to be honored and respected. Now, it was at this point that Paul became conscious of the division in the Sanhedrin between the Pharisees and the Sadducees (v. 6). He appealed to the Pharisees, not to cause inner strife, but once again to attempt through his own personal identification as a Pharisee, to win them all to the Lord. However, they continued to point their attention to the apostle Paul, and to protect him. A fight was about to break out between the Sadducees and the Pharisees, so the commander took him from the Sanhedrin to the Roman stockade! It is at this point that we turn from the circumstances and consider Paul and his Lord.

Verse 11 gives us hope with these words, "And the night following." Those are significant words because they bring to mind a host of things that only the night hours amplify. One of the night-hour thoughts was the disastrous failure of the day. His claim of sincerity had been insulted. His passion for righteousness had been defeated. His purpose of testimony had been frustrated. And what was the result? Paul was overwhelmed with a sense of failure in Jerusalem.

He was confronted with doubts as to the future of his ministry. Now, on what basis do we declare these things? On the basis of his experience, through which he had passed. On the basis of what would seem natural to any human heart. On the basis of what Christ had said to him. Paul had come to Jerusalem bearing gifts, in order to reach his kinsmen. His hopes were to preach in Rome, but failure brought despair, dejection, and doubt. It constituted what must have been one of the darkest nights in Paul's life, but the scene changed: "The Lord stood by him" (v. 11). The fact of His presence—it was not a voice or vision, it was not an angel or a promise, IT WAS THE LORD HIMSELF. The significance is that the Lord was familiar with Jerusalem. He too had been there, buffeted, bruised, broken, and alone. BUT He had been victorious over those very experiences. The Lord knew all about dejection, despair, and doubt, and He had a word for Paul's plight: "Be of good cheer" (v. 11). He had a word for Paul's feeling of failure in Jerusalem: "Thou hast testified of me in Jerusalem" (v. 11). There may have been failure in method and in policy, but his motive was pure: he had testified (v. 11). And He had a word for his fear of the future: "So must thou bear witness also at Rome" (v. 11). What a night that was, especially after such a day! Strange, it is the reverse from the usual; we think of the daytime as holding the answers, the clarity, the encouragement; BUT not so here. In the night, "The Lord stood by him" (v. 11). And He'll stand by you too—with encouragement, direction, and faith. STANDING SOMEWHERE IN THE SHADOWS.

The Jews Plot Against Paul Acts 23:12-35

The theme of this chapter, thus far, could be summarized in the benediction so often used by the apostle Paul, "The grace of our Lord Jesus Christ." As to the present, Jesus ever brings us, in the hours of darkness, the cheer of His nearness. When He does so, prisons become sanctuaries, and dark nights become golden days. Now, in the rest of this chapter, we have the story of how the first word of the Lord spoken in the night was vindicated and the last word was fulfilled. There are three matters of interest in the remaining verses of this chapter: Paul's mental mood, his surrounding circumstances, and the over-ruling Lord.

The night had passed, the intimate presence of Christ had gone, the voice no longer sounded in his ears, and he was still in prison. Conscious of the increasing hostility outside, he was face-to-face with multiplying difficulties, yet everything had changed! There was perfect assurance, and this man never wavered again through all the perils and trials that grieved and tried and brought suffering upon him. Ever after, in this man's attitudes and activities, there was poised and balanced judgment in evidence. There was no recurrence of dejection, and no more sadness on account of failure. He had no further doubts as to the issue of God's dealings with him. "He had passed into the realm of a great and dignified peace and quietness and confidence, because he dared to believe what His Lord had said to him in the quietness of that one night," as G. Campbell Morgan graciously stated.

Consider his surrounding circumstances! Forty men were plotting and pledging themselves to neither eat nor drink until Paul was dead. Then remember his loneliness; there was no help from the church, and there was no message sent to him from the local church leadership. In Peter's case, the church prayed, but there was no one in Jerusalem for Paul to turn. The only "friend" seemed to be the chief captain, Claudius Lysias. The determined hostility of the men outside was inspired by religious fanaticism; the most dangerous form of hostility. Thus, there was no change of former conditions—no ray of earthly light broke in upon the darkness. Yet, he was steadfast and strong. The Lord had been WITH him and assured him to "be of good cheer" (v. 11). And the music of that anthem was singing itself out in his soul while men outside plotted his death. The Lord had set His seal of approval upon his testimony in Jerusalem, and He had declared Paul would witness in Rome. Paul knew that no hostility could prevent God's purpose.

Thus, in this Scripture passage, a theme prevails that can minister to us today: the over-ruling Lord. It is not obvious to the eyes of sense; in fact, it is a series of events in a commonplace story. The first instrument of God's use is Paul's sister's son. We know nothing about him, and he never appears again in Scripture narrative. He overheard the plot against Paul's life, and the unseen Lord took ahold of this youth for the ultimate deliverance of the apostle. The next prominent person in this story is Commander Lysias. The heart of this man is moved toward Paul to deliver him from the riotous surrounding of the turbulent Jews. Through the actions of the commander, the Lord saved Paul from the more than forty men waiting to kill him the following day. Commander Lysias called up 400 soldiers and seventy horsemen to give Paul safe passage under cover of night.

Through the night, he rode in the midst of this army as far as Antipatris. The danger zone passed, 400 of them went back to Jerusalem, and Paul went on to Caesarea riding in the center of seventy of the Roman cavalry. That is how the Lord took care of him. The account of this situation that Paul faced ends with him "kept in Herod's judgment hall" (v. 35). It was a prison, but a prison in a palace. It was the Lord's provision for His servant.

Paul wrote about this in his letter to the Ephesians, "One Lord, one faith, one baptism. One God and Father of all, who is above all, and through all and in you all" (Ephesians 4:5-6). Look back over this story at the sequence of events: the clandestine meeting, the inquisitive boy who cared to hear the story and tell it, the caring Lysias, and the protective Romans. Who is it who commissions all of these in their special part? IT IS THE LORD! And in our commonplace experience of life, it is not a loose-ended, unplanned existence, beloved! He will keep us "in the king's palace" if He must. We look at our lives, and at times, it is all confusion. There is no hope in circumstance; there is no help in man. But the Lord is committed to us, that we might know His peace. He will use the small things to save us, like the curious boy. He will compel the great things to our service, like the Roman soldiers. It is a commonplace story indeed, but it is alight with the glory of the over-ruling Lord!

Paul, in Chains, Gives His Defense of the Gospel

Acts Chapter 24

Paul is in trouble with the Jewish leaders and was bound in chains for two years. This chapter unfolds the charges brought against him and the beginning of his defense to the ruling authority. Although in chains, he managed to avoid demise because of God's favor upon him.

With Dad being in ministry on a Bible college campus for twenty-five school years, there was bound to be a story or two about a student getting himself/herself into trouble. Let me tell you about one that involved my somewhat innocent dad. Dad earned the moniker "Pope Jones" in his latter days at Trinity Bible College from a like-minded, Jesus-lovin', sarcasm-lovin' student, Steph (Heil) Wahl. This picture of him in pope regalia ended up in his office and various other places around campus. Jordy Nunez, a student of his during his "Pope" days, has this story to tell:

> There was a hall with all of the portraits of previous presidents at Trinity. There was an empty spot reserved for the president at the time. Someone had gifted Brother Jones a picture of him in pope regalia. We schemed and, in the middle of the night, placed Brother Jones's pope picture in that empty spot. He loved it and laughed so much; however, leadership frowned upon the prank.

So, join me in that hallway to enjoy his humor, and most likely a nugget of scriptural truth as well.

* * *

Paul Bound at Caesarea Acts 24:1-16

This chapter covers a period of two years while Paul is in Caesarea to be tried by Felix, the Roman governor. It is, by the grace of God, a time of rest for Paul: imprisonment in favorable circumstances. It was a curious bunch of accusers who descended upon the court of Felix. The inspiration of the accusation was made evident by the presence of Ananias, the high priest. That fact alone is indication of the diabolical source of Paul's opposition. Ananias was an elderly man. He had come from Jerusalem, at least seventy miles away, in great haste, to the Roman court. He brought with him an orator, one knowledgeable in the order of the court (a lawyer), Tertullus.

Note Tertullus's typical lawyer-like approach in verses 2-4. The charge against Paul was three-fold. It is important to note these in the light of Paul's defense in verse 16. They first described him as "a pestilent fellow" (v. 5). Now, that in itself is a serious charge. It was meant to be a defamation of character in order to prejudice his case in the mind of Felix. The term "pestilent fellow" suggests that Paul was a man of very base morals; in fact, no word in the original language could blast Paul's character more!

Upon introducing him as such, the charges were laid out. He was described as "a mover of sedition among all the Jews throughout the world" (v. 5). No doubt that claim referred to the trouble at Ephesus and Philippi, but the charge was groundless. He was also accused of being a "ringleader of the sect of the Nazarenes" (v. 5). And, lastly, they claimed he "also hath gone about to profane the temple" (v. 6). The first and the third claims are very serious charges. These then were the charges laid on Paul before Felix. Naturally, there was an element of truth in all of this with respect to his notorious ministry for Christ. And the thought for us here is in *our* activity for Christ. Is there enough evidence to convict us of being totally committed to Him, as was Paul?

Now, the defense of Paul himself is a singular illustration of his ability with similar courtesy and flattery as that of Tertullus (v. 10). His defense was based upon the basic Roman tenet that those who accuse ought to be present and prove their case. For example, there was a distinction between accusation and proof.

Having thus denied the charges and demanded proof, Paul proceeded to tell the testimony of his own religious experience. And in a very interesting manner, he declared, "I confess unto thee, that after the way which they call heresy, so worship I the God of my fathers" (v. 14). In the light of the accusation, it was a brilliant defense. He declared his religion was their religion carried to its ultimate conclusion. He argued that this "way" was according to the law and in harmony with that which was written in the prophets. He declared his religion as one of personal conviction, and so must be ours in our court. Thus, his defense was first biblical and then one of personal experience; written in the law and prophets, "I confess" (v. 14).

Furthermore, he said that he practiced it diligently, "I exercise myself" (v. 16). People are conscious of their physical health, appearance, etc., and also their mind, education, and improvement. BUT how's your spiritual condition? "Therefore I always exercise and discipline myself, mortifying my body (deadening my carnal affections and worldly desires) endeavoring in all respects to have a clear, blameless conscience" (v. 16, AMP).

Let's break down this verse of Paul's credibility, because credibility as a Christian is of utmost importance to the believability of the gospel. Tertullus had just leveled his slanderous oratory in words that brought Paul's witness seriously into question. And Paul answered with a pure heart. He was honest with himself, with God, and with others. And so must we be the same in order to have a credible witness of the gospel.

Now, the reason that we must be honest with ourselves is because that is where truth is first realized and from which it is nurtured and developed. Paul said, "I exercise myself" (v. 16). As Jeremiah warns us, "The heart is deceitful above all things, and desperately wicked" (Jeremiah 17:9). The truth is that I must be honest with myself before I ever have any kind of relationship with God. The awesome thing is that God always responds to our honesty about ourselves with love, mercy, and grace!

For Paul to then say "To have always a conscience void of offence toward God" (v. 16), was important in his defense because the Jews were trying him for heresy and sedition in his ministry for God. And it is just as important for us today to be honest with God. Some folks act as if God were deaf, mute, and stupid. But hear this from Hebrews, "Neither is there any creature that is not manifest in his sight: but all things are naked and opened unto the eyes of him with whom we have to do" (Hebrews 4:13). According to that, can we afford to be anything but honest with Him?

Finally, our Christian credibility depends upon us being honest with others, obviously! And Paul mentions that also in his defense statement here. The believer in Christ today must be as credible as the gospel he or she represents. How can this be in a day of credibility gaps? Romans 13:13-14 is a good rule of thumb and holds the essence of our credibility: Jesus! "Let us walk honestly as in the day; not in rioting and drunkenness… But put ye on the Lord Jesus Christ."

Notice the sequence of this verse; we must be honest with self, God, and then man. And the truth is that each one of these should affect the credibility of the next.

Paul's Continuing Defense Before Felix Acts 24:17-27

Paul's defense at the court of Felix continued with his reason for being in Jerusalem. "I came to bring alms to my nation, and offerings" (v. 17). He emphatically denied that he had made insurrection. He described the peaceableness of his visit there. Thus, the defense of Paul consisted, first of a claim for justice, and then, a telling of his own story, whereupon Felix, with an apparent understanding of "the way," deferred Paul's case for two years.

During that time, he kept Paul prisoner, but with liberty and privilege. This is noteworthy when we observe the kind of man he was; and this is the study that will reveal some truths perhaps about ourselves. Felix was a curious picture of conviction and confusion. Interestingly, his name means "happy, reckless abandonment to pleasure." He was a freed slave, one who had risen from the lowest ranks in the most corrupt city at that time. He had forced his way into power with his brother. The character of Felix is remarkably revealed, not in biblical history, but by the Roman historian, Tacitus, who wrote of Felix, "Through all cruelty and licentiousness, he exercised the authority of a king with the spirit of a slave." Significantly, there is no despot so cruel as a slave when he is put on a throne, much like Hitler. And history reveals that he was eventually recalled to Rome because of his cruelties. He was corrupt, adulterous, sensual, and lustful. He had three queens. One of his queens, Drusilla, had left her husband at his persuasion. She bore a son to Felix, but both perished in the eruption of Mt. Vesuvius.

However, the overriding message to Felix is that you cannot "play" with the Spirit of the Lord. Felix would periodically call for Paul to come and talk with him concerning faith in Christ, according to verse 24. And Paul spoke to him the truth, "And as he reasoned of righteousness, temperance, and judgment to come" (v. 25). Righteousness revealed Felix as an unjust, dishonest ruler. Temperance revealed him as an ungoverned libertine. He lived a fast life, filled with immorality. Fleshly satisfaction was his consuming interest, and Paul's message concerning JUDGMENT TO COME caused Felix to tremble. "He was terrified" (v. 25, ASV). Felix was not the first, or the last, to come under the convicting power of the Holy Spirit, and his response reveals some interesting truths for us. Procrastination in the face of truth will drive us from it. "Go thy way for this time; when I have a convenient season, I will call for thee" (v. 25).

Two years passed for Paul while Felix repeatedly put off the conviction of the Holy Spirit. If he had responded to his own terror and allowed that to lead him to truth, the news would have been different. BUT he didn't. Instead, he put conviction away from him! Another truth to be learned from this story concerns the folly of indecision. Indecision always produces hardness in the face of truth. And hardness of heart is more hopeless than any of the particular sins such as drunkenness, lust, or immorality. This truth is taught in many places in Scripture. And many lives emphasize the experience today to their own undoing and ultimate damnation.

Paul's Trial

Acts Chapters 25 & 26

Paul, in trouble and in bonds, faced different authority figures to see what must be done about this trouble maker. Standing before Festus, the Roman procurator, and then Agrippa, the Jewish authority, Paul was either passed along by divine intervention, or somewhat dismissed. But, in both cases, Paul unashamedly shared the gospel and his personal testimony.

Let me tell you about a time when Dad was thought to be in trouble but had a secret weapon of lineage favor. Dad attended North Central Bible College in Minneapolis, Minnesota (now North Central University) in the late '50s, where my grandpa, T.J. Jones, was a renowned Bible professor, book enthusiast, and also the dean of students. My grandpa, being fully British, was dignified, distinguished, and full of decorum. A little intimidating, to say the least, along with a role on campus that could bring down an unruly student. One day, my dad dropped by Grandpa's office to pick him up to go home for the day. He jumped out of his souped-up car to wait for Grandpa by the entry. Another student saw Dad get out of his fancy car and said to him, "I wonder what Dean Jones would do if he saw you get out of that car!" Remembering the times, the 1950s proved to be a decade where honoring your elders and submitting to authority was a given. So to possibly offend the Dean of Students by parading your fancy car around campus was alarming! But just as alarming, the moment the words were out of that student's mouth, my grandpa came out of the building, walked alongside my dad to said car, and got in. Dad most likely had a smirk, enjoying the irony, and the student most likely had a jaw-drop moment!

Wouldn't it be great to go back even further in time and hear the British preacher, T.J. Jones, give his words of wisdom on Scripture? Well, the apple didn't fall far from the tree.

* * *

Paul Before Festus in Caesarea Acts 25:1-27

This chapter is preparatory to Paul's final address to his captors before he reached Rome. The setting is still Caesarea. Felix was succeeded by Porcius Festus as the Roman procurator in that area. Immediately following, an attempt was made by the Jews to have Paul brought to Jerusalem. Now, this is significant in light of the fact that two years had elapsed since the end of chapter 24, and there was a new high priest in Jerusalem. But their hostility toward Paul remained. That says something to us of the perpetual evil of a man's nature and Satan's wickedness.

However, an interesting intervention took place on Paul's behalf. Verse 4 tells us that Festus declined to bring Paul to Jerusalem. Now, here is an interesting sequence of events, which reveal the touch of divine power that God's will might prevail. "And (Festus) desired favour against him (Paul)" (v. 3). Then he seemed to change his mind in verse 4, "But Festus answered, that Paul should be kept at Caesarea." He waffled again in verse 9, "But Festus, willing to do the Jews a pleasure, answered Paul, and said, 'Wilt thou go up to Jerusalem, and there be judged of these things before me?'" (v. 9). How do we explain his indecisiveness? He is either unbalanced, or it is the intervention of the divine, that He might fulfill His word to the apostle in Acts 23:11: "So must thou bear witness also at Rome." It is the same power that blinds the eyes of the enemy, opens the eyes of the servant, makes the guards at the tomb as dead men, and puts the quaternion of soldiers in suspended animation. It is God's intervention for His servant. This intervention ended with Paul's appeal to his Roman citizenship.

God loves to bless His children, show them favor, and move on their behalf in ways only He can! I can look back and see several of these moments, big and seemingly inconsequential, where God's handiwork is evident—from keeping my dad and his family safe during WWII while living in London, to orchestrating my grandpa, T.J. Jones, living here in America during the war and ending up in Minneapolis, Minnesota where, many years later, my parents would meet; from seeing God guide my dad in his life in ministry, going from pastoring to teaching, back to pastoring and then teaching again; and to watching God's call on my life unfold from a six-year-old little girl, just "knowing" that she was going to marry a pastor one day, to not only marrying a pastor but becoming a pastor myself. All the times that God, as I like to say, just "shows off" for us with blessings that are needed, and very much appreciated, are little reminders of how much He loves us personally! God moved on my family's behalf when my sister Heidi was deathly sick; He changed the course of events and she ended up only spending a few days in the hospital, and fully recovered. Only God! And then, God showed off again when he blessed my family with a home that was perfect for us, and more than we even prayed for, with a bankruptcy still on our credit report. He even threw in a doggie door for our beloved canine and a pool for our girls, just because He could! Only God! What are some ways that God has intervened for you?

Back to Paul; he was willing to face charges if they were true, but not the Jewish charges, as he testifies in verse 10. His defense is laid out in verse 8, that he did not break any of the Jewish laws, desecrate the temple, nor offend Caesar. Thus, his appeal is to Caesar, who had abrogated to himself the right to final decision in cases of citizenry. Therefore, Festus had no choice in light of Caesar's power, "Unto Caesar shalt thou go" (v. 12).

The scene then changed to a meeting with great pomp before Agrippa and Bernice, which set the stage for Paul's address and witness of his salvation, and continues in chapter 26. Agrippa and Bernice are an interesting pair. Agrippa II was the last of the great Herods. His grandfather had murdered the infants at the birth of Jesus. His grand-uncle had murdered John the Baptist. His father, Agrippa I, had executed James the apostle, and had also laid hands on Peter. It is interesting to note that each of these men had died or been disgraced soon after these events—somehow the destinies of his house had always been mixed up with the faith and fate of Jesus. Agrippa was, by virtue of office, a guardian of the temple. He appointed the high priest, but he was also a vassal of Rome. Bernice was living in open sin with Agrippa. She was his own sister, and also a sister of Drusilla (the wife of Felix).

Now, in all of this, there are two facts of interest and value. The first is this: the appeal of the apostle to Rome and Caesar. Some have assessed his appeal to be wrong action on his part. He loved his countrymen, but they had violated every principle of justice, and he appealed to the final court of human authority that had always treated him justly. He had been repeatedly cared for by that authority, even though the Jewish mob threatened and the religious leaders plotted to kill him. The principles underlying this appeal are revealed in the book of Romans.

> Let every soul be subject unto the higher powers. For there is no power but of God: the powers that be are ordained of God. Whosoever therefore resisteth the power, resisteth the ordinance of God: and they that resist shall receive to themselves damnation. For rulers are not a terror to good works, but to the evil. Wilt thou then not be afraid of the power? do that which is good, and thou shalt have praise of the same: For he is the minister of God to thee for good. But if thou do that which is evil, be

> afraid; for he beareth not the sword in vain: for he is the minister of God, a revenger to execute wrath upon him that doeth evil. (Romans 13:1-4)

The second fact of interest is the matter in which Festus himself seemed to discover as the supreme matter in this whole difficulty with Paul, and is found in verse 19: "One Jesus, which was dead, whom Paul affirmed to be alive." Indeed, Festus. It is the supreme matter, and it involved an interplay of theological problems. The Sadducees were the persecuting priests; and the Pharisees were intellectual believers but practical unbelievers. And Paul, to whom the resurrection of Jesus was an accomplishment and a fact—HE WAS ALIVE! And if Paul had not believed that "ONE JESUS" was alive, not a single chapter would have been written! It was that conviction that sustained him. AND THE TRUTH ABIDES TODAY!

Lift the resurrection from this chapter, this book, human history, and only the cross is left. But, without the resurrection, the cross has no meaning, no power. It all hinges on that! Romans 8:11 reinforces this, "But if the Spirit of him that raised up Jesus from the dead dwell in you, he that raised up Christ from the dead shall also quicken your mortal bodies by his Spirit that dwelleth in you." Take away the resurrection, and the cross is a colossal tragedy—a blunder. But this Jesus who was dead is alive FOREVERMORE! Paul knew it, and so do we! Glory to God!

Back at Trinity Bible College, it is nearing the end of the semester at this point, being in Acts 25. Dad was always up against either the longing to see family and participate in Christmas traditions in the Fall Semester, or the distraction of the inevitable budding romance and excitement of summer plans in the Spring semester. Regardless, he still had important things to get across to the Acts students in these latter chapters. It is with this need to overcome distraction, along with the conviction for the point being made of the importance of the resurrection of Jesus Christ, that he would have pounded the lectern for emphasis and shouted that last sentence with Holy Spirit fervor! His voice would have even lilted into an upper range, breaking out in a chorus of praise, as he ended this section with his signature, "Glory to God!"

Paul and Agrippa Acts 26:1-32

Our attention in this chapter is focused on the two men confronting each other: the one seated in the "dignity" of his kingly office, the other standing as a prisoner. Agrippa and Paul were face to face. The one a king, robed and enthroned; the other a prisoner, chained and arraigned. The one an expert in all the technicalities of the Hebrew economy. The other equally expert in the same technicalities, but with a great knowledge of the spiritual values and intentions. The one given over to sin and impurity; the other glorifying in the deliverance from sin. The one an enslaved king; the other an enthroned prisoner. Now, with Agrippa having given him permission to speak, Paul made what Luke terms "his defense." This chapter falls into three sections, which constitute Paul's defense: his address to Agrippa, his testimony, and Jesus's messiahship.

First is his address to Agrippa in verses 2-11. His plea for a patient hearing suggests his memory of previous interruptions; and, indeed, his address this time was never finished because Festus interrupted him. Beyond the usual niceties of his introductory remarks, there is a passion for the soul of this man, Agrippa, that he might see things in a spiritual light. This man, so mighty and magnificent in many respects, for instance his physical presence and his mental ability, is in dire need, spiritually. Verse 3 tells us that Paul complimented Agrippa as an expert in the technicalities of the Hebrew economy. Upon addressing Agrippa in this most gracious manner, Paul gave his testimony. And that is what it is; it is not merely a defense! What an amazing heart Paul had for the lost when, with any opportunity given him, he shared his testimony in an appealing way for each specific hearer.

He made no reference to the charges that had been brought against him by his own countrymen. They probably weren't even there! This was an official Roman court function, and Paul's defense was one of explanation of the reason for the change in his own life! The whole of his address before them was one of testimony; and that must be the strength of any experience in God. It can be theological, it can be doctrinal, it can be orderly, or ethical; but it MUST BE experiential. His witness to the city of Corinth is this, "And last of all he was seen of me also as of one born out of due time" (1 Corinthians 15:8). And all through Paul's life and writings, it is openly evident that he had come face-to-face with his Savior.

Herein is one of the most concise and experiential testimonies of conversion of the born-again experience, as Paul testifies in verses 12-19. He was on his way to persecute the Damascus Christians. He recalled that he was exceedingly mad against them, but by the marvelous powers of the risen Christ, his next response to the world is in verse 19, "I was not disobedient unto the heavenly vision." Think about what a powerful testimony it is that knows no condemnation. Furthermore, he stated that by the help of God, he had witnessed of Christ unto that very day. And his witness is that Christ would suffer, be the first born from the dead to never die again, and be brought as light to all. What a magnificent message! Throughout his appeal, his primary target was Agrippa.

Six times, Paul paused in his testimony to refer by name or direct reference to Agrippa. Here again, Paul is connecting and appealing to his hearer personally.

Jesus had so changed Paul's heart with His personal interaction on the road to Damascus; how could Paul do anything but connect and appeal to each person he had the opportunity to share his testimony with? How has God changed your heart? How has He connected with you personally to show His love for you? And, has this divine connection moved you to share your experience with others?

Now, Paul's great and final thrust here, in this third section, is in the fact of the demonstration of the messiahship of Jesus. That which was the central hope of Israel has been fulfilled in ONE who demonstrated His messiahship by His actual resurrection from the dead. Paul's Christianity was the logical and necessary sequel to the past. Upon the interruption of Festus, in verse 24, Paul changed his approach from testimony to conclusion, commitment, and crisis.

Paul's fervor for the lost is seen here in his earnestness to "seal the deal" with King Agrippa. He was in front of him; this was his opportunity, and his call to convince his fellow Jew of the messiahship of Jesus could not be quieted! With Festus calling Paul's sanity into question, whether a real accusation or one of hyperbole, Paul must have seen his opportunity coming to a close and wanted to make the most of it. Thus his need to conclude and call King Agrippa to a moment of personal crisis. Being committed to Jewish prophecy, the fact that it was played out in the Person of Jesus Christ warranted a response.

In verse 27, Paul addresses Agrippa directly, "King Agrippa, believest thou the prophets? I know that thou believest." In essence, he was saying, 'Agrippa, you know the story of Jesus, and you believe the prophets; put them together and find the logical conclusion that, by your own will, you can choose Christ for yourself.' Paul was trying to do for Agrippa what Agrippa must do for himself. Now, Agrippa's response has been the focal point of commentators for centuries. Was he convinced? Was he making fun of Paul?

Let's look for a moment at the king's reply, "Almost thou persuadest me to be a Christian" (v. 28). The Amplified version says it like this: "In a short time [and with so little effort] you [almost] persuade me to become a Christian." Without having been in the room with Paul, Festus, and Agrippa that day, it certainly is hard to decipher the king's heart by his response. However, I think we can look at the other interactions between Festus and Paul, and Agrippa's response to and about Paul, for some additional insight on this. Festus was aggravated and shouted an accusation at Paul: "Thou art beside thyself; much learning doth make thee mad" (v. 24). He definitely had a strong reaction to Paul's claims, and Paul's strong response to Festus shows us the need he felt to defend the gospel. And Paul's response back to Agrippa had almost a pleading feel to it, not one of defense like that of his response to Festus.

Now, look at King Agrippa's response to Paul's question. There is no shouting or raising of his voice like there was with Festus. Maybe convicted, but Agrippa does not seem to be angry at Paul's question. After Festus's and Agrippa's gracious synopsis of Paul having done nothing worthy of death, Agrippa adds a comment to Festus that shows sympathy: "This man might have been set at liberty if he had not appealed to Caesar" (v. 32). That response does not seem to be from one that is making fun of someone else. I think Paul, and God, got to King Agrippa!

We cannot definitively say how that turned out, but our last consideration in this chapter is of Paul. It is illustrative of his whole life! It was a moment of high inspiration when the surging tides of the Christ-life leaped from his own heart to the heart of Agrippa. Verse 29 exposes this passion of Paul, "I would to God, that not only thou, but also all that hear me this day, were both almost, and altogether such as I am, except these bonds." Oh God, give us a like passion for the souls of men! What a supreme picture of Christianity. After Agrippa and Festus talked, Paul was on his way to Rome!

Paul's Proverbial and Actual Storms

Acts Chapter 27

Paul really displayed his fortitude in Acts 27. On his journey to Rome, Paul had quite the ride on the seas! It started with a nor'easter, followed by the throwing of supplies and belongings overboard to save the ship. The shipmates found themselves all but shipwrecked; some swam to shore and some floated on pieces of the ship. Sometimes, life looks like this for us, and we find good, solid truth from my dad in this chapter regarding attitudes during our storms.

I remember one such trip that the Joneses had, not on the seas, but still full of "fun" surprises. It all started the day before we were headed out to Anaheim, California for the Assemblies of God General Council. Everyone was preparing for the trip, except the family station wagon. It decided to "give up the ghost," as Dad would say. It died and necessitated Dad having to find and buy a car the day before we were to leave! Of course, it was a station wagon, and I remember, from my sickbed, being very excited to ride in the new-to-us beige station wagon for our family road trip.

The next day, all seven of us: Mom, Dad, Wendy, Jimmy, Heidi, me, and Adam, loaded up into the car, and we were off to California. Full car, to be sure! What could go wrong? Remember me being excited from my sickbed the day that Dad was buying the car? Oy! So, my sickness spread through the family in the form of throwing up, and the like. Luckily, only one family member threw up in the new-to-us car, and thankfully, we contained it. The good news is that once we arrived in California, the flu bug had run its course, and we were able to enjoy our time together there.

So, join us on the road for some real-life application of walking with Christ.

* * *

Paul's Journey to Rome Acts 27:1-44

A grouping of verses scattered over the last ten chapters of this book are gathered up in Acts 28:14, "So we went toward Rome." It is the "Reader's Digest" version, by Luke, of the momentous happenings in this chapter of their journey there. Remember Paul's words in Acts 19:21, "I must also see Rome"; they were spoken in Ephesus just before the uproar. Again, the mention of Rome appears in Acts 23:11: "So must thou bear witness also at Rome." Out of a lonely night in Jerusalem, after the scourging and buffeting, into a quiet cell, the Lord spoke to his servant. And then in Acts 25:12, "Unto Caesar shalt thou go" was said by the Roman governor who was in subconscious cooperation with the will of God and the desire of the apostle. Lastly, the words of an angel bear witness to Paul's destiny of Rome, "Thou must be brought before Caesar" (v. 24). This chapter is the culmination of events that bring Luke to that comment in Acts 28:14, "So we went toward Rome."

The heart of the message for us here is found in verses 21-25. By his experience and declared faith in God, the apostle Paul brings together the facts of faith and the facts of life. He applies the blessing of God to the blasts of life experience. A poet expresses the all-too-common malady:

> We find it easy to pray,
> to sing all day
> when our cup runneth over with joy,
> but when things go wrong,
> we often lose our song
> and feel like sitting down to cry.

Paul's experience could have been like that, but it wasn't! And his authoritative testimony was, "I believe God, that it shall be even as it was told me" (v. 25). Now, for some reason, in very pictured language, Luke describes the journey and the subsequent dilemma of their ship. Verses 2-14 tell us that sailing from Caesarea to Rome in the last of summer, they came near the Island of Crete. Then, in the late fall of the year, they suddenly met head-on with a "tempestuous wind" (v. 14). A wind of tempestuous forces, "a northeaster" (AMP), is how it is described. So characteristic was this storm that it was named "Euroclydon" (v. 14). It was not unusual for such a wind at that time of year. Needless to say, the storm rendered them helpless. Verse 17 tells us that they braced the ship so that it would not break up, actually binding it with cables. It worsened, and verse 18 tells us that they threw the freight overboard. Note this significance: it is good not to have too much stuff on board in the storm. The next day, the furniture and tackling went into the sea, verse 19 tells us. And finally, in verse 20, Luke laments, "When neither sun nor stars in many days appeared, and no small tempest lay on us, all hope that we should be saved was then taken away."

What a hopeless situation! None of us is immune to the storms of life—the troubles, trials, and turmoil. Paul was right in the middle of trouble, but notice that he IS NOT A VICTIM OF THE TROUBLE! For in the middle of the storm, he exuded an authority that was far greater than any rage of the elements. His "speech" to his captors started with the jab of 'I told ya so.' He says in verse 21, "Sirs, ye should have hearkened unto me." But then, his encouragement and direction, "And now I exhort you to be of good cheer: for there shall be no loss of any man's life among you, but of the ship" (v. 22).

Those are strong words, Paul! Is he out of his head? Is he sick? No, but HE KNOWS TO WHOM HE BELONGS! He testifies of this in verse 23, "For there stood by me this night the angel of God, whose I am, and whom I serve." And there is the basis of his authority in the storm! Do you know to whom you belong? Listen, folks, "The angel of the LORD encampeth round about them that fear him" (Psalm 34:7). "The Lord knoweth them that are his" (2 Timothy 2:19). "I pray for them…for they are thine… and thine are mine and I am glorified in them" (John 17:9-10). We are chosen in Him, kept by Him, and more than conquerors through Him. I BELONG TO GOD! And the apostle affirms that, in the light of apparent destruction. So, I say to you all, CHEER UP, WE'LL MAKE IT BECAUSE WE BELONG TO GOD!

Now, the matter that adds to the authority of His ownership of us is that if we truly belong to Him, we will serve Him, "Whose I am, and whom I serve" (v. 23). And when a man draws his authority in the midst of a storm from such a Source, there is strength and power to override anything. Thus, his testimony in verse 25, "Wherefore, sirs, be of good cheer: for I believe God." Listen, there is no argument to that kind of testimony! It rings with surety, with convincing positive assurance. Paul experienced a meeting with a visitor from heaven.

There were some truths that were present, which gave Paul the authority of testimony regarding the predominance of God's will. Let's look at them in verses 10, and 23-24. It starts with the prophetic word regarding the voyage, "Sirs, I perceive that this voyage will be with hurt and much damage." Then, in verse 23, Paul encounters an angel of God with a message of hope. Finally, the promise from the divine messenger in verse 24 that "Thou (Paul) must be brought before Caesar." Paul was convinced, in the light of all this and in the height of the storm, that he would have gotten to Rome, even if he had to walk on the bottom of the sea! "I believe God" (v. 25) rings out Paul's assurance and authority. And like Paul, our testimony can be just as sure. Some folks are theoretical believers, but practical atheists. But we can stand with those of the ages—on the authority of God's Word, in the face of anything—and declare, "I BELIEVE!"

There are some other significant verses in chapter 27 that take us from the sure faith of Paul's announcement in verse 25 to their eventual shipwreck on the island of Melita. For example, verse 40 tells us their fate, "And when they had taken up the anchors, they committed themselves unto the sea." We cannot fight the storms of life in our own power. We must commit ourselves to the providence of God. Let's look at the evidence of that in the details of Paul's life. Verse 42 tells us that "the soldiers' counsel was to kill the prisoners." "But the centurion, willing to save Paul, kept them from their purpose" (v. 43). Again, the apparent providence of God is revealed. Paul WOULD get to Rome! The centurion commanded "that they which could swim should cast themselves first into the sea, and get to land: and the rest, some on boards, and some on broken pieces of the ship. And so it came pass, that they escaped all safe to land" (vv. 43-44).

Melita Ministry and Paul in Rome

Acts Chapter 28

Well, here we are, already at the end of the momentous book of Acts! The world was never the same after these events documented by Luke. So, the end of Acts finds Paul, as a prisoner, on his way to Rome to defend the faith. But first, the sailors found themselves run up on shore after several days on the stormy sea. After some eventful time on Melita (also known as Malta), they finally made their way to Rome, where Paul passionately strove for the Roman souls with the power of God and his own testimony.

As the men encountered the people of Melita speaking a different language, sounding like gibberish to the sailors and prisoners on board, it made me think of my dad and his silly gibberish, and the exasperated response from my mother every time. Our home, like any other home, had silly moments, almost always initiated by Dad. One "act" that played out over and over again went something like this:

> Dad: "I'm gonna go shake a tower" (which we all knew meant "take a shower." See what he did there?)
>
> Any Jones kid in earshot: smirk, eye roll, or chuckle—or all three
>
> Mom: "Oh David, you'd better stop mixing your words up like that, or one day you're going to do that from the pulpit."
>
> Dad: Proud-of-himself smirk

That story, of course, was not biblical wisdom or insight—or was it? Proverbs 17:22 encourages us with, "A cheerful heart is good medicine, but a broken spirit saps a person's strength" (NLT). And he read through the book of Proverbs every month. So, let's dive in with him to this last chapter to see what jewels of wisdom he has for us.

* * *

Ministry on Melita Acts 28:1-10

Now, there are two very obvious manifestations of God's power recorded in this chapter about their stay on Melita, which was inhabited by people commonly referred to by both Romans and Greeks as barbarians. They were so named by the Greeks because they could not understand their language. The term "barbarian" means "those who say bar-bar-bar." This term is used three times by the apostle Paul (see Romans 1:14; 1 Corinthians 14:11; Colossians 3:11), as well as here in Acts 28:4. The word does not mean that they were an uncivilized people, rather, they were neither Greek nor Roman. Interestingly enough, the name Melita means "refuge," and indeed it was!

A remarkable event happened involving a venomous snake on the island, and another example of God's providence. "A viper came out by reason of the heat, and fastened on his hand" (v. 3, ASV). "And he shook off the beast into the fire, and felt no harm" (v. 5). The American Standard Version puts it this way, "And took no harm." The implication here is that he refused any harm. He did this by the same power of God by which he declared his faith in the midst of the storm. There is, through every situation of Paul's journey to Rome, the unmistakable presence of Christ: in Jerusalem, in Caesarea, in the violent storm, and finally, on the Island of Melita.

My dad never had an encounter like this with a snake, however, a student of his tells of a victorious incident with a bee. As told by the student, Alfonso Macedo:

> I remember in class one day, a big bee made its way into the classroom, and some folks were freaking out. The bee was going right in Bro. Jones's direction. He told us to calm down, rebuked the bee, and told it to leave. The bee literally turned as if it was being handled by a remote, and left the classroom. I remember my jaw dropping, and he just kept on teaching like nothing happened. I thought to myself, 'I'm going to try that!' Only, my bee didn't turn around!

The providence of God is a marvelous point of faith! It is not fatalism, for fatalism has no point of reference. Fatalism says, 'Whatever will be, will be'; but PROVIDENCE says, 'I BELIEVE IN GOD!' Providence sits down to a meal in the midst of the storm (Acts 27:35). Providence holds the venomous beast fixed to the arm and shakes it off, taking no harm (vv. 3, 5). Providence accepts the presiding presence of Christ as a fact of life, and the events that come our way are simply the unfolding and developing of God's great plan.

Namely through the viper incident, the barbarians of Melita are brought to a place of willingness to listen to Paul's message of Christ. "They changed their mind" (v. 6) from believing that he was a murderer to saying that he was a god (vv. 4, 6). There was also the healing of Publius's father. Publius was the chief man of the island, who apparently owned an estate near the place of Paul's shipwreck. With no apparent witness as yet on Melita, that was an open opportunity to reach the people through their leader. The story is told in just one sentence, but it is a grand illustration of the power of Christ working through Paul, "And it came to pass, that the father of Publius lay sick of a fever and of a bloody flux: to whom Paul entered in, and prayed, and laid his hands on him, and healed him" (v. 8). Verse 9 tells us that healing opened up a ministry to the entire island. God was there to prove the power of the risen Christ; supporting the Word spoken in exhortation years before, as noted in Luke 10:19, "Behold, I give unto you power to tread on serpents and scorpions, and over all the power of the enemy: and nothing shall by any means hurt you."

Paul in Rome Acts 28:11-31

This passage constitutes the last page of the first chapter of the history of the Christian church. We have followed, according to the plan of the risen Lord, the witnesses in their work in Jerusalem, in Judea, in Samaria, and unto the uttermost part of the earth. Luke tells the story of a generation and the movement from Jerusalem to Rome, and there he ends. But the end it is not; the book is a fragment; it is incomplete. Having followed this movement, the church witnessing in Jerusalem had seen its failure and its victory, and having followed this man of God, through journeyings, and through many perils, we finally get to Rome.

Now, we could observe the power of this gospel in this "queen of cities," sprawled out on her seven hills, roads running out to the whole earth; but as we prepare for its development before us, the book is over! There is no further record! And why not? Because more was unnecessary. The same story will be repeated in every decade and century until the Lord shall come. Enough was written to reveal the secrets of power, to reveal the perils and the pathway, and to provide all that was necessary for the church to fulfill its mission until the consummation of the age. But this last page is full of interest because we arrive at Rome. Rome, at this point, was under imperial despotism; perhaps the worst of all: Nero. Rome was a crumbling power. Rome, at that time, was the center of paganism with all its miseries and vices and follies. The significance of Paul's need to preach the gospel in Rome is now obvious: two million people, and half of them slaves. Also present is the consistent attempt to hinder him from coming.

Thus, into that great center of paganism, where the amazing and awful power of Rome was manifest, passes Paul the apostle of Jesus. Now, his first activity upon arrival in Rome was that of allying together those of the Jewish community, as stated in verse 17. Upon their response to his invitation, he proceeded to explain his situation and declare to them the gospel.

He testifies in verse 20, "Because that for the hope of Israel I am bound with this chain." THE HOPE OF ISRAEL! Now, that statement is significant in light of the fact that, for the Jews in Rome, these Christians were a break with Judaism. But Paul's constant contention is that Christianity is not a break with Judaism, but a fulfillment of the claims of Judaism. Thus, the gospel of Christ! This fact was the basis of Hebrew teaching: the Hope of Israel. Indeed, the hope of the whole world. That successful first meeting was followed by a more formal assembly.

Verse 23 tells us that all day long, Paul preached, argued, and reasoned "concerning Jesus, both out of the law of Moses, and out of the prophets." And the reactions were the same as today, "Some believed the things which were spoken, and some believed not" (v. 24).

The following comments in verses 26-27 are the prophetic response of mankind to the gospel in any age. It is the unthinkable fact that of all who hear the gospel, some will reject it. Their only hope! As far as our text is concerned, it thrusts the gospel to the gentiles. The apostle reminds the Romans of this in his book to them.

> I say then, Have they stumbled that they should fall? God forbid: but rather through their fall salvation is come unto the Gentiles, for to provoke them to jealousy. Now if the fall of them be the riches of the world, and the diminishing of them the riches of the Gentiles; how much more their fulness? For I speak to you Gentiles, inasmuch as I am the apostle of the Gentiles, I magnify mine office: If by any means I may provoke to

> emulation them which are my flesh, and might save some of them. For if the casting away of them be the reconciling of the world, what shall the receiving of them be, but life from the dead? For if the firstfruit be holy, the lump is also holy: and if the root be holy, so are the branches. And if some of the branches be broken off, and thou, being a wild olive tree, wert grafted in among them, and with them partakest of the root and fatness of the olive tree; Boast not against the branches. But if thou boast, thou bearest not the root, but the root thee. Thou wilt say then, The branches were broken off, that I might be grafted in. Well; because of unbelief they were broken off, and thou standest by faith. Be not highminded, but fear: For if God spared not the natural branches, take heed lest he also spare not thee. (Romans 11:11-21)

Now then, this whole book of Acts is the story of God's final striving with the Hebrew people. And here is the final appeal, the words Paul quotes in verses 26-28—the words that were originally spoken by the prophet Isaiah. And the declaration is that they themselves closed their eyes because they would not see. Therefore, God had made them blind and given them over to their own hardness of heart. But, in spite of the reaction of some, verse 30 gives ministers hope as Paul continues his ministry; and so must we: "Preaching the kingdom of God, and teaching those things which concern the Lord Jesus Christ" (v. 31). The message goes on; the power is unfailing; the Savior is still blessing.

Throughout my growing-up years, as a searching young adult in the throes of mid-life and ministry (sometimes alongside my dad and sometimes with him cheering me on), I can testify of this same heart and hope for people. He, like Paul, had life-changing encounters with Jesus, and so convinced of God's life-saving and life-giving power, my dad strove for people to understand His love for them and to grasp the wisdom and life-giving words in the Scriptures. I also saw my dad never give up on people, me included. Did he get frustrated with people's nonchalant response to the gospel? Yes! Did his soul cry out for the souls of those he loved, who were not living in the freedom that Christ died to give us? Ever so much, yes! Yes, he had angst with people, however, I have heard so many stories from students, ministers, and congregants of how my dad believed in them and saw something in them that they did not; it was THAT that made a difference in their walk with Christ. Again, me included! Everyone needs encouragement along this path of Christian service, and my dad was gifted at it. Glory to God, as Dad would say!

Wrap-Up

Well, there you have it, folks! You basically just sat through my dad's Acts class—timeless truth, life application, meaningful revelation, all mixed with his renowned British wit. I hope you learned and enjoyed it as much as I enjoyed putting it together! When I began this project, I was quite overwhelmed. If you have ever prepared a Bible study lesson or a sermon, you know that awesome weight you feel of handling the Word of God correctly. Well, handling both the Word of God and Brother Jones's words with accuracy and meaning had me watching out for the proverbial lightning strike from the heavens—times two! Ha ha! I jest (I am David Jones's daughter, after all). I truly enjoyed my time studying both the Word of God and my dad's words.

It was all the more meaningful after my dad passed away mid-project. Every time I worked on it; it was like spending time with my dad. I could hear him say some of the jokes and exclamations in my head, and I would laugh or smile in remembrance every time. Truly precious moments! If you knew my dad, either as pastor, professor, or friend, I hope you enjoyed a trip down memory lane. If you didn't know my dad, I hope you enjoyed "meeting" him through his commentary and the stories about him.

Appendix A: Deacon Nomination Process

In my dad's experience, he found that the deacon nomination process needed to be improved. So he came up with the process laid out here. He submitted the idea, with an article, to the Assemblies of God publication: Advance. That is included here, along with the necessary "worksheet" for the process. Below is the resolution that was added to the bylaws of the church he pastored at the time.

Worksheet Instructions:

1. Input the names of all eligible members for the role of deacon.
2. Give worksheet to six church members, detailed in the resolution below.
3. Have each assigned member prayerfully rate the eligible members on the worksheet.
4. Once all worksheets are submitted, tally the results, and the most qualified members will rise to the top. Those that do will be confirmed by the voting members at the annual business meeting.

Nominating Committee for Board Members Resolution

A nominating committee shall be appointed annually by the official board for the purpose of presenting a slate of qualified candidates for the office of board member to each annual business meeting. This committee shall consist of three board members including the pastor, and three members of the assembly who do not serve on the board.

A plan for nominating deacons

DAVID L. JONES
Pastor, Mount Zion Assembly, Owatonna, Minnesota

Our churches need the best leaders, both in administrative and spiritual areas. Many churches have suffered needlessly because of a consistent failure to present to the annual business meeting the most qualified members as candidates for deacon. Who is qualified? Who will allow his name to be presented to the voting members?

Out of the particular dilemma of the Early Church, God gave its leaders a means by which to elect a "deacon board" to assist the ministry. "Men full of faith and of the Holy Ghost" is the distinct measure laid down by the Spirit of God through those believers.

Many churches have had to live with problems conceived in such statements as, "I nominate Joe Black. He doesn't come very much; but maybe if he's a deacon, he will become more faithful."

Another mistake is the assumption that because a man is a good businessman he will be a good deacon. Thank God for businessmen who are "full of faith and of the Holy Ghost," but this is not always the case.

Variations of these examples have created problems in many churches. The resulting chaos is often difficult to unravel without hurt feelings or alienated members.

A variety of annual business meeting situations over the past 20 years stirred a desire in my heart for some meaningful and sensitive way to deal with this matter of presenting to the voting constituency of the church the most qualified nominees for deacon.

I began by providing in our church bylaws for the appointment of a nominating committee for deacons. The bylaw read something like this:

> "A Nominating Committee shall be appointed annually by the official board for the purpose of presenting a list of nominees for deacon to the annual business meeting of the church. This committee shall consist of the pastor, two deacons, and three other persons from the membership of the church."

When the nominating committee meets, each member is given a duplicated worksheet listing the names of every eligible male church member. The worksheet includes five areas in which each person is evaluated: spirituality, faithfulness, leadership, maturity of life, and involvement in the church ministry as a whole.

Each committee member is to evaluate each person in the five areas on a 1 to 10 basis: i.e., 1 equals poor, 10 equals excellent. When the evaluations are completed, the scores are totaled, then compiled on a master sheet. The worksheets are destroyed to maintain confidentiality.

Those members with the highest scores are contacted for permission to place their names in nomination on the agenda and ballot of the business meeting. At this point the pastor can share with each nominee his own ideas, and the nominee can gain some further understanding of the office.

In assessing this method over the past few years in three separate church situations, we observe some definite benefits: (1) The worksheet produces by natural evolution the most qualified nominees; (2) each of the areas of evaluation is quite self-explanatory to the committee; (3) in the process of the nominating committee's work there is no discussion of personalities, thus no provision for gossip or useless talk about an individual; (4) with this procedure, evaluation is between the person whose name is listed, the committee member, and the Lord.

Obviously the smaller church with a limited membership would have some difficulty with this procedure, but a church of 25 to 30 members or more would find it a useful tool to solve an oftentimes knotty problem. One committee member who has a variety of experience in church and community leadership made the comment, "I was a little skeptical at first, but it is the smoothest operation I've ever seen." △

"I nominate Joe Black. He doesn't come very much but maybe if he's a deacon he will become more faithful."

NOMINATING COMMITTEE "Worksheet"

Evaluate each person on a basis of 1 - 10 i.e. 1 = poor, 10 = excellent.	SPIRITUALITY	FAITHFULNESS	LEADERSHIP	MATURITY of Life	INVOLVEMENT in the church ministry as a whole	TOTAL

Appendix B: A Sample of Dad's Handwritten Teaching Notes

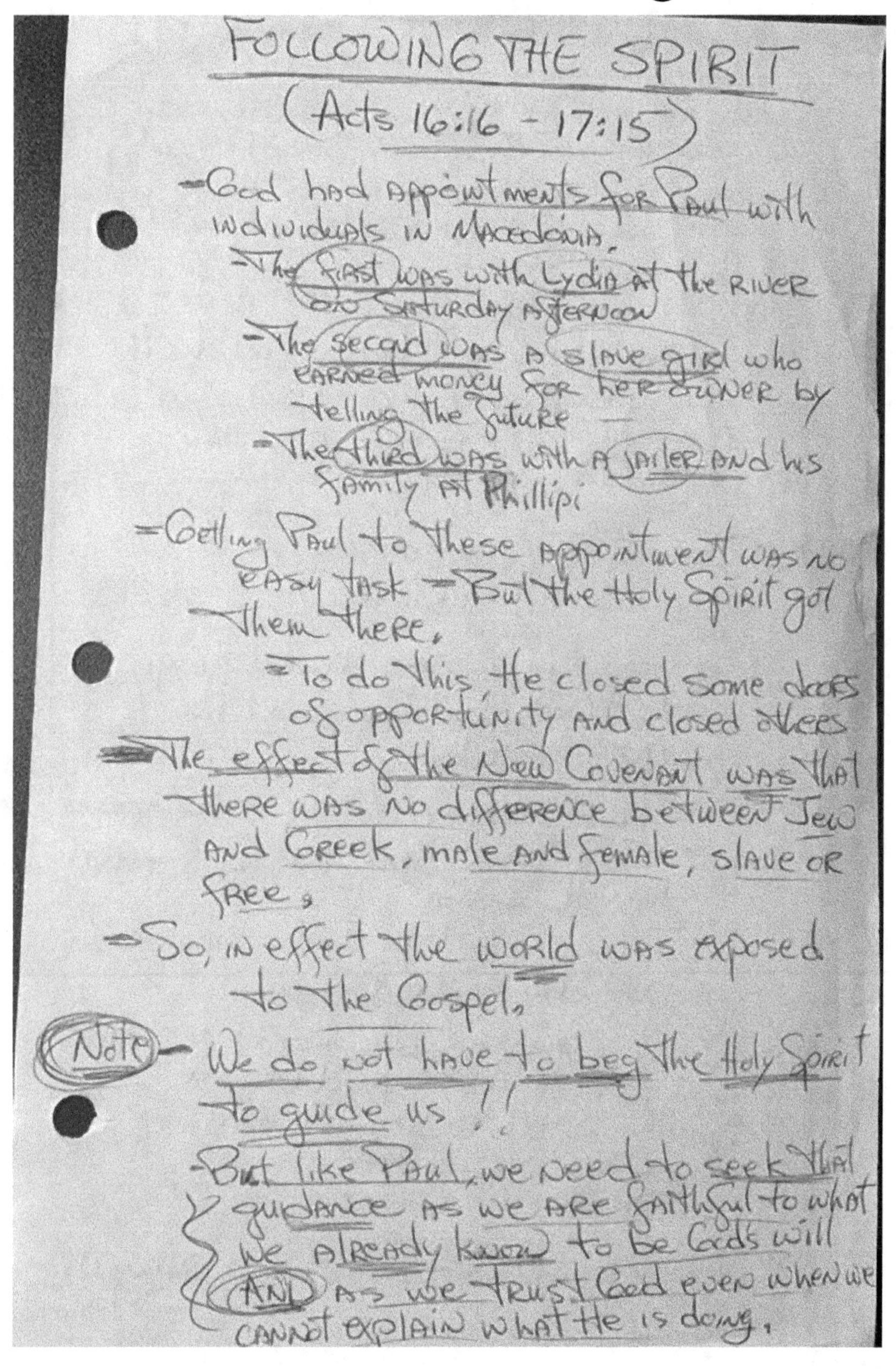

FOLLOWING THE SPIRIT

(Acts 16:16 - 17:15)

- God had appointments for Paul with individuals in Macedonia.
  - The first was with Lydia at the river on Saturday afternoon
  - The second was a slave girl who earned money for her owner by telling the future —
  - The third was with a jailer and his family at Phillipi
- Getting Paul to these appointment was no easy task - But the Holy Spirit got them there.
  - To do this, He closed some doors of opportunity and closed others
- The effect of the New Covenant was that there was no difference between Jew and Greek, male and female, slave or free.
- So, in effect the world was exposed to the Gospel.

Note - We do not have to beg the Holy Spirit to guide us!!

- But like Paul, we need to seek that guidance as we are faithful to what we already know to be God's will AND as we trust God even when we cannot explain what He is doing.

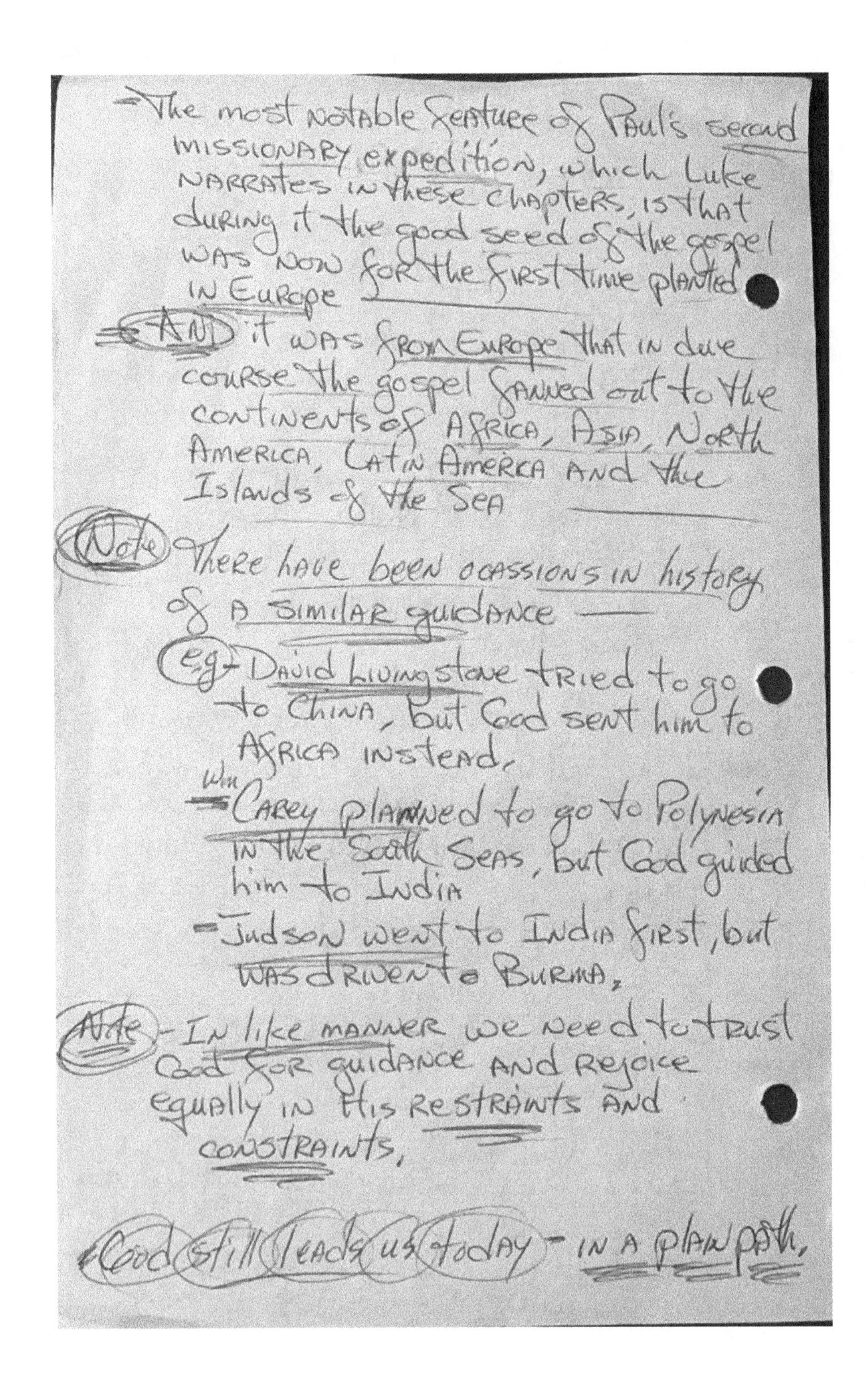

- The most notable feature of Paul's second missionary expedition, which Luke narrates in these chapters, is that during it the good seed of the gospel was now for the first time planted in Europe

= AND it was from Europe that in due course the gospel fanned out to the continents of Africa, Asia, North America, Latin America and the Islands of the Sea

(Note) There have been ocassions in history of a similar guidance —

(e.g.) - David Livingstone tried to go to China, but God sent him to Africa instead.

= Wm Carey planned to go to Polynesia in the South Seas, but God guided him to India

- Judson went to India first, but was driven to Burma.

(Note) - In like manner we need to trust God for guidance and Rejoice equally in His restraints and constraints.

God still leads us today - in a plain path.

Meet the Authors: Jennifer Courtney

Jennifer (Jones) Courtney, daughter and granddaughter of two preaching and teaching greats, is a third-generation minister, spanning almost 100 years of a Jones in full-time ministry. She is grateful for her spiritual heritage and loves that God has called her to continue the tradition of cherishing and spreading the message of God's Word. She has been pastoring with her husband since 1994, starting in youth and young adult ministries, and now lead pastoring churches alongside her husband. She is ordained with the Assemblies of God, serving as the discipleship pastor at her current church, and teaching future ministers at the Minnesota School of Ministry. She loves her craft room, her green Mini Cooper (named Mr. Bean) and all things winter and snow. She lives with her husband, Dan, in Central Minnesota and has two adult daughters, Allison and Megan.

Meet the Authors: David Jones

David Lancaster Jones, born in England in 1938, grew up like a proper British chap, and became the wise, witty, and sarcastic preacher and professor everyone knew affectionately as Brother Jones. Before he joined the church triumphant in 2021, he knew that his daughter was getting his life's work published. He was an ordained minister in the Assemblies of God for over fifty years and was a favorite pastor or professor of many. Over twenty-five years of his ministry career was spent pastoring churches in Minnesota, North Dakota, Wisconsin, and Nebraska. The rest of his ministry career was spent at Trinity Bible College in Ellendale, North Dakota, instilling into future ministers a love for God's Word and the enormous honor and responsibility of sharing that with others. You couldn't be in a class or congregation of his without appreciating the depth of his biblical wisdom or laughing at a witty comment you didn't see coming. He was one of a kind! He was married to his high school sweetheart, Mary G. Jones, for sixty years before she went to heaven in 2019. Together they raised five children: Wendy, Becky, Heidi, Jennifer, and Adam, along with being foster parents to over 100 children.

Printed in the USA
CPSIA information can be obtained
at www.ICGtesting.com
LVHW010058131023
760672LV00061B/1452